World War I and the Origins of U.S. Military Intelligence

James L. Gilbert

ROWMAN & LITTLEFIELD
*Lanham • Boulder • New York • London*2012

Published by Rowman & Littlefield
A wholly owned subsidiary of The Rowman & Littlefield Publishing Group, Inc.
4501 Forbes Boulevard, Suite 200, Lanham, Maryland 20706
www.rowman.com

Unit A, Whitacre Mews, 26-34 Stannary Street, London SE11 4AB

British Library Cataloguing in Publication Information Available

Library of Congress Cataloging-in-Publication Data

The hardback edition of this book was previously cataloged by the Library of Congress as follows:

Gilbert, James L. (James Leslie), 1943-
    World War I and the origins of U.S. military intelligence / James L. Gilbert.
    p. cm.
    Includes bibliographical references and index.
    1. United States. Dept. of the Army. General Staff. Military Intelligence
Division—History. 2. World War, 1914-1918—Military intelligence—United
States. 3. Military intelligence—United States—History—0th century. I. Title.
    UB251.U5G55 2012
    940.4'8673—dc23

                                                          2012015810

ISBN 978-0-8108-8459-5 (hbk : alk. paper)
ISBN 978-1-4422-4918-9 (pbk : alk. paper)
ISBN 978-0-8108-8460-1 (ebook)

∞™ The paper used in this publication meets the minimum requirements of American National Standard for Information Sciences—Permanence of Paper for Printed Library Materials, ANSI/NISO Z39.48-1992.

Printed in the United States of America

Contents

Foreword

Today, intelligence and security play an upfront role in America's war against international terrorism and in support of US Army deployments worldwide. This hasn't always been true. Evolution of military intelligence has often taken place at an excruciatingly slow pace, with periods of retreat and restarts. It took more than 125 years before the War Department recognized intelligence as a permanent member of its general staff; another 25 years before intelligence would play a significant role during peacetime; and still another 20 years before it became a separate branch within the Army that provided intelligence specialists with their own career path.

World War I serves as a prominent marker in the development of military intelligence. For the first time, military intelligence was left with an organizational blueprint, beginning with the War Department and extending down to army, corps, and division. Such terms as G2 would become a fixture within the Army's vocabulary. World War I also witnessed the introduction of new disciplines that have, to this day, remained the backbone of Army intelligence: counterintelligence, technical intelligence, and document exploitation, to name a few. World War I is also important because it would forever link intelligence to technology. Observers in airplanes using cameras and operators at intercept stations foreshadow today's dependence on emerging technologies and information systems to find and target an elusive enemy.

Regardless of the changes that have occurred within military intelligence since World War I, there has remained one constant throughout the years—the dedication of the men and women themselves. In the early days, individuals and their personalities were more apt to show through the tapestry of war; the growth of the national security bureaucracy has often hidden the human element. Still, the same spirit and devotion to excellence demonstrated by those who served as pioneers in their respective disciplines continues to characterize military intelligence professionals of today and to foster a legacy of service and sacrifice.

John D. Thomas, Jr.
Major General, USA (Retired)

Preface

During World War II, military intelligence played a defining role in operational planning within the Pacific and European theaters that would lead to victories on the battlefields and ultimately shorten the war itself. The Army was able to accomplish this because of the groundbreaking efforts of intelligence and security specialists in World War I. Unfortunately, within intelligence literature, World War I has been the forgotten war, and the few books that have been prepared on US Army intelligence contributions during the Great War have been singular in purpose, focusing on only one aspect of the effort. As significant and spectacular as a particular system and activity may have been, it still paled when compared to the organizational and operational achievements as a whole. This book is an attempt to provide the larger picture and to connect the various parts. It begins by depicting the lack of an intelligence presence during the years leading up to World War I.

The organization of the book was aided greatly by the natural division of intelligence itself between the home front and overseas. I was very dependent on the writings of both Generals Dennis E. Nolan and Ralph Van Deman and tried to keep the emphasis where they had placed it. One area I did not focus on but that did receive greater attention during the war was the publication of various intelligence reports. However, in retrospect, the subject matter of these documents was very repetitious, ranged widely between the mundane and the speculative, and often did not seem to touch directly on the conduct of the war.

As always, I was dependent on former colleagues for advice and assistance. Romana Danysh, Thomas Hauser, and Karen Kovach were particularly helpful. Special thanks goes to Michael Bigelow, the historian of the US Army Intelligence and Security Command, for granting me access to many of the photos used in the book, as well as kudos to Robert Bills for his technical support. Thanks to the librarians and archivists at the National Archives and Records Administration (NARA), the US Army Heritage and Learning Center, and my local library in Fairfax County who patiently retrieved dozens of books on interlibrary loan. Finally, thanks to my wife, Marilyn, who not only encouraged me but added her editorial skills to the project.

Photos originated from the Library of Congress (LC), National Security Agency History Office (NSA), the US Army Intelligence and Security Command (INSCOM), and the NARA. One of the photos is copyrighted and came from Brown Brothers. I am hopeful that this summary will serve as a useful introduction to the rise of military intelligence in the 20th century. As always, I alone am responsible for any mistakes.

1

Steps to War

"Spare no pains, no cost, to gain information of the enemy's movements and designs; whatever sums you pay to obtain this end, I will cheerfully refund."

—General George Washington

The history of US Army intelligence leading up to World War I consisted largely of isolated stories in which the actions of individuals and visionaries would play as important a role as official Army initiatives. The first advocate for exploiting information was none other than George Washington, who had, as a young officer, witnessed firsthand the consequences of intelligence failure; following the French and Indian War, Washington would dedicate himself to studying all available books on the subject. For most of the Revolutionary War, General Washington, as commander of the Continental Army, would also serve as his own intelligence chief—creating spy rings, applying deception, and ordering that all plans be kept as secret as possible. Trenton and Yorktown, two of Washington's greatest triumphs on the battlefield, were aided by intelligence and secrecy. Unfortunately, those who came after him did not learn from Washington's example of practicing the art of knowing one's enemies and saw no need to establish a permanent intelligence organization within the new republic's War Department. Apart from the lack of vision on the part of its military commanders, America did not feel threatened by enemies on its borders and thus saw no need for an early warning mechanism. Being a democracy, the United States also did not acquire a tradition of court intrigue and dependence on foreign alliances—conditions that spawned the use of trained spies and secret communications among European nations.

1

Each time a major war broke out during the 19th century, commanders in the field depended on observation and reconnaissance as their chief means of information gathering; management of intelligence collection within major army headquarters was left in the hands of veteran officers who possessed neither training nor special talents. This would hold true for both the North and South during the Civil War, but the conflict did witness the first attempt by the Union at centrally collecting information for the purpose of informing its leadership in Washington, D.C., as to the current status of the enemy's forces. In peacetime, the Army's primary focus remained on the frontier, where it provided order and protection during America's long movement westward, and subsequently came to rely on a number of intelligence tools in fulfilling its mission. To chart new territory, the Army utilized topographical engineers; to pacify the Plains Indians, the Army depended on the reconnaissance skills of its cavalry and scouts, eventually establishing a Corps of Indian Scouts in 1866.

In 1885, the War Department finally took its first step toward organizing a viable intelligence agency when the adjutant general created the Military Information Division (MID) in order to answer questions on foreign military matters for the secretary of war. The term *information* was selected instead of *intelligence* because in the 19th century, the latter term was often equated with the day's news, as evidenced by a number of papers employing the term as part of their title. MID's first home was located in three offices on the first floor of the ornate State, War and Navy Building (now the Eisenhower Executive Building) next to the White House. Other, more subtle factors were also at work that reinforced the decision to organize the division. A number of reformers believed that gathering information on Europe's forces would potentially benefit the War Department's own plans to transform the Army into a more professional organization. The new MID also ensured that the Army kept pace with the Navy, which had recently established an Office of Naval Intelligence to collect data on emerging technology from maritime powers.[1]

In the 19th century, the Army occasionally dispatched military observers overseas, such as during the Russo–Turkish War, but the longest of these assignments was for only six months. On September 22, 1888, Congress passed an act that provided for a more permanent means of collecting and classifying military information from abroad, and in turn, gave MID its first real function. In the future, the War Department would appoint officers as attachés who would be entitled to transportation and computation of quarters while on duty, plus the assistance of a clerk to help with day-to-day correspondence. On March 11 of the following year, the first two military attachés departed the States: one destined for the US legation in London and the other to Berlin. Soon, other officers were on their way to the capitals of Austria–Hungary,

Russia, and France. Once settled into their new duty stations, the attachés set about to obtain a wide variety of data thought to be of value to the US Army; the information falling into two broad categories: general and technical or scientific.[2]

During the coming years, MID's mission and capabilities continued to grow, eventually forming four branches. One dealt with digesting incoming reports from attachés and using the information to publish books, monographs, and maps for distribution within the Army; among the early publications was Major Theodore Schwan's *Organization of the German Army*. Another branch monitored the strength of the National Guard as well as prepared plans for its mobilization. A third was assigned the task of watching the northern border, frequently sending officers on hunting and fishing leave for the purposes of visiting and mapping the Canadian wilderness. The last branch kept close tabs on countries within the Caribbean, and on the eve of the Spanish–American War, would dispatch several officers undercover to Puerto Rico and Cuba.[3]

Having served as an instructor at the Fort Leavenworth School, forerunner of the US Army Command and General Staff College, Colonel Arthur Wagner was best known as an advocate for professionalization of the Army's leadership; later he would help to establish the Army War College. Wagner also played an equally important role in the development of military intelligence by promoting the thinking that all modern armies should have a viable organization to collect information. He subsequently authored a book on the subject—*The Service of Security and Information*—the first of its kind in the US Army. Wagner also published a second book, *Organization and Tactics*, in which he called for the Army to assign an intelligence officer to each major field headquarters. In 1896, the arrival of Colonel Arthur Wagner as chief of MID marked an important moment in the organization's development; unfortunately, during the Spanish–American War, the Army's commanding general in Cuba kept Wagner from putting into practice many of his revolutionary ideas. Apparently, Major General William Shafter believed that Wagner's proposed Intelligence Bureau was, in actuality, an attempt by the War Department to spy on how the war was being conducted in the field, not to collect information on the enemy.

By the turn of the century, America was demonstrating to the world that it was a rising power. In the aftermath of the Spanish–American War, the United States liberated Cuba and assumed responsibility for the Philippines. In 1898, the United States also acquired the Hawaiian Islands, further extending its presence in the Pacific, and in 1903, it gained the rights to construct the Panama Canal, which would eventually link the world's two great oceans. Coinciding with these dramatic changes, Secretary Elihu Root modernized the War Department in 1903 by establishing a General Staff, which was divided along three functional lines: administration, intelligence, and plans as modeled by the French.[4] Of the 44 officers assigned, 6 were given over to intelligence, the so-called Second Division, which absorbed MID's missions. Although this restructuring gave intelligence an elevated status, the Second Division remained far from its modern equivalency; the division still operated only for purposes of the General Staff and possessed no authority to influence the organization of intelligence within the larger Army.

In light of its international obligations, the United States finally began to grow its standing Army over the next 10 years until it reached 100,000—a fourfold increase—yet still miniscule when compared to the major powers of Europe. Paradoxically, its intelligence capacity would virtually disappear over the same period. In 1908, the Second Division, now situated in the Lemon Building not far from the White House, underwent a series of organizational changes that unfortunately would prove its undoing. The Third Division, which had oversight of operational planning and was the major consumer of information generated by the Second Division, was relocated to Washington Barracks (now Fort McNair) situated in the southwest corner of the District of Columbia. Given limited means—one automobile—to courier documents between the two divisions, the chief of staff Major General J. Franklin Bell signed off on the recommendation that the Second and Third Divisions be merged at Washington Barracks. Bell's decision was believed to have been prejudiced by an incident that took place several years before in the Philippines where he had suffered the embarrassment of having his support for a certain matter openly overruled in favor of a position held by the local intelligence element.[5]

In any event, the Second Division did not go quietly but strenuously objected to the recommendations and pointed out that it existed to serve all of the War Department, not just operations. The division's staff members also departed with the consolation that an ad hoc committee of War Department senior officers agreed with their position. Irrespective of these arguments, the Third Division was subsequently renamed the War College Division, and residual functions of the Second Division consolidated within a paper organization called the Military Information Committee, whose members were members in name only and were preoccupied with their normal day-to-day duties.

It is easy to dismiss the absence of a permanent intelligence element within the War Department on the eve of the Great War. The long delay in acquiring an authoritative command over the Army and its lack of a General Staff were certainly key factors that had discouraged such thinking. Still, it is hard to understand the failure by the Army leadership to see the need for routine intelligence reporting on developing situations internationally and the need for such basic tools as maps, especially when the United States became responsible for security interests in the Pacific and the Caribbean.

Although the War Department was once again without an active intelligence organization, the number of attachés assigned grew over the years to cover most of the European nations along with Mexico, Japan, and a number of countries in the Caribbean basin. However, without someone within the War Department to assist them, they lacked any professional guidance on what type of information the Army actually wanted collected. A member of the General Staff later acknowledged the consequences: "the collecting, digesting, and filing of military information of foreign countries . . . appears never to have been carried on continuously," and the "work of attachés is without proper supervision and guidance, and therefore to a large extent, the value of their work is lost."[6]

As far as any intelligence effort in the field on the eve of the Great War in 1914, the Army possessed only the Military Information Division in the Philippines, where for 15 years it had gathered information on local guerrillas, managed informers, and created maps. Besides monitoring the activities of potential Filipino insurgents, the small intelligence element helped to expose the occasional attempts by the Japanese to conduct espionage in hope of fomenting unrest within the islands. The Philippines also served as a staging area for several trips by officers traveling incognito to China to map railroads and other lines of communications. Interest in China had grown since the European powers, Japan, and the United States had acquired a commercial stake in the country and had deployed an international force to quell an anti-foreigner rebellion on the part of the Chinese.[7]

Elsewhere within the Pacific region, Army Lieutenant A. Seone and Commander Joseph Thompson of the US Navy Medical Service conducted a two-year reconnaissance of Japanese fortifications and coastal facilities while disguised as South African naturalists, which gave them cover as they traveled about to collect specimens for their research. Finally, the Army began language classes in both Japan and China for a handful of officers on a rotating basis. Ironically, on the eve of war in Europe, the Army's limited collection efforts were in the Pacific, and in the eyes of its handful of intelligence officers, Japan posed the greatest threat to US interests.[8]

THE SIGNAL CORPS

The US Army also possessed a second intelligence player—the Signal Corps, begun in 1860 under the able leadership of General Albert J. Myer. As a medical doctor, Myer had first acquired an interest in communications when he created a sign language for the deaf. In the Army, Myer developed a wig-wag system that employed flags and torches during the Civil War to relay messages in a timely fashion from high atop towers and elevated platforms. Using their telescopes, Signal Corps personnel also possessed an extended view of the landscape. While stationed on a mountain, Signal Corps personnel had first warned of General Robert E. Lee's army crossing the Potomac River and advancing into Maryland during the Gettysburg campaign. The Confederate Signal Corps took its mission a step further by reasoning that all collected information required transmission, and thus intelligence should logically fall under its control. Consequently, the Confederate Signal Corps not only carried out its day-to-day communications responsibilities but also ran the South's spy nets inside the Union capital of Washington, D.C. In the 1890s, the Army Signal Corps, which by then called itself the Service of Information, would dust off the same argument in an unsuccessful bid to bring the Military Information Division under its direct control.[9]

Balloons had seen limited action in both the Civil and Spanish–American Wars. Consequently, as the Signal Corps entered the 20th century, its leadership maintained an interest in, but not a commitment to, the use of balloons for the purposes of observation and command and control of troops in the field. In 1907, the environment began to change under the new chief Signal officer, Brigadier General James Allen and his assistant, Major George O. Squier, who had the distinction of holding a doctorate in engineering from Johns Hopkins University and was already considered a pioneer in electrical communications. On his own, Squier began to study aeronautics and followed the progress of the Wright brothers and their heavier-than-air flying machine. In August, General Allen named Squier chief of the newly created Aeronautical Division with the mission of all matters pertaining to military ballooning, air machines, and kindred subjects. Four months later, the Army solicited bids for a two-passenger craft that could fly at least 40 miles per hour in a sustained flight. Because the Signal Corps did not possess sufficient funds to sponsor the trials, the Board of Ordnance and Fortification agreed to provide the necessary funds.

On September 3, 1908, Orville Wright and his aircraft arrived at Fort Myer, Virginia, just across the Potomac River from Washington, D.C., to undertake the first flight from a military installation, achieving several new records in the process, but on September 17, disaster struck shortly after takeoff with Wright at the controls and Lieutenant Thomas Selfridge as a passenger. (Selfridge was chosen for the initial tests because he and fellow officer Benjamin Foulois had already piloted cigar-shaped balloons with motors.) One of the two pusher propellers split, cutting a guy-wire that collapsed the rudder, causing the aircraft to plummet to the ground. Wright was seriously injured and Selfridge lay dying—the first air pioneer to make the supreme sacrifice; the historical marker would read "in an effort to aid man's endeavor to fly."

The tragedy would fail to deter the Army in its quest for an airplane, and almost a year later in July 1909, the Wright brothers returned to complete a round trip between Fort Myer and Shooters Hill (now the site of the George Washington Masonic National Memorial) overlooking the city of Alexandria while maintaining a speed of 42 miles an hour. To mark Shooters Hill, the Signal Corps inflated one of its stored balloons and tethered it to an unmanned pylon. First Lieutenant Benjamin Foulois was the lone passenger on the flight, and President William Howard Taft was among the crowd on hand to witness the historic event. On July 30, 1909, the Army awarded the Wright brothers a $30,000 contract to provide an aircraft and to train a handful of pilots.[10]

Lieutenant Foulois was not among those who received training from Wright, but he would be the one sent with the 40-horsepower aircraft to Fort Sam Houston, Texas, with the following instructions: "Take plenty of spare parts, and teach yourself to fly."[11] Given only $300 in congressional funding, Foulois soon had to dip into his own pocket to finance maintenance and employed a local blacksmith to forge parts; following several crashes, the lieutenant decided it was in his best interest to install the first seatbelt made from a saddle strap. Still, these early steps by Foulois and his enlisted assistants, known locally as the "crazy birdmen," were considered crucial ones. In 1911, Major H. A. Erickson interested the Army leadership in combining photography with the airplane when he submitted superb aerial photos of the San Diego area. The same year, other milestones were achieved, for instance, night flying and the development of a more powerful scout plane (Wright Type C) that contained room for an observer along with wireless and photographic equipment.

The years 1912 and 1913 were equally important ones in the early history of Army aviation. Congress allotted an appropriation of $125,000 for the purchase of five new aircraft and the formation of an aero company at Fort Sam Houston. For the first time, the War Department established the designation of aviator with performance standards as well as an increase in pay. In 1913, the aero company would evolve into the 1st Aero Squadron (Provisional), which, on paper, consisted of 20 officers and 90 enlisted men. An Army pilot and his observer also completed a cross-country flight from Texas City to San Antonio 200 miles away, establishing a new two-man record, but more importantly for intelligence purposes, on the return flight the observer made a sketch map that measured 18 feet in length, reinforcing the aircraft's potential value as a reconnaissance platform.[12]

Although not as dramatic as the aircraft, the Signal Corp experienced advances in communications, most notably the coming of the wireless that held long-term implications for intelligence. Known initially as the wireless telegraph, the system allowed for the transmission of Morse code by electromagnetic waves rather than wires. The discharge of a spark across a gap caused by the pressing of a telegraph key generated the electromagnetic waves that relayed the message. The Signal Corps first used the wireless in 1906 during military operations involving US Army troops in Cuba. However, dissipation of energy over the broadband limited how far signals could travel. Further advances in continuous wave technology coupled with the invention of the vacuum tube were necessary before wireless telegraphy would evolve into radiotelephony.[13]

Although private inventors and the Navy led the way, the Signal Corps proved adept at repackaging emerging technologies for military uses. Yet at no time did the Signal Corps give thought to future exploitation of these emerging technologies for intelligence purposes, despite the fact that during both the Civil and Spanish–American Wars, Army personnel had gained important information through the use of wiretapping of telegraph lines. The hasty deployment of elements of the Army's V Corps to Cuba during the Spanish–American War had been attributed to a Signal Corps wiretap of a cable from Spain relaying news that its main fleet had been dispatched to the port of Santiago de Cuba.[14]

If the Signal Corps lagged behind in new technologies, one could sympathize and attribute it to the absence of congressional funding; but the Signal Corps' lack of progress in the area of cryptology, the study of making and breaking codes, was less understandable as it was at the very heart of the branch's mission—communications. Perhaps one reason for the inattention was that cryptology had been historically associated with diplomacy rather than military affairs. Just prior to World War I, the Signal Corps had at its disposal the War Department Telegraph Code, a bulky code designed primarily to save telegraph charges, not to safeguard messages. Because of its administrative nature, the Telegraph Code did not possess the necessary vocabulary for use under actual combat conditions, but it did have a substitution table of encipherment to pass classified messages. Unfortunately, too often communicators employed their own homemade systems—an additive or subtractive method—in an attempt to garble sensitive communiqués. For instance, during the Spanish–American War, signal personnel simply used the number of the year 1898. For nonheadquarters elements in the field, the Signal Corps devised a handheld, celluloid device called the Army Cipher Disk, based on the simple principle of mono-alphabetic substitution. The concept was more than 400 years old, and the disk itself resembled one used by the Confederate

Army during the Civil War. Realistically, it offered about the same degree of security as toy secret rings later found in cereal boxes. The failure of the Signal Corps to protect communications had left the Army's secrets open for all to read.[15]

WAR IN EUROPE

Events had transpired long before 1914 to set the stage for conflict in Europe and to make the forthcoming war appear inevitable. Germany had embarked on a total armament program under Kaiser Wilhelm II, whose saber rattling and martial strutting would have been comical if the consequences were not so dire. France, with the continent's second largest army, still remembered its bitter loss to Germany in 1870 that had given rise to the Third Republic. The spark that finally lit the powder keg of Europe occurred at just before 11:00 A.M. on June 28, 1914, in the streets of Sarajevo in Bosnia, a southern province of Austria. Gavril Princip, a member of a secret society called the Black Hand, fired into the open car, killing the visiting Archduke Francis Ferdinand, heir apparent of the Austro–Hungarian Empire, and his beloved wife, Sophie—all for the cause of a greater Serbia. In the aftermath of the assassination, failure of Europe's diplomats to avert war, flawed strategies embraced by its military leaders, and a series of entangling alliances would soon bring the powers of Germany, France, Russia, and Great Britain into the conflict.

Halfway around the world, President Woodrow Wilson responded by embracing America's long-standing policy of keeping out of Europe's wars. Wilson proclaimed, "Force will not accomplish anything that is permanent, I venture to say, in the great struggle which is now going on, on the other side of the sea," and he went on to urge that Americans remain neutral in thought as well as deed. The problem for Wilson was that United States could not or would not enforce its neutrality. In theory, Americans should have been able to trade equally with all belligerents, but the British proceeded to announce the whole of the North Sea be considered a military area and that all ships must consequently first stop in Dover for sailing directions through the minefields. This pronouncement flew in the face of international law that placed the North Sea outside of territorial waters, plus the fact that the British list of what was contraband continued to grow until it conveniently excluded all items even remotely of value to the Central Powers. From 1914 to 1916, American exports to France and Great Britain rose from $750 million to $2.5 billion; at the same time, they would drop from $345 million to $2 million for the Central Powers. Germany, which was not a sea power, proceeded to launch U-boats to counter the blockade and reduce the delivery of materiel to the Allies. The principles that President Wilson publicly expounded would soon fall victim to the battle for control of the seas.[16]

From the start of the war, Americans followed events in Europe with a watchful eye. Over time, such acts as a German U-boat sinking the British liner *Lusitania* that resulted in the drowning of 1,198 persons, among them 128 Americans, began to sway public opinion in favor of the Allies. Support was also growing for the preparedness movement, in which young volunteers began to train seriously at General Leonard Wood's camp in Plattsburg, New York, for a war they believed would soon involve the United States. Yet there were still vocal minorities who remained either pro-German or arch-isolationists, and Wilson successfully campaigned for reelection in 1916 on the slogan "He kept us out of war."

The coming of war in Europe may have ironically saved the attaché system. In early 1914, the Army leadership was attempting to address the severe shortage of available officers by reducing the number of those in detached status. In response, Brigadier General Hunter Liggett, president of the War College, wrote the most amazingly short-sighted proposal to his superiors. In it, he recommended the elimination of attachés in Spain, Italy, Austria–Hungary, and Belgium and the designation as temporary the positions situated in Russia, Switzerland, the Balkan states, and Turkey. Finally, if the US Army was to undertake major field exercises, then all attachés in Europe along with officers studying in France and Germany faced the prospect of immediate recall.

Fortunately, with the announcement of war, cooler heads in the War Department prevailed. Not only were the 16 existing positions worldwide saved, but observers were added to supplement the work of the attachés in Europe so that the latter could continue to pursue their normal duties. Six new officers sailed for France, six more to Germany, three to Austria–Hungary, and five to Japan. All went well, except for the element in France, where authorities refused to allow non-Allied personnel to accompany French armies into the war zone. The head of the US delegation in Paris lamented that the courtesies offered were "practically the same as those extended to small unimportant countries, such as, for example, Ecuador and Siam."[17] One of the Americans attached to the French mission was 38-year-old Captain Marlborough Churchill, an artillery officer and distant relative to Winston Churchill; Captain Churchill was destined to hold several key leadership positions within military intelligence.

TWO CAPTAINS

With the nation itself, just three short years away from entering the war, there were no indications that Captains Dennis E. Nolan and Ralph Van Deman would soon lead the largest intelligence organizations in the history of the United States and that these would be comprised of hundreds of soldiers and civilians. Apart from holding the same rank, being rather tall and wearing glasses, the two held little in common. Nolan and Van Deman were acquainted with each other, serving briefly together in the Philippines and later within the Second Division of the General Staff.

The junior of the two, Nolan, was a son of an Irish immigrant who worked in the gypsum mines of western New York. Originally studying to become a schoolteacher, Nolan took a late appointment to the US Military Academy when it became available. From the start, he seemed destined for greater things; Nolan starred on the athletic fields of West Point and held a position of leadership among the cadets. He also married well—Julia Dent Sharp, the daughter of a recognized military family and niece of First Lady Julia Grant. During the Spanish–American War, Nolan demonstrated bravery under fire when he received two decorations that were later replaced with Silver Stars. He would return to the academy where he taught history and coached the football team to its greatest season to date. Nolan also prided himself as an administrator—a position he held on several occasions. In the Philippines, Nolan served as acting adjutant general to newly appointed Brigadier General John J. Pershing and in various capacities in the civil government where he made the acquaintances of those who would later become instrumental in his selection to lead intelligence. While in the islands, Nolan also experienced firsthand the trials of an intelligence officer when a local native he recruited as an informant was unfortunately hacked to death by suspicious neighbors. The outbreak of war in Europe in 1914 found Captain Nolan and his wife at Fort Seward in Alaska—a bittersweet time for the family, having to adjust to the recent loss of their young son due to illness while celebrating the arrival of a new daughter.[18]

Captain Ralph Van Deman possessed more of a scholarly bent as evidenced by his impressive academic credentials; his career began as a member of the Ohio National Guard where he organized its first signal detachment. After Van Deman graduated from Harvard, he stayed on for a year to read law and then returned to his native state of Ohio to obtain his medical degree before finally accepting his Army commission. In 1895, while attending the school at Fort Leavenworth for infantry and cavalry officers, Van Deman became acquainted for the first time with Colonel Wagner; two years later, he would serve under Wagner when he became head of MID. Having been exposed to Wagner's vision was enough to convince Van Deman to become a lifelong advocate for a viable intelligence system within the Army. He would have his first opportunity to turn theory into reality during the Philippine insurrection when he worked within the Bureau of Insurgent Records. In time, local authorities selected Van Deman to reorganize the bureau into the Military Information Division of the Philippines; this he accomplished by adding mapping functions and organizing spy rings. By doing so, Van Deman would create the field intelligence organization that his mentor Wagner had planned but failed to accomplish in Cuba during the Spanish–American War.[19] While assigned to the islands, Van Deman experienced firsthand what would become his life's passion—counterintelligence. He personally directed a band of paid, undercover Filipino agents, who on at least one occasion learned of a plot to attack sections of Manila and to assassinate key military leaders. The same agents successfully identified the hiding place of the attackers along with the names of many of their contacts inside the city, making possible the quick dispersion of the guerrillas. From the Philippines, Van Deman also traveled incognito to China to help map railroad lines emanating from Peking. By 1907, Van Deman had returned to Washington, D.C., to serve again in the Second Division, only to be present at its demise 12 months later. When the year 1914 dawned, Van Deman was once more back in the Philippines—the only place where Army intelligence remained a reality.

In 1915, Major Dennis Nolan received orders for Washington, D.C., where his superiors assigned him the task of assembling a threat estimate to justify the War Department's preparedness plan. Having no current intelligence estimates to draw from, Nolan relied on three outdated documents for his figures: a 1914 almanac of the world's armies, a shipping register from the same year, and the Army's own Field Service Regulations. The result was either ingenious or laughable, depending on how seriously Nolan actually believed his own math. Utilizing Nolan's calculations, it was possible for Germany to deploy to the United States a force of 435,000 men and 91,457 horses and mules in only 15.8 days, thus overwhelming America's current army. As absurd as the proposition was on its face, the finished product accomplished what the War Department leadership wanted—rationalization for an expanded force. Nolan's next assignment would be the promotion of national conscription.[20]

Also in 1915, the War College Division created the Military Information Section as one of its two major subelements, but it was purely window dressing for the sake of preserving congressional funding. Apparently, Congress still had an appropriations line designated for the Military Information Section, General Staff; funds were divided between $11,000 for contingencies and $15,000 for observers and attachés. The War College assigned the new paper organization "General Staff work," an eclectic mission statement consisting of 10 functional areas ranging from writing histories to working legislation issues—only one actually dealt with intelligence matters.

On the positive side, the president of the War College, Brigadier General Montgomery M. Macomb, attempted to correct a major deficiency—publication and dissemination of valuable information to the Army. His plan consisted of sending documents to the Command and Staff School at Fort Leavenworth, where its staff would be responsible for printing and distributing the studies. Unfortunately, the first document selected just happened to be one originally obtained from a major European power by a military attaché who had pledged under the strictest of confidences to keep its contents secret. Following this debacle, the War College quickly retreated from the publishing business.

When Major Ralph Van Deman was reassigned to Washington, D.C., in 1915, he discovered that "he was the only officer in the War College Division who had had any training or experience in what we now designate as military intelligence."[21] Van Deman immediately began a letter-writing campaign to reverse the status quo. In March 1916, Van Deman put down on paper the role that military intelligence should be performing within the General Staff and urged that it immediately reestablish a separate and viable Military Information Division. General Montgomery M. Macomb promptly signed off on Van Deman's proposal and forwarded it to General Hugh L. Scott, chief of staff, for his approval.

General Scott, a veteran of the wars in the West and a recognized authority on the Plains Indians, did not respond directly to Van Deman's paper but did surprisingly fulfill in April a long-term goal of military intelligence. Within the continental United States, the Army divided itself into six geographic departments. For the first time, the chief of staff directed that each departmental commander establish an intelligence element within his headquarters as circumstances dictated. Their subordinate posts and commands were also to name their own intelligence officers (IO). The duties of these officers included the creation of information files and indexing of maps. Although the original orders referred to the new departmental intelligence offices as branches of the War College, this linkage on paper never became one in reality. Instead, all of the departmental intelligence offices operated autonomously, similar to the MID organization in the Philippines.[22]

The same legislation in 1916 that increased the Army's authorized strength to 175,000 also contained a provision that specified half of the officers assigned to the General Staff could not at any time be stationed or assigned to or employed upon any duty in or near the District of Columbia.[23] This meant that of the 41 officers assigned to the General Staff, only 19 could be in the Washington area. At the very time the War College's staff fell to nine officers, its onetime dormant Military Information Section began to experience a dramatic rise in mail. To process the incoming requests and documents, Brigadier General Joseph E. Kuhn, the acting president, directed in late 1916 that classes at the college be canceled and that all available personnel be used to conduct an extensive study of military intelligence reports from abroad so the information compiled might be imparted to the troops.

SMALL STEPS BY THE SIGNAL CORPS

The Signal Corps, in the meantime, recognized that the war presented an opportune time to solicit more funding for its fledgling aviation element and used as its rationale the need to keep pace with the various European armies. After all, the total military aircraft of Britain, France, Italy, Russia, Germany, and Austria–Hungary had quickly mushroomed to over 2,000. In stark contrast were the 30 aircraft that at one time or another had been in the US Army's inventory; the number included one that was now in the Smithsonian Institution and 20 others destroyed in accidents or condemned, leaving only 9 operational planes. To sum up the government's prevailing attitude, one congressman allegedly remarked, "Why all this fuss about airplanes for the Army—I thought we already had one."

In a pamphlet, the chief signal officer, Brigadier General George P. Scriven, outlined the potential role of airplanes in reconnaissance—a role that was presently being demonstrated in the skies over the battlefields of Europe. To satisfy these goals, Scriven believed that 18 squadrons were necessary. The War College issued a separate report indicating that three types of aircraft were essential if the Army's needs were to be met: scout aircraft to conduct long-range reconnaissance and to battle enemy aircraft, ordinary reconnaissance aircraft, and a third category for destroying the enemy's combat forces and related materiel.

To correct the deficiency, General Scriven boldly requested a little over $1 million, but the secretary of war reduced the request to $300,000. Congress would cut the amount by another $50,000; all in all a pittance, but still almost twice the amount of the previous year. While the chief signal officer contended for more money, his Aviation Section and school each were suffering through scathing reviews by the Army's inspector general and an investigating officer appointed by the General Staff. One result of these probes was the reappointment of Colonel George O. Squier as the head of the Aviation Section. Fresh from his tour of duty as an attaché to London, Squier brought with him firsthand information on state-of-the-art aviation as well as numerous contacts with emerging European leaders in the industry. During his stay overseas, Squier secretly undertook several trips to the frontlines where he observed firsthand the performance of airplanes under actual combat conditions, including the use of cameras; this would lead him to report that for strategic and tactical reconnaissance the aircraft had become indispensable.[24]

Prior to US involvement in the war, the most significant accomplishments in Army cryptology could be attributed to one officer—Captain Parker Hitt. An imposing figure at 6 feet 4 inches, Hitt was a former engineering student at Purdue University. Following service in the Spanish–American War, where he won his commission, Hitt settled into a teaching position at the Army Signal School at Fort Leavenworth. While assigned to the training center, Hitt embraced the study of cryptology, soon becoming the Signal Corps' foremost authority on the subject. His wife, Genevieve, shared in his avocation, and throughout their marriage, they often corresponded by means of a sophisticated strip-cipher device that he had invented.[25]

In 1915, Hitt recorded his knowledge for the purpose of training other officers—the *Manual for the Solution of Military Ciphers*—which he offered for sale at the Fort Leavenworth school for a sum of 35 cents. More importantly, Hitt's primer was the first book on cryptology ever published in the United States, and it covered ciphers up to polyalphabetics (mixed alphabets) in difficulty. Compared to Europe's military codes and ciphers, the book was outdated when it went to print, but its contents still proved useful. Hitt wrote in a style that gave understanding and clarity to the novice, and when listing the various factors that led to success in cryptanalysis, he demonstrated a certain refreshing honesty by citing the role played by luck. Captain Hitt also used his publication to advocate the establishment of cryptologic offices within field headquarters, outlining their duties and pointing out how the Army's own transmissions could be made more secure. Finally, he called for the creation of an agency to conduct interceptions of enemy communications.[26]

THE FIRST SHOTS IN THE INTELLIGENCE WAR

Intelligence organizations of the Central Powers became involved in an unofficial war against America long before their armies exchanged shots. Count Johann von Bernstorff, German ambassador to Washington, was in the inevitable position of nursing President Wilson's desire to keep America neutral while at the same time overseeing Germany's efforts to sabotage US war materiel before it reached Allied hands. Von Bernstorff was the ideal person for the assignment because he spoke English without an accent and had married an American. To assist him, Ambassador von Bernstorff employed a number of lieutenants: Captain Franz von Papen, military attaché; Captain Karl Boy-Ed, naval attaché; Franz von Bopp, consul general in San Francisco; and Doctor Heinrich Albert, commercial attaché. Albert handled the money and was personally responsible for putting many of Bernstorff's plans into action. Unlike Europe, where German intelligence had planted professional agents in countries long before the outbreak of war, this had not occurred in the United States. The absence of a trained intelligence network would, from the start, hamper Germany's intelligence and sabotage plans and cause them to be less effective than hoped. A second problem for the Germans was that the British were routinely reading the diplomatic traffic between Berlin and North America, having obtained a copy of their code.

On New Year's Day, 1915, Germany launched its sabotage campaign by bombing the John A. Roebling wire-cable manufacturing plant in Trenton, New Jersey. Two days later a detonation tore a gaping hole in the S.S. *Orton* docked in Brooklyn. Over the next four months, saboteurs detonated other explosions at ammunition plants in Haskell and Pompton Lakes, New Jersey, and Allon, Illinois. One ship carrying munitions caught fire at sea, and crews on two others discovered unexploded bombs. In August 1915, the British released documents revealing the role of Austro–Hungarian Ambassador Constantine Dumba to the United States in fomenting strikes at munitions factories. Following Dumba's recall in December, US authorities captured would-be saboteur Robert Fay, who implicated the German attachés, Franz von Papen and Karl Boy-Ed, forcing their quick departure.[27] Fay, who was an experienced mechanic, was best known for having built a sabotage device that could be attached underwater to the rudder post of a ship while at a pier; a clock piece served as the timer.[28] There were much more than ships at risk; German agents also attempted to inoculate horses bound for France with glanders disease and anthrax bacilli.

Two of the early German saboteurs are of particular significance: Both were among the most effective, and Army counterintelligence would later play an important role in their apprehension. Doctor Walter Scheele was a German chemist sent to the United States in 1893 to acquire technical intelligence on American's munitions industry. When war broke out, he invented a cigar-shaped sabotage device (usually a four-inch lead pipe) with a copper disk that divided two packages; one half held sulfuric acid that slowly dissolved the disk and then penetrated the second package of chlorate of potash or picric acid, resulting in a fire.[29] Mass production of the device took place aboard German vessels interned in New York harbor, and it took little skill to place these on nearby ships bound for Europe and to set them to ignite 15 days later or when the ship was out in international waters. On several occasions, crews put out the fires before they could do large-scale damage, but still proceeded to deliver the doused munitions. This led Allied gunners to begin reporting duds and premature explosions, giving credence to the rumor that US munitions were somehow inferior.

A member of the Imperial German Navy, Lothar Witzke, had found himself interned when the light cruiser that he had been on was scuttled in Chilean waters less it fall into the hands of the British. Witzke would eventually make his way north to San Francisco. Soon thereafter, he became a member of Germany's most prolific sabotage team and was personally involved in its greatest singular act of destruction. At the Lehigh Valley Railroad's Black Tom Island terminal on the New Jersey side of the Hudson River, close to the lower end of Manhattan, a large amount of munitions was awaiting shipment to the Allies. In the early morning hours of Sunday, June 30, 1916, Witzke and his companion were responsible for a huge explosion that ripped through the depot, scarring the Statue of Liberty with shrapnel, leaving the New York City skyline awash in light, knocking late-night revelers in the city off their feet, and waking people as far away as Maryland. Its shockwave caused the deaths of five people, including that of a sleeping 10-week-old infant who died when violently thrown from his crib in nearby New Jersey.[30]

Besides the threat from foreign agents, the United States faced a number of groups who were openly pro-Central Powers, such as veterans of Germany's armed forces. Others were anti-British, among them those from Ireland and India. To counter these, the Department of Justice, the Secret Service, and bomb squads of various large cities soon found themselves on the front lines. The New York City Bomb and Neutrality Squad was led by Inspector Thomas J. Tunney, who was described as a scrapping Irishman; Tunney and his men proved particularly adept in working the docks to capture saboteurs and their would-be assistants—many of them recent immigrants from Ireland now working as longshoremen. His greatest triumph was exposing the connection between Paul Koenig, chief of security for the Hamburg–America Shipping Line, and von Papen who was directing the sabotage campaign. During the investigation, Tunney and his team of detectives conducted various types of surveillances that included shadowing of suspects, using undercover operatives, and deploying telephone taps.[31] Yet despite all these early efforts to safeguard the nation, no other country during the war would come close to the United States in terms of the amount of losses of materiel suffered at the hands of saboteurs; all the while, the Army possessed no means to protect itself against the growing threat.

AN EARLY TEST SOUTH OF THE BORDER

As early as 1915, it had become obvious to a number of pro-German agents that sabotage alone could not prevent the United States from shipping goods and arms to the Allies. Franz von Rintelen, a former representative of the Deutsche Bank in Mexico, wrote, "Should Mexico attack the United States, the United States would need all the arms it can produce and would not be in a position to export arms to Europe." Meanwhile, Mexico had exchanged the incompetent government of General Victoriano Huerta for another led by Venustiano Carranza, but the staid Carranza soon faced a revolutionary threat in the form of the wild and colorful Pancho Villa. To offer support in case of war with the United States, German agents would make contacts with any and all groups that might hold power in Mexico: General Huerta, who was exiled to Spain, officials of the Carranzista government (the so-called Constitutionalists), and persons associated with the revolutionary Pancho Villa.

To discredit Carranza, Villa tried to draw the United States into intervening in Mexico. Carranza himself had employed the same tactic when he used the US occupation of the port of Vera Cruz as an excuse to criticize his predecessor. On January 11, 1916, Villa's band held up a train carrying 17 recent college graduates from California traveling south to Mexico to open a mine. Although the Americans journeyed under a safe conduct pass issued by Carranza, it did not stop Villa's men from murdering 16 of the young engineers. The Santa Ysabel massacre quickly drew the attention of the Wilson administration and the US public, but Villa wanted more. Consequently, on March 9, he raided and set fire to the town of Columbus, New Mexico, killing 17 soldiers and civilians in the process. Some evidence exists that a German agent, Felix A. Sommerfeld, who had exchanged his life as an engineer for one of a soldier of fortune and an arms dealer, was involved in buying guns for Villa for use during the cross-border raid.[32]

Although attempts by agents to stoke open hostilities between the United States and Mexico produced more smoke than fire, Germany would get partially what it wanted—US military intervention into Mexico. On March 15, 1916, Brigadier General John J. Pershing led a Punitive Expedition of 6,000 soldiers across the Rio Grande to bring Pancho Villa to justice. Authorities also called up thousands of National Guard troops to help protect the borders in the event of a repeat attack by Villa. In the coming months, US forces would penetrate more than 300 miles into the state of Chihuahua, where they endured mountainous terrain, a late blizzard, and sandstorms.

With two small exceptions, the intelligence phase of the expedition confined itself to south of the border. An information officer with the expedition routinely sent copious reports back to the War College in the form of telegrams. Here, another officer read the incoming mail, but no evidence exists that anyone in authority ever acted on the information. Van Deman recalled that while at the War College, he discovered a table piled high with such telegrams that had never been filed. From time to time, the border command intercepted ciphered messages emanating from Mexico.[33] Most originated with the Constitutionalists because they had access to wireless sets, but occasionally, from agents associated with Villa. The intercept stations passed on all unreadable coded messages to Captain Parker Hitt, who used various methods to decode them, including the Mexican Army Cipher Disk, which employed four numerical alphabets placed on a revolving disk. General Pershing appointed Major James A. Ryan, 13th Cavalry, to lead the "service of information." Ryan had previously served as an associate professor of modern languages at the US Military Academy and was proficient in Spanish. His successor was Captain Nicholas W. Campanole, who spoke Spanish as his native tongue as well as several other languages, including, of all things, Japanese. Regardless of who was in charge, intelligence faced numerous obstacles; foremost was the lack of maps. Coupled with this, the state of Chihuahua was also Villa territory and the people were either friendly to the rebel leader or simply hated Americans; even the jingle of silver often did not elicit the desired information. Another reason many Mexicans did not choose to cooperate was simply their lack of knowledge as to events outside their immediate area.

Although not easily obtained, intelligence derived from humans remained the primary source. Occasionally, US patrols performing reconnaissance duties made contact with American prospectors, ranchers, and Mormon colonists. As far as Mexican prisoners or civilians were concerned, it was often hard to determine whether they were telling the truth. Colonel George H. Dodd, Commander of the 2nd Brigade, once became so frustrated that he impressed two locals into service on the threat of their immediate execution. Whether by design or ignorance, the two reluctant guides then proceeded to lead Dodd and his men on a long, roundabout way to their destination, thus preventing Dodd's surprise attack from fully succeeding. A frequently used method to derive intelligence from prisoners or townspeople was to question them separately. After comparing all stories, a US officer could usually arrive at some semblance of the truth. Despite the obstacles, Major Ryan was able to assemble a small trustworthy band of agents and civilian scouts who each received a designator such as "Agent J" or "Messenger O." Among their successes, two of the individuals gained access to Villa's camp in September and reported that his forces amounted to 800 men. After the campaign was over, one of Ryan's spies produced a signed note that recommended US authorities grant him citizenship based on his invaluable service to General Pershing.[34]

The Punitive Expedition would be the last time the Corps of Indian Scouts would see action. Lieutenant James Shannon commanded a detachment of 20 Apache scouts and was forced to deal with their unique approach to the campaign. To the Indians, a Mexican was a Mexican; they did not see the fine line of political loyalties. In one instance, having sighted a company of Carranzista soldiers, First Sergeant Chicken gave the following command to his men, "Heap Mexican. Shoot 'em all!" Lieutenant Shannon had all he could handle to rein in his men. On another occasion, the scout's actions spoiled what could have been an even larger victory. Approaching a camp of Villistas, the Indian scouts were supposed to hit their objective at full gallop, but when they heard a shot fired, they quickly abandoned their horses and began firing back far out of range. Apparently, it was not a part of the Apache's nature to receive fire without returning it immediately, and no amount of commands could persuade them otherwise. Still, the Indian scouts utilized their exceptional tracking skills in helping to hunt down Villa's army as well as the occasional US deserter.[35]

While the Indian scouts were on their way out as intelligence collectors, US Army aviators received their baptism under fire during the Punitive Expedition. The 1st Aero Squadron, under the command of Captain Benjamin Foulois, showed up with 11 officers, 84 enlisted men, 1 civilian, 8 planes, and 12 trucks. On March 12, the first flight over Mexico went off without a hitch, but because the 1st Aero Squadron possessed the only mechanically qualified personnel on hand, authorities initially diverted them to assemble wagon bodies on truck chassis for the expedition, as well as to serve as drivers until the Army could hire civilians.[36]

On March 19, General Pershing ordered the pilots to fly all eight of the aircraft to Casas Grandes to receive their first assignments. None of the planes made it. One had to turn back because of engine trouble; the others faced the daunting prospect of landing at night—only three were unscathed. Unfortunately, this became a trend, and by April 20, only a single JN4 or Jenny remained operative. The aircraft simply lacked the power to work in the mountainous terrain, and the airframe proved too fragile for the daily rigors of a sustained campaign. This forced Captain Foulois to report that due to terrific vertical air currents and whirlwinds, which at times drove the aeroplanes within 20 feet of the tree tops, the pilots were unable to cross the Sierra Madre Mountains. Remarkably, Foulois was able to arrange for a quick delivery of four more powerful aircraft, but the V-8, 165 hp Curtiss R-2's would have several defects of their own to correct—the most difficult was obtaining wooden propellers that would not warp or split.[37]

Pershing had good reason to write that the airplanes were of no material benefit, either in scouting or a means of communications. Most amazingly, no US pilot lost his life in spite of repeated forced landings. On two occasions, pilots found themselves with a disabled plane in uncharted territory, days on foot from any American base. Despite suffering from thirst, hunger, and wounds, they still managed to reach safety. From time to time, pilots also faced hostile crowds who threatened to destroy parked aircraft by throwing stones, and on one occasion, Foulois spent a night in the local jail—the first US aviator to become a prisoner of war.

Despite these challenges, Army aviation achieved a number of important milestones. Between March and August, pilots of the 1st Aero Squadron flew 540 missions, covering over 19,500 miles. A typical mission was to scout the Carranzista troops, whose intentions were of increased concern to the Expeditionary Forces. "Pershing would get a bit of information saying that there were 350 [Carranzista] cavalry over at such and such a ranch. He'd send us out, and we'd fly over there, and we would fly low around the corral of this ranch. If there were only five horses in there, why chances were that there weren't any cavalry there." The squadron also experimented with an automatic camera, manufactured by the Gem Engineering Company of Philadelphia for the purpose of producing serial strips—excellent for mapping purposes.[38]

The Signal Corps witnessed no new breakthroughs in the area of communications as evidenced by its having to resort to carrier pigeons. The only telegraph line ran along railroad tracks but was controlled by the Carranza government and placed off limits to Americans. The corps laid hundreds of miles of so-called buzzer lines, but the noninsulated telegraph lines were unreliable under certain weather conditions. For good reason, the wire was often referred to as the "please don't rain wire." The widespread deployment of motor vehicles during the Punitive Expedition was just as revolutionary as the airplane. The Signal Corps experimented with radio-tractors—White Company trucks carrying wireless sets—but the mountains and dependence on French-made radio parts greatly undercut the receivers' effectiveness.[39]

Located at Pershing's headquarters and the rear supply base in Columbus, New Mexico, the primary mission of the radio-tractors was to transmit messages, but beginning in June, they also picked up communiqués emanating from Carranza forces that were quickly passed on to General Pershing. Messages revealed the locations of the Mexican government's soldiers so that Pershing could avoid them, particularly late in the campaign, when tensions flared between the two governments. Intercepted transmissions also provided insights as to where Mexican forces thought Pancho Villa was situated. Pershing reported that his staff "took up the study of code messages and soon was able to decipher any code used in Northern Mexico."[40] An overstatement, but coded messages between Mexican Secretary of War Alvaro Obregon and his generals were routinely broken. In addition, the Americans also began tapping telegraph wires to gain intelligence, but when Mexican officials learned of the practice, they lodged a formal protest to the US Department of State.

By the fall of 1916, a Mexican–American commission and the pending reelection of President Wilson neutralized the affair. The last of the US troops withdrew in February 1917 as the focus of the US public had shifted to events surrounding the war in Europe. Most histories label the Punitive

Expedition a failure because of its inability to bring Pancho Villa to justice. In his book, *Blood on the Border*, Clarence C. Clendenen arrives at a much different conclusion: "it should be sufficient to point out that the Villistas were surprised in every single encounter. The Punitive Expedition was not a single slow column plowing through the Mexican wilderness. Pershing's method of operation, rather, was a series of small, mobile forces that moved as fast as the Mexicans, or faster, and could live off the country for long periods of time."[41] Just months away from the US involvement in Europe's war, the US Army had benefited from the early shakedown, especially the National Guard units that had been mobilized. In addition, several important future leaders emerged—most notably, General Pershing, who was previously unknown to the US public. As far as intelligence was concerned, aviation would prove the big winner by making Congress aware of its need for much greater appropriations.

NOTES

1. Ralph H. Van Deman, *The Final Memoranda* (Wilmington: Scholarly Resources, 1988 [1949]), 3–4.
2. John P. Finnegan, *Military Intelligence* (Washington, DC: Center of Military History, 1998), 12.
3. Ibid., 13.
4. James Hewes, *From Root to McNamara* (Washington, DC: Center of Military History, 1975), 5–6.
5. Van Deman, *The Final Memoranda*, 23–24.
6. Finnegan, *Military Intelligence*, 16.
7. Van Deman, *The Final Memoranda*, 11–12.
8. Ibid., 21; Bruce W. Bidwell, *History of the Military Intelligence Division* (Department of Army, 1961), pt. I, chap. IX, 10.
9. Rebecca Robbins Raines, *Getting the Message Through* (Washington, DC: Center of Military History, 1996), 82–83.
10. Benjamin D. Foulois, *From the Wright Brothers to the Astronauts* (New York: McGraw-Hill, 1968), 60–65.
11. Ibid., 2.
12. Maurer Maurer, *The US Air Service in World War* (Washington, DC: Office of Air Force History, 1978), Vol. II, 19, 22.
13. Robbins Raines, 105, 126.
14. Ibid., 89.
15. James L. Gilbert, "US Army COMSEC in World War I," *Military Intelligence* 14 (1988): 24–25.
16. Chad Millman, *The Detonators* (New York: Little, Brown, 2006), 6.
17. Bidwell, *History of the Military Intelligence Division*, pt. I, chap. X, 183.

18. Karen Kovach, *The Life and Times of Dennis E. Nolan* (Fort Belvoir: US Army Intelligence and Security Command, 1998).

19. Marc B. Powe, "American Military Intelligence," *Military Review* (December 1975): 17–30; Michael E. Bigelow, "Van Deman," *Military Intelligence* (December 1990): 38–40.

20. John P. Finnegan, *Against the Specter of a Dragon* (Westport, CT: Greenwood, 1974), 50.

21. Van Deman, *The Final Memoranda*, 19–20.

22. Bidwell, *History of the Military Intelligence Division*, pt. I, chap. X, 19.

23. Ibid., 24–25.

24. Maurer, *The US Air Service in World War*, Vol. II, 55–57.

25. David Kahn, *The Codebreakers* (New York: Macmillan, 1967), 321–322.

26. Parker Hitt, *Manual for Solution of Military Ciphers* (Fort Leavenworth, KS: Press of the Army Service Schools, 1916); Kahn, *The Codebreakers*, 323.

27. Thomas J. Tunney, *Throttled!* (Boston: Small, Maynard, 1919), 151.

28. For his crime, Fay would spend less than a month in prison before he escaped, eventually making his way to Spain.

29. Jules Witcover, *Sabotage at Black Tom* (Chapel Hill, NC: Algonquin Books, 1989), 91.

30. Millman, *The Detonators*, 91–93.

31. Tunney, *Throttled!*, 8–9.

32. Frederick Katz, *The Secret War in Mexico* (Chicago: University of Chicago Press, 1981), 413.

33. Van Deman, *The Final Memoranda*, 19.

34. Clarence C. Clendenen, *Blood on the Border* (London: Macmillan, 1969), 332–333.

35. James A. Shannon, "With the Apache Scouts in Mexico," *Cavalry Journal* 27 (April 1917): 546.

36. Clendenen, *Blood on the Border*, 316.

37. Foulois, *From the Wright Brothers*, 134–135.

38. Clendenen, *Blood on the Border*, 319; Foulois, *From the Wright Brothers*, 134–135.

39. Robbins Raines, *Getting the Message Through*, 150.

40. David Hatch, "The Punitive Expedition," *Cryptologia* 31, no 1. (January 2007): 41.

41. Clendenen, *Blood on the Border*, 358.

2

America Enters the War

"I want to say—I cannot say too often—any man who carries a hyphen about him carries a dagger which he is ready to plunge into the vitals of the Republic. If I can catch a man with a hyphen in this great contest, I know I will have got an enemy of the Republic."

—President Woodrow Wilson

As war clouds darkened over America in early 1917, General Joseph E. Kuhn, president of the War College, opened discussions with the chief of the Militia Bureau regarding the possibility of National Guard officers receiving intelligence training. After due consideration, chief of staff General Hugh Scott authorized the sending of a confidential letter to the adjutants generals of all states, the Territory of Hawaii, and the District of Columbia instructing them to appoint intelligence officers. Time was allowed for many of these officers to receive nominal instructions so that they, along with those assigned similar duties within the six geographic departments, left the US Army with at least a token intelligence organization on the eve of America's entrance into the war.[1]

By February 1, the German admiralty reasoned that the launch of unrestricted submarine warfare should keep American goods and munitions from reaching Great Britain and eventually force the island nation out of the war altogether. In the interim, such action would bring the United States into the conflict, but the only thing the United States could offer immediately was its Navy, and Great Britain already controlled the seas, at least above the waterline. So by the time the United States could raise and train an army, the war would be over. Such thinking validated those in America who had long argued for preparedness. Had the United States possessed a sufficient number of divisions ready for immediate deployment, Germany most likely would not have been as quick to choose war. Two days later, President Woodrow Wilson responded to Germany's decision by severing diplomatic relations and announcing the arming of America's merchant ships.

The sinking of the Cunard liner *Laconia* along with an American steamer and three freighters in a month's time made war inevitable. To compound America's grievances, the White House received word from the British that it had decoded a diplomatic telegram from the German foreign secretary, Arthur Zimmermann, to his country's representative in Mexico. For more than a year, British cryptanalysts had labored within Room 40 inside the Old Admiralty Building in London to read the German-to-Mexico link; this had led to the breaking of a coded message that contained an enticement to the Mexican government to join in war against the United States, with the promise that it might reoccupy the lost territories of New Mexico, Texas, and Arizona. To add insult to injury, Germany had transmitted its diplomatic messages by using US diplomatic channels in Berlin or via a wireless station at Sayville, Long Island—a courtesy the White House had extended when hostilities first broke out in Europe. President Wilson's response to Germany came at 8:30 on the evening of April 2 when he delivered his war speech to Congress; only one phrase would be remembered: "The world must be made safe for democracy." Four days later, congressional members overwhelmingly passed a joint resolution declaring hostilities against the Central Powers.

Among the military intelligence personnel affected by the prospects of war were those attachés within nations belonging to the Central Powers (Germany, Austria–Hungary, and the Turkish Empire). In January, the War Department directed Captain Richard H. Williams, a coast artillery officer, to return home at once. Williams had been the only foreign attaché to be assigned to the Turkish Army during the ill-fated Gallipoli Campaign by the British; later he accompanied the Bulgarian and German armies in their offensive against the Rumanian–Russian forces. Consequently, the German government had no intention of letting Williams go so that he could use his knowledge against them in the forthcoming war. The Germans first required that he go back to the United States via Berlin, where for eight days Williams told of being subject to everything but an x-ray to ensure authorities that he carried no sensitive documents with him.[2]

German authorities finally granted Captain Williams permission to depart, but by this time it was the 11th hour and hostilities were now at hand. The Danish ship bearing Williams to Sweden had no more than left the harbor in Copenhagen when word was received that Germany and the United States were officially at war. German authorities immediately dispatched a ship to intercept the transport and take Williams into custody. Somehow, the US officer was able to elude the search party; from Sweden he traveled through Norway and Iceland before arriving back in the United States. Having evaded detention, Williams appropriately received from his friends the new nickname of "Houdini," after the famous escape artist.

MILITARY INTELLIGENCE SECTION

Following the declaration of war by the United States, the governments of Great Britain and France began sending delegations to the United States to coordinate its future role in the war. Among the first to arrive were Allied intelligence officers. Naturally, Army officials directed these representatives to the War College, where only courtesies were exchanged, as there was no active intelligence organization with which to hold talks. With the blessing of General Kuhn, Captain Ralph Van Deman went to see the chief of staff in person on several occasions in an attempt to persuade him of the necessity for a separate military intelligence department. Because America's new allies possessed extensive intelligence organizations, Van Deman reasoned that it was only logical that the US Army would want to follow suit; however, General Hugh L. Scott assumed the stance that should the Army need intelligence in the future, all that would be required was simply to ask the British and French for the desired information. Van Deman paraphrased Scott's thinking: "Here, we are now ready for service—we would be pleased if you hand over to us all the necessary information concerning the enemy which your intelligence services have obtained."[3] For good reason, General Scott had never been known as a visionary; former President William Howard Taft once describing the general's mental processes as "wooden to the middle of the head." However, Van Deman did not believe Scott's lack of appreciation of intelligence to be unique but one probably shared by a majority of US generals.

Besides turning a deaf ear, the chief of staff also specifically forbade Van Deman from approaching the secretary of war. Regardless of the consequences, Van Deman remained resolved to see the matter through, even if he had to use an envoy. The first person whom Van Deman confided in was "one of the best known and respected women novelists of the United States." Edith Wharton, author of such classics as *Ethan Frome* and *The Age of Innocence*, is the most likely candidate for the unnamed lady.[4] Wharton had been a longtime champion of the American Volunteer Ambulance Corps in France; more importantly, she had a friend in British intelligence and would have been fully aware of the crucial role it was playing in the war. Van Deman first met Wharton while escorting her on an inspection tour of nearby military installations at the request of Secretary of War Newton D. Baker. Wharton had undertaken similar visits to Allied camps at the behest of French generals during her frequent visits overseas. Understandably, Van Deman's new confidante expressed dismay that the US Army should lack an intelligence organization of its own and readily agreed to take up the matter with the secretary at the earliest possible opportunity. As insurance, Van Deman also availed himself of a second messenger—a longtime acquaintance—the superintendent of the district police, Raymond Pullman, who happened to eat breakfast every morning at the same club as Secretary Baker.

On April 30, the president of the War College received the anxiously awaited phone call ordering Captain Van Deman to report at once to the secretary of war. For the next half-hour, Van Deman described in as much detail as time allowed the role being played by Allied intelligence and the problem that the lack of an American counterpart posed. At the end of the briefing, Secretary Baker advised Van Deman that he should expect orders within 48 hours, assigning him the task of establishing an intelligence organization. This was somewhat out of character for Baker, as he tended not to interfere in military matters. On May 3, the Army War College responded to the secretary's directive by creating the Military Intelligence Section (MIS), which no longer would employ the term *information* but instead adopted the term *intelligence* in keeping with the British tradition. Its mission would be "the supervision and control of such system of military espionage and counterespionage as shall be established . . . during the continuation of the present war."[5] Not only would Van Deman be given the task of organizing the branch, but being the only person immediately available with any knowledge whatsoever of military intelligence organizations and their activities, he would also serve as its first head. Van Deman soon rose to the rank of colonel, but having crossed the chief of staff, he would witness his promotion to general officer temporarily scuttled.

Whether by design or accident, the War College, not the War Department, prepared the order that created the MIS. This would undercut the MIS's authority because it allowed Van Deman no direct access to the chief of staff and left the MIS without any leverage when dealing with other members of the staff, thus delaying responses for assistance and cooperation. Van Deman's immediate supervisors sympathized with the situation and attempted to redress the matter on several occasions—General Joseph Kuhn with General Scott and later Colonel P. D. Lockridge with Scott's replacement, Major General Tasker H. Bliss—each time without success. In his refusal to approve the recommended changes, Chief of Staff Bliss did serve notice that Van Deman should notify him of potential problem areas. Van Deman resolved to take full advantage of this offer. Among other things, he pointed out to the chief of staff that the MIS possessed no authority to implement security practices. For instance, the MIS staff had learned that certain suspicious persons were requesting copies of the "Army List and Directory," a monthly publication containing the name, rank, and address of every officer in the Army coupled with information on various organizations, their missions, and locations, but the adjutant general vigorously resisted MIS's recommendation that it suspend the issuing of the publication until the end of the war. In this particular instance, the opposition would become less and less defensible, and eventually, Major General Henry P. McCain, the adjutant general, acceded to MIS's wishes.

In setting up the MIS, Van Deman turned to Allied counterparts for their advice and assistance—in particular, Lieutenant Colonel C. E. Dancey of the British Military Mission. Subsequently, Van Deman chose to structure his organization after the British model because the French employed a separate civilian agency for portions of its counterintelligence mission; this coupled with the American Expeditionary Forces (AEF) having already selected the British system as their blueprint. As a starting place, Van Deman utilized the mission statement contained within the general order that organized the MIS; for the internal structure, he relied heavily on the British model, which called for the creation of functional subsections as needs arose and resources became available. Consequently, some missions existed in embryonic form within another section long before they became separate entities. For instance, military attachés played an important role from the beginning and contributed to various mission areas, but MI-5 (Military Attachés) would not officially come into existence until March 1918.

By the end of 1917, the MIS possessed the following structure: MI-1 Administration (Personnel and Office Management); MI-2 Collection and Dissemination of Foreign Intelligence; MI-3 Counterespionage (Military); MI-4 Counterespionage (Civilian Sector); and MI-8 Cable and Telegraph (Making and Breaking of Codes). During the course of the war, military intelligence used the French term *counterespionage* and a British term *negative intelligence* interchangeably to represent the discipline of counterintelligence, the craft of keeping one's secrets from foreign intelligence services.

The MIS began with only two enlisted soldiers and a handful of civilians—so small a staff that it was located in an office overlooking the War College library. Given permission to select his own assistants, Van Deman chose Captain Alexander Coxe, who had served with him in the Philippines and China, and Major A. P. Ahern, recently retired from the War College. Any success enjoyed by the MIS could in part be attributable to their administrative skills. At the height of its existence, the MIS would never have more than six regular officers assigned. This left the MIS hunting for individuals who possessed a specific area of expertise from the civilian sector, commissioning them in either the National Army or Officers Reserve Corps, and then permitting them to select their own staff; in this manner, they were more likely knowledgeable of others who were qualified in their respective field. Initially, most received commissions in the Signal Corps because there were numerous unused billets in its Aviation Section, but over time, the MIS turned to any and all branches that held available slots.[6]

This informal approach worked for the most part but occasionally had its glitches. For instance, when several new officers reported to the War Department—one a Rhodes scholar, the second a former embassy official, and the third a recognized world traveler—there was initial confusion on how to utilize such qualified individuals. Consequently, the receiving office temporarily put them to work filing documents. In time, someone in the chain of command suspected there might be a mistake, so he began checking around and soon discovered that Van Deman had been eagerly awaiting their arrival. In another instance, Van Deman personally chose the prominent New York attorney Nicholas Biddle to be in charge of his city's MIS office—a logical choice due to Biddle having served as special commissioner to the NYC Police Department. When his paperwork finally showed up at the War Department, none of the approving officials had an inkling why an applicant with his credentials would want to become an officer in the Signal Corps and nearly turned him down. It took the intervention by future Supreme Court Justice Felix Frankfurter, who happened to be working in the War Department and was Van Deman's close friend, to resolve the issue. Despite the occasional hiccup, nearly 300 officers were slowly but steadily added over the next year and half to the MIS staff. By the war's end, the MIS would secure the services of 1,200 civilians (excluding the personnel working at the MIS branch offices). Beside clerks and typists, the civilian force included investigators, a guard force, and various maintenance personnel. Budget-wise, the MIS received well over $1 million for expenditure in fiscal year 1918 alone.[7]

The need to obtain information from those already involved in the intelligence war was high on the agenda of the new MIS. Naturally, the MIS began with agencies that had similar missions, such as the domestic branch of the Office of Naval Intelligence and the Bureau of Investigation within the Justice Department, both with a piece of the counterintelligence pie. Eight years earlier, the attorney general had created the Bureau of Investigation to assist in the investigation of corruption and other violations of federal law, but in late 1916, he had assigned the agency several hundred additional agents to keep watch on German sympathizers. Consequently, upon declaration of war, the bureau moved quickly to arrest a number of the more militant suspects. The *Literary Digest* reported that during the last week of September 1917 alone some 90 persons were arrested or interned. On the other hand, the navy did not organize its domestic branch until May 1917, and like the MIS, would be starting from scratch. A third player with whom the MIS exchanged liaison officers from the beginning was the State Department, because it too shared a need for foreign intelligence. Besides conducting formal liaisons, MIS personnel soon began informal contacts at the working level.

As the need arose, MIS staff members established communications with various counterparts within the Departments of Justice, Treasury, Interior, and Commerce. Interestingly, the secretary of treasury specifically forbade his Secret Service, which protected the president, ferreted out counterfeiters, and exposed land fraud, from coordinating with the MIS. Despite the prohibition, the head of the Secret Service still acknowledged the requirement to be informally in touch. As the nation mobilized, the MIS soon added wartime agencies such as the Food Administration, Committee on Public Information, War Trade Board, War Industries Board, National Research Council, and Censorship Bureau to its list. The MIS also conferred with numerous Allied missions on the home front as well as intelligence agencies abroad on a case-by-case basis. By the war's end, the MIS had 21 officers who were devoted full time to liaison work and were routinely in touch with 16 Army staff elements and departments plus 28 other military and civilian agencies.

THE BIGGER PICTURE

The War Department was responsible for procuring and training the personnel to fill the intelligence officer positions at home and overseas. Unfortunately, the MIS lacked sufficient manpower as well as authority to select personnel on its own or even to determine the qualification guidelines. In July, the adjutant general directed departmental commanders to name 160 men to undergo officer training for intelligence assignments, using the following broad instructions to guide their selection process: "a young college instructor with language ability." As demonstrated in at least one case, it was fairly easy to circumvent the system. Asked if he knew French, a future intelligence officer later confessed that he had a ready reply, "Well, Sir, I made a great many trips to Paris and never had any difficulty getting around." Little did the approving officer suspect that this supposed "command of the French language consisted primarily in telling the taxi drivers to take me either to the railroad terminal at Gare du Nord or to the Moulin Rouge."[8]

One responsibility that the MIS did handle concerned the applications for the new Corps of Interpreters, which was established on July 4 with an initial allotment of 58 officers and 72 sergeants. Intelligence took over the recruitment process after the War Department had commissioned a handful of officers without proper screening. To test applicants, the MIS established an examination station in Washington, D.C., and convened local boards across the country. Over the course of the war, interpreters provided crucial language support to the AEF overseas, to the War Department staff, and within the various departments inside the continental United States, often working side by side with intelligence specialists.

When it came to the AEF general staff, Major Dennis E. Nolan confessed that he was taken back by General John J. Pershing's decision to name him intelligence chief, as he had not actively lobbied for a leadership post.

> Several days after Major James G. Harbord [recently appointed Pershing's chief of staff] had established his office in the State, War and Navy Building, he called me on the telephone and invited me to come to his house that night for dinner, specifying that he preferred that I come after dark in order that no one might know of my visit. When I arrived he informed me that I had been selected to head the Intelligence Section of the General Staff and that I should report to him in the morning to begin organizing my part of the expedition. I was surprised and delighted to go with Harbord as Chief of Staff for I had served with and under him for 4 years in the Philippine Constabulary.[9]

At the conclusion of the visit, the two officers raised a toast to the success of the AEF.

Nolan was quick to admit that he brought with him limited intelligence expertise. With only two weeks before he was to sail to France, Nolan attempted to use his time prudently by taking Van Deman's advice to consult Lieutenant Colonel C. E. Dancey from the British embassy. During the follow-on discussions, Nolan learned firsthand of the important role being played by military intelligence, as well as how to organize his new staff and make use of intelligence products; he later termed the information received from these early meetings with Dancey as being most helpful.

On May 28, Major Nolan prepared to set sail on the S.S. *Baltic* from New York harbor along with General Pershing and other members of his staff. The day itself was foggy, cold, and rainy, and the sendoff was anything but auspicious. According to one officer who witnessed his fellow passengers arriving in their less-than-up-to-date civilian clothes, "We looked more like a group of Methodist ministers from the Middle West going to a convention than we did like a group of General Staff officers about to organize the greatest expedition in which American soldiers ever took part."[10] To top it off, the officers had recently received their shots for typhoid, paratyphoid, and smallpox that made them feel even worse than they appeared. Plans called for the voyage to be a secret, but as a clerk of the White Star Line explained with a smile, "There's nothing confidential about this expedition."

Accompanying Nolan was a handful of officers assigned to intelligence. Due to the rush and lack of orders, a few of Nolan's officers were forced to pay their own way and were listed during the trip as war correspondents. Because he was the junior member of the General Staff, Nolan did not enjoy the luxury of selecting his own men, but rather received those unclaimed. As it turned out, most of his staff had done quite well in the General Service Schools, and a number of them were graduates of Harvard. The man whom Nolan termed a great find was Captain (soon to be colonel) Arthur L. Conger, a former instructor at Fort Leavenworth; he also enjoyed a broad academic background and had studied in Germany, spoke the language, and possessed a good understanding of its army. Conger held the distinction of being extremely knowledgeable of Civil War history, and on two separate occasions, had addressed the American Historical Society. It was Conger's reputation of being difficult to work with that had led other staff to pass him over. Fortunately, his temperament seemed to have been misjudged, because his fellow intelligence officers would in time find him to be quite agreeable.

Perhaps the most significant outcome from a brief stopover in London and the War Office was that Pershing and British Prime Minister David Lloyd George immediately took a disliking toward each other. Nolan also remembered how America's new Allies expressed surprise regarding the small size of the US delegation and kept asking where all the younger officers were. Eventually, Pershing and his party landed at the port of Boulogna sur Mer in France. Soon after, General Pershing officially let Washington know that he would conduct the war and that it was the job of the War Department to supply him. This demarcation would hold for the duration of the conflict. In a similar manner, there would be no initial attempt to join the efforts of the MIS with those of the AEF intelligence staff. Van Deman's emphasis would be on counterintelligence for the reason that it was impossible for the MIS to play an active role in directing intelligence gatherers an ocean away; this task would be left to Nolan. Over time, there would be a greater sharing of information, but for the immediate, Nolan and Van Deman each remained focused on his own Herculean task of creating a viable intelligence organization.

After studying the British and French armies, General Pershing chose what he called a "square" structure, with each division composed of two infantry brigades and each brigade having two regiments. (US divisions each had 979 officers and 27,082 enlisted men, more than twice the size of a British or French division.) To address information and security needs, he judiciously decided that intelligence staffs should be included down to the brigade level.

It was also fortuitous that the officer sent by the War College to prepare the actual "Tables of Organization" for all corps, divisions, brigades, regiments, and battalions was well versed in the requirements of military intelligence.

A COUNTERINTELLIGENCE PROBLEM

In the three months leading up to America's entry into war, the *Washington Post* alone ran over 30 stories concerning the threat of spies and saboteurs. Typical of the headlines were "Spy Stole Navy Code," "100,000 Spies in Country," "Justice Department Unable to Cope," "US Aviator Is Spy," and "Spy Plot Widespread." The *New York Tribune* wrote that "Spies are everywhere! They occupy hundreds of observation posts . . . they are in all the drug and chemical laboratories." Not surprisingly, when President Wilson asked Congress to declare a state of war, he mentioned the activities of German agents within the United States as part of his indictment. "From the outset of the present war [Germany] . . . has filled our unsuspecting communities and even our offices of government with spies and set criminal intrigues everywhere afoot against our national unity of counsel, our peace within and without, our industries and our commerce." Wilson went on to state that he believed German-born Americans to be loyal citizens, but "if there should be disloyalty, it will be dealt with a firm hand of stern repression." The president had set the tone for what would follow.

What America and Van Deman did not know was that the danger of Germany directing spies and saboteurs on America's home front had already suffered a devastating blow when diplomatic relations were severed and Ambassador Johann von Bernstorff and other officials were sent packing. Thus, he and his staff were no longer present to direct and fund the efforts of their agents. For this reason, the last major act of sabotage on American soil was the one that destroyed the Kingsland, New Jersey, plant on January 11—three months before the declaration of war. The early morning explosion at the Canadian-owned munitions plant killed 17 employees, set off over 500 shells destined for Russia, and caused an estimated $4 million worth of damage. The man responsible was Kurt A. Jahnke, a German saboteur who had previously teamed with Lothar Witzke to pull off several major acts of destruction in the United States.[11]

Although not confronted with a coordinated threat, Army counterintelligence still had a very real security challenge to deal with—one posed by pro-German individuals and groups, lone agents, and German intelligence, which still had hopes of launching a war of terror from nearby Mexico. Members of the new MIS staff were literally brought face to face with the potential threat in the summer of 1917 when authorities in Denmark intercepted a large shipment of weapons destined for use by saboteurs in the United States. The items consisted of dispatch cases, field glass cases, fountain pens, and imitation lumps of coal, all loaded with dynamite and equipped with fuses. Also in the haul was carborundum, a very hard abrasive used in sabotaging automobile and airplane engines. Upon removing the fuses, Danish authorities had promptly shipped the items off to Washington, D.C., and the MIS for further examination. For several days, Van Deman recalled feeling very uncomfortable while performing his day-to-day duties with enough explosives in his office "to blow that part of Washington into bits."[12]

DISTRICT OF COLUMBIA

Because of a lack of available resources, Van Deman did not begin waging the counterintelligence war indiscriminately but rather proceeded in concentric circles of priority—the first being Washington, D.C., where a series of events transpired in the early days to test the capabilities of his small office. Buildings that housed members of Army agencies possessed little physical security. For example, the State, War, and Navy Building had a front desk with guards but no means of discriminating between regulars and visitors. At other facilities, janitors pulled double duty as night watchmen. The security risk was real as evidenced by the story of a young officer who showed up at the Ordnance Department demanding a list of all the facilities in the western United States where high explosives were stored. Fortunately, the civilian in the office indicated that no files were releasable without the authority of the colonel who had requested the documents. Frustrated, the officer left without having secured the data. A follow-up call to the colonel revealed that not only had he not sought the documents in question, but also the name and description of the mystery officer failed to match anyone in his organization. Naturally, the War Department transferred the matter to MIS hands, which in turn alerted local and military police to cordon off the city to thwart the spy's escape, but the first case in which MIS members played spy catchers would end in failure. British intelligence later informed the MIS that decoded German messages revealed the sought-after information had been intended to aid a sabotage campaign being planned out of Mexico.[13]

In response to this incident, the MIS dressed its officers in civilian clothes and dispatched them to a number of buildings occupied by the War Department staff between the nighttime hours of 2200 and 0400. Here, they searched tabletops and unlocked desks for documents marked Confidential; upon discovering unsecured notes listing safe combinations, the night visitors proceeded to open the locked containers in search of more papers. The next morning, MIS staff called the various offices that were raided the night before, requesting the documents taken. When told that the papers in question were missing, the intelligence officers identified themselves, explained how they came by the documents, and promised their immediate return. The results of the exercise were subsequently briefed to the Army's leadership who quickly implemented MIS's recommendations for a guard system.

Next, the MIS took steps to increase security awareness surrounding the numerous clerks and typists employed by the Federal Civil Service. Daily, the federal government indiscriminately dispatched thousands of these employees to various government offices, where some of them worked with sensitive documents. None of the workers possessed a security clearance to handle such information, and no procedures were in place to ensure an office manager that the arriving clerks were who they claimed to be. Loyalty checks appeared out of the question, so the MIS did the next best thing by implementing a personal identification card with photograph. The counterintelligence staff of the MIS also established a system by which anyone observing a civilian engaging in suspicious behavior or questionable associations could report the incident for possible follow up.

Captain Harry A. Taylor, formerly of the Metropolitan Police of New York City, assumed charge of what became MI-3C. Intended at first to perform guard duties, it was quickly transformed into resolving the counterespionage problem within the District of Columbia, the capital being the nerve center for the war effort and logically a priority target of enemy spies. Personnel of MI-3C initially operated out of an office at 310 E Street, NW, under a sign designed to conceal its real purpose: "Personal Improvement Bureau." To fill MI-3C, Van Deman sent out a call for personnel with the necessary investigative skills; the vast majority coming from the New York City and Boston Police Departments or private detective agencies. The MIS furnished the new recruits with civilian clothes and lodging in a private house in the southeast part of the city; only their direct chain of command actually knew the names of all MI-3C members.[14]

Over the course of the war, the unit processed over 6,500 cases and conducted detailed loyalty investigations on some 900 War Department civilian employees. One of the MI-3C's most unusual assignments originated from the State Department, which wanted to know the intent of General Alvaro Obregon's visit to Washington, D.C., so Army agents conducted surveillance on the Mexican revolutionary leader. Looking back, Van Deman believed that this elite element (eventually totaling 5 officers, 41 enlisted and civilian agents, 4 clerks, and 16 enlisted men) was the true forerunner of the Army's famed Counter Intelligence Corps of World War II and the Cold War.[15]

Among the civilians was Anna W. Keichline from Bellefonte, Pennsylvania; an architect by profession, she would have the distinction of being the first woman agent.[16]

CORPS OF INTELLIGENCE POLICE

While addressing the counterintelligence threat on the home front, Van Deman received a request to help recruit the necessary personnel to solve the security problem facing the AEF. After his arrival in France, Colonel Dennis E. Nolan had become apprehensive about the possible dangers that US troops were to face from enemy agents. It was a concern shared by his fellow Allied intelligence officers, so in early July 1917, he wrote the adjutant general requesting that "fifty secret service who have had training in police work [and] speak French fluently" be provided. (Actually, the numbers included 25 who could speak French and 25 who could speak both French and German.) He also added that it was essential that they be men of high character and with courage and unquestioned probity. This called for a category of intelligence personnel not previously anticipated, but in August, authorization was approved, creating a 50-man Corps of Intelligence Police (CIP) that consisted of enlisted soldiers who would serve with the rank, pay, and allowances of sergeants of infantry. Soon a six-week probationary period was established before a new recruit could actually acquire the rank of sergeant. Nolan also requested officers to serve in various counterintelligence roles, but for these, no special recruitment was undertaken. Instead, they would be filled from the larger intelligence officer pool.

Colonel Van Deman immediately ran into difficulty in his quest for qualified CIP candidates. Private detective offices seemed as good a place as any to begin the search, but when informed of the Army's requirement for honest French-speaking investigators, the head of the well-known Pinkerton Detective Agency quickly dismissed the idea, "There ain't no such animal."[17] Eventually, the War Department dispatched a junior officer to New Orleans and New York City where he placed advertisements in the local papers. The lieutenant signed up all personnel who could pass the Army physical and answer a few simple questions in French and then promptly shipped them off to Fort Jay on Governors Island in New York harbor for a month's training as infantrymen.

Here, the Army outfitted the new recruits with distinctive green-corded campaign hats and collar brass marked "IP" for Intelligence Police. On an occasion, the green hat bands would provoke a hostile response on the part of some military policemen who harbored anti-Irish feelings. Each soldier would undergo target practice with a .38 caliber revolver and a day of judo. The only things they lacked before sailing for France were the actual tools needed to perform their mission: intelligence skills and civilian clothes. One positive outcome of this initial shakedown was the discovery and dismissal of a suspected radical within the ranks—the soldier having previously served time for his role in a violent demonstration against the capitalist John D. Rockefeller.[18]

COUNTER-SUBVERSION

To raise the necessary human resources to fight the war, Congress had enacted the Selective Service Act on May 18, 1917, creating the draft that swept up US citizens and resident foreign nationals alike, including those from enemy countries. Of every 100 men who served, 77 were in the National Army, 10 in the National Guard, and 13 in the regular Army. Twenty-four million men would eventually register, and over the course of the war, 3 million would actually become members of the armed forces. As one of its first assignments, the MIS researched the attrition rate of French and British officers who were wounded or killed; in this manner US authorities could estimate how large a replacement pool was needed.

Nearly 13 percent of the first 1917 draft (1,243,801) were aliens of some sort. In response to reports and rumors of possible acts of disloyalty, the adjutant general ordered that all organizations confidentially report the names of German nationals and those of Germany's allies, and that company commanders be given primary responsibility for alerting authorities regarding the presence of enemy sympathizers, but not all enemy aliens were given the same priority. Because the immediate focus was on the number of Germans registering for the draft, it took another six to seven months before the federal government could identify Austrians, Hungarians, Turks, and Bulgarians.

These figures influenced Van Deman's thinking that the number-one counterintelligence threat was internal, and he made sure that the threat was spelled out in the counterintelligence manual: "Enemy agents are in the military service, not only in the ranks, but in our offices, arsenals and munitions plants."[19] It went on to say that the National Guard and the National Army were particularly vulnerable, and indicated that the enemy's goal was to plant an agent in each regiment. If there was further need for justifying a strong counterintelligence effort, the Allies themselves were voicing concern about receiving US troops on French soil without some guarantee that no Central Power spies were within their ranks. The British even took the initiative of sending Lieutenant Colonel H. Pakenham to Washington to assist the MIS on this and other counterintelligence matters; the French followed suit with the appointment of Lieutenant M. Bourgeois.

General Marlborough Churchill, Van Deman's successor, later elaborated on the rationale that drove the MIS to create MI-3, whose mission was to conduct counterespionage within the Army: "neither the Department of Justice nor the Secret Service of the Treasury was adequate to do all the investigation required." He further expressed the belief that investigating members of the military was repugnant to most in the service, but if required, "we want it done by agencies under our own control, and not by unsympathetic civilian bureaus."[20] This was a viewpoint undoubtedly shared by the Army leadership if not publicly voiced.

In October, Van Deman initiated phase two of his counterespionage strategy by ordering all intelligence officers just assigned to newly activated divisions to travel surreptitiously to Washington, D.C. Here, Van Deman proceeded to lay out his plan for keeping America's Army safe by providing each officer with instructions on how to establish a covert surveillance plan within his division down to the company level. An assistant to the division intelligence officer would actually oversee the pyramid surveillance system, which began with recruiting two operatives called "silent watchers" unknown to each other within each company. Their responsibility was to observe any suspicious behavior on the part of their fellow soldiers and to report all findings to the next higher echelon. Division intelligence was then to consolidate all reports and forward them to MI-3B. To assist the officers in the field, the MIS issued a publication titled "Instructions for the Organization and Maintenance of the Counterespionage Service within Military Units," which spelled out in detail how to classify suspects. Van Deman later extended the program to regular Army divisions and military posts and installations.

As the system began to churn out names that required follow-up investigations, it soon overwhelmed the existing MIS resources. To supplement the efforts of his overworked officers, Van Deman hired civilians and recruited volunteers. Although civilian investigators remained an important part of the force, it became increasingly difficult to find competent persons willing to work for $4 a day plus expenses. In November, he requested that the Army provide 250 enlisted soldiers of the Corps of Intelligence Police to assist the MIS in its counterespionage campaign. Fortunately, the draft had swept many former insurance agents, lawyers, and teachers into the Army, who would have been ideal for performing background checks. An unforeseen consequence was that many of the MIS civilian investigators would choose to exchange their suits for CIP sergeant uniforms.

Although the actual figures are a best guess, MI-3B claimed responsibility for handling more than 10,000 such investigations during the course of the war, but many of the cases would undergo only superficial review before being returned to the originating unit for final disposition: discharged, internment, commission withheld, court-martialed, or case dismissed for lack of evidence. The only action ever taken against regular Army officers was to have them reassigned to isolated posts where their opportunities for mischief might be reduced to a minimum. Someone being stationed in the middle of Alaska was considered just as neutralized as someone being held in the disciplinary barracks at Fort Leavenworth.[21]

The MI-3B subsection also assumed responsibility for men whom the AEF shipped to the United States due to suspected disloyalty or negative influence on fellow soldiers. One conscripted division alone sent 800 malcontents back. Once back in the United States, the soldiers faced actions that ranged from continued observation to early discharge under presidential authority, but it would take nearly five months before military intelligence could correct major flaws in the process—the transfer of a soldier back home without an intelligence representative ever having reviewed the case and minus sufficient records for MI-3B to conclude the investigation.

One of the individuals returned was a soldier named Baron von Schrack, once an officer in a crack German regiment. Hard times had forced him into the spying business and an assignment to England. For personal reasons he deserted and departed for America, where he eventually took on an assumed name and became a sergeant in the cavalry. A follow-up investigation found that von Schrack was indeed telling the truth, so the onetime German lieutenant was commissioned as a captain in US military intelligence—the ideal assignment for a soldier with his unique skills and background.[22]

THE CIVILIAN SECTOR

From the beginning, the Wilson administration saw the nation's involvement in the war as affecting every segment of the population. Consequently, President Wilson, aided by his supporters in Congress, enacted a body of emergency wartime legislation calculated to manage the threat on the home front as well as any opposition. In the president's words, "It is not an army that we must shape and train for war. It is a nation." The Espionage Act of June 15, 1917, defined punishments for those who willfully interfered with the war effort, caused dissension in the armed services, or obstructed recruitment. Eleven months later, Congress added the Sedition Act, which made it illegal to utter, write, or publish any disloyal, profane, scurrilous, or abusive language intended to cause contempt for the Constitution, the flag, or uniform of the armed forces and to curtail the production of war materials. Over time, the government would prosecute some 1,500 people under these acts. These sweeping pieces of legislation also encouraged Van Deman to begin to address security threats within the civilian sector that directly or indirectly impacted the Army's ability to fulfill its mission.

By November, Van Deman launched the final stage of his counterintelligence plan—MI-4 (Counterespionage among Civilian Population) under the leadership of Major Herbert Parsons. Its mission was to trace the actions of enemy agents and the activities of disloyal civilians within in the continental United States and overseas, but MIS personnel possessed no arrest powers and would be very dependent on the Department of Justice. In the end, MI-4's operations often proved to be as vague and indeterminate as its mission statement, and its functions varied greatly depending on the place and time. MI-4 documents summed it up this way, "problems arose, threatened and vanished, and expediency necessarily overruled precision."[23]

MI-4B was by far the most important subsection because it oversaw various counterintelligence branches established across the United States, and it was among the branch offices that almost all CIP investigators were ultimately assigned. The so-called branches consisted initially of the following: New York City, Philadelphia, Pittsburgh, Chicago, St. Louis, New Orleans, Hoboken (New Jersey), Salt Lake City, San Francisco, Los Angeles, and San Juan (Puerto Rico)—each representing a major city or point of embarkation. The New York City branch began with 23 former members of the metropolitan police department's Neutrality and Bomb Squad, and would eventually have twice the manpower as the next city. In his book *Throttled!*, Thomas Tunney noted that because many of the key personnel of the local military intelligence branch had previously worked for the police, it "made possible a degree of cooperation in spy-hunting in New York which would have been impossible to develop within a short time."[24] The New York City branch, with headquarters at 302 Broadway, divided itself by the type of investigation (graft and espionage); by organization with which it conducted liaison (port control, Red Cross, American Protective League, etc.); by groups requiring monitoring (socialists, Industrial Workers of the World, Bolsheviks, etc.); and finally by geographic area covered.

New York City was by far the busiest of the field branches; for one reason, Germans, at the turn of the century, comprised one of the city's largest groups of immigrants. Over the course of the war, the New York City branch claimed responsibility for 400 arrests, including acquisition of a former spy who had escaped from a British prison and turned to impersonating an officer of his Majesty's Light Horse Brigade; then there was the case of shutting down an antiwar printing operation run by Bolsheviks. The New York City branch's first espionage case involved a small exporter in Brooklyn who, as part of his business, routinely sent telegrams to Amsterdam. Upon closer examination, it was discovered that the dates and quantities of goods ordered corresponded remarkably with the sailing times of various transports.

The investigation that posed the greatest threat to homeland security involved a bomb plot that stretched from New York City to San Francisco. Over the course of the war, the Germans called for the independence of India from Great Britain and had constituted the Indian National Committee in Berlin—all to help stir the anti-British sentiment. To German intelligence, the United States seemed an ideal place to foment such unrest, as it was home to many who had recently migrated from India to seek a new life. Members of the New York City Police Department Bomb Squad were the first to become engaged in tracking a radical Hindu group living in America; when many of these same policemen later transferred to the MIS, they received permission to see the investigation to its successful conclusion. The Hindus regularly communicated to Berlin for funds, often by using a simple substitution code; on other occasions, they employed a code that referenced a word in a book by using the number of the page—potentially much more difficult to break. Fortunately, they chose a small German–English dictionary, which was widely sold, so Army cryptanalysts were able to crack the code with ease. These messages would eventually lead to intercepting and searching a ship bearing weapons destined for Indian revolutionaries in America. The end result was the conviction of 135 Hindus for violation of the Neutrality Act; coinciding with the investigation, officials exposed an elaborate scheme that was funded by Germany to promote uprisings in British colonies throughout the world.[25]

Army counterintelligence also viewed Philadelphia as a prime target for enemy agents because it covered a portion of New Jersey and Delaware where munitions were being manufactured; to perform its mission, the Philadelphia branch had personnel permanently assigned to 13 smaller cities within its tri-state jurisdiction. Among the branch's case files was an incident involving bombs set off at the homes of prominent Philadelphia citizens by a group calling themselves "the American Anarchists." However, such acts of terror were the exception. More often, cases involved events that in retrospect seemed to pose little real danger or to possess any relevancy to the war effort. For instance, a William A. Robinson, who was living within his stepfather's country of Germany, elected not to return home upon declaration of war but instead began working for the German Red Cross. He immediately fell under suspicion when intercepted correspondence revealed that he was using every means available to obtain money from an estate being held by the Commercial Trust Company of Philadelphia. Finally, there was the case of the Pocket Testament League, which benignly distributed New Testaments to US troops. In the process, members of the league wrote on a card each soldier's name, unit, and church preference; the card was then passed on to his denomination so it could continue to correspond with the serviceman. When confronted by the MIS that the accumulated data posed a risk, league officials agreed to destroy their files under the watchful eyes of government officials.

All field branches would eventually fall under the organizational umbrella of the intelligence staff belonging to one of the Army's six departments. In the continental United States alone, there would be more than 500 individual offices, varying greatly in size depending on their mission; for instance, there were the lone intelligence officers assigned to censorship offices, Army camps, and disciplinary barracks. Near the end of the war, the six departments grew to nine when the Army separated the Eastern Department into three parts and added the Panama Canal Zone.

Within each of the departments, the leadership gave priority to the larger security issues unique to its particular region. In his *History of Military Intelligence Division*, Bruce W. Bidwell spells out the different types of threats. The Eastern and Northeastern Departments focused on enemy aliens and foreign radical groups such as the Sinn Fein; the Central Department monitored the activities of various pro-German societies and individuals; and the Southern Department, which included Texas, naturally paid foremost attention to potential enemy agents crossing the border with Mexico. The Southeastern Department kept an eye on the reaction of blacks to the war effort.

The black community was among the groups meriting special attention by MIS early in the war because African Americans were divided on what exactly their involvement should be. Furthermore, the nation's leadership was concerned over the recent outbreak of several major riots, including one in East St. Louis that had killed 46 citizens. To confirm whether or not actual threats existed that might disrupt the war effort, the MIS chose two extremely capable African American servicemen to travel separately throughout the country, mostly in the north. Stateside, undercover counterintelligence agents normally received a monthly allowance of only $55 plus service pay—far from enough to cover day-to-day expenses. The two soldiers reported a handful of instances concerning pro-German groups attempting to exploit existing discontent, but there was no evidence of direct German involvement. The MIS representatives were also responsible for countering any antiwar propaganda messages through one-on-one conversations and by speaking at various public and church meetings. In his *The Final Memoranda*, Van Deman acknowledged the fine job they had performed and was apologetic for the lack of formal recognition.[26]

In the Western Department, labor unrest was the Army's number-one subject of interest, giving special attention to the activities of potentially violent groups, such as the radical Industrial Workers of the World (IWW).

To assist them, the regional MIS had a thousand-member Volunteer Intelligence Corps, composed of civilians who possessed their own badges and credentials. In one instance, Army counterintelligence infiltrated the IWW by using one of its agents disguised as a laborer; over time the undercover operator was able to gain access to some of the inner councils. During the coming months, the Army worked closely with the Justice Department, which would eventually prosecute more than 100 members of the labor movement.

THE ADVENT OF YARDLEY

In an extremely shortsighted use of its personnel, the Army did not assign its most accomplished cryptologists, Captain Parker Hitt and Major Joseph Mauborgne, to positions where their unique skills could be utilized. Like Hitt, Major Mauborgne had prepared a number of insightful articles on code breaking, including solving the British Playfair field cipher. Ironically, both officers would conceive of cipher devices that, if they had been developed, could have greatly aided in securing US combat communications.

At the outbreak of hostilities, the War Department received numerous letters from amateur cryptologists offering their services. One came from a George Fabyan, who would present the Army with a unique opportunity. Fabyan was an eccentric philanthropist who had established a think-tank called Riverbank in Geneva, Illinois, just west of Chicago. Among his odd mannerisms was the suspending of furniture from the ceiling by chains and purchasing unclaimed freight and luggage that he proceeded to examine with a childlike curiosity. Fabyan's eclectic interests were also reflected in the facilities of Riverbank itself, a working farm but with a tea garden, zoo, and Dutch windmill. Riverbank served as a home to scholars who received free rein to study a variety of Fabyan's pet subjects, among them cryptology, because Fabyan believed that a code was contained in Shakespeare's plays that would reveal who the real author was. There is little evidence that anyone on his staff actually shared Fabyan's theory, but Riverbank opened up for several of them a completely new world of codes and ciphers to which they would eventually dedicate their lives. Riverbank cryptologists included William F. Friedman, who was Russian by birth and a graduate of Cornell University where he had studied genetics; his wife, Elizebeth Smith Friedman, was a student of literature; and J. A. Powell, former director of the University of Chicago Press.[27] On behest of the Signal Corps, Major Mauborgne journeyed to Riverbank to witness Fabyan's operations firsthand; following his visit, Mauborgne quickly wrote back to the War Department that it should take immediate advantage of Fabyan's offer to decipher captured messages.

But all the plans for Riverbank proved premature and did not factor in the arrival of 28-year-old Herbert O. Yardley. Born in a small town in Indiana, Yardley followed in the footsteps of his father, a railroad telegraph operator, and moved to Washington, D.C., in 1912 to work for the State Department as a clerk and telegrapher in its code room. Yardley had demonstrated from an early age that he was too bright and too ambitious to remain in his current position forever. While on night shifts with little to do, he busied himself by studying how the department's codes were constructed, among them a 500-word message between President Wilson and his closest advisor and confident Colonel (honorary) Edward M. House. Finding US codes too simple, he turned next to more challenging foreign samples: "I knew most of the telegraph operators in Washington, and got some of them to steal a few coded diplomatic messages of various governments; these I practiced on."[28] Each success reinforced in Yardley's mind the obvious—he was gifted and he had found his calling as a cryptologist. His first major accomplishment was to prepare a 100-page paper that would lead the State Department to adopt a new method of encoding its messages.

With the announcement of war, Yardley took his crusade for greater utilization of cryptology to the War Department and eventually found himself face-to-face with Van Deman. Although Yardley remembered the small office and staff as being anything but impressive, he was in awe of Van Deman, whom he described as being Lincoln-like in appearance with a "heavy-lined face" and "deep eyes." Yardley proceeded to remind Van Deman that all of Europe's Great Powers possessed large and established staffs to read foreign codes and that "it was immaterial to America whether I or someone else formed such a bureau, but such a bureau must begin to function, and at once. . . . How except by reading the secret messages of foreign governments was she to learn the truth?" Yardley concluded by arguing that the German army was using wireless transmissions in code to direct the movement of their ground forces. "These messages must be intercepted. Who would attempt to solve them? General Pershing would demand a cryptographic service in France. Who would train cryptographers for this venture?" Van Deman responded to the questions by saying that he liked Yardley's confidence well enough but not his age. However, in the end Van Deman set aside any misgivings and told Yardley to report for duty on Monday morning.[29]

While establishing the American Cryptographic Bureau, Captain Yardley sought knowledgeable personnel to staff the effort.[30] Yardley first called on the Allies to send help but received only silence in return. His next step proved a crucial one—the offering of a commission to John M. Manly, a quiet-spoken scholar, who headed the English Department at the University of Chicago, and was destined to become a leading authority on Chaucer.

Regarded as an expert on literary ciphers, Manly had also routinely corresponded with the Riverbank staff. As a rule, Yardley, who had only briefly
attended college, looked down on academics because in his thinking many of
them did not possess the unique gift of "cipher brains." Regardless, Manly
would soon become Yardley's closest associate and would bring along former colleagues and university staff who helped to fill out the cryptologic
organization.[31] Yardley initially planned to divide the effort. In this arrangement, he was to attack enemy codes while Manly focused on ciphers. (Codes
were groups of letters and numbers that represented words or terms; ciphers
usually substituted letters for an equal amount of plain text.)

America had no more than entered the conflict when the War Department learned it had far more to worry about than the threat posed by spies
and sabotage. The British informed the assistant secretary of state that the
confidential communications being transmitted to Europe and General Pershing lacked protection. The Germans were reading the United States mail by
laying induction wires several hundred feet alongside the transatlantic cable
so that telegraph operators onboard U-boats could copy the messages; this
was probably why the Germans decided not to sever the cables.[32] A Signal
Corps officer would confirm the Allies' suspicions by duplicating the German system. The Germans also possessed a photographed copy of the War
Department's telegraph codebook. Apparently, one had been lost or stolen in
1916 during the Punitive Expedition to Mexico, but it was a moot point due
to the code being subject to cryptanalytic attack anyway.

Instead of turning to the Signal Corps for answers, the War Department
handed the problem off to its newest member—the Military Intelligence
Service—to solve. Perhaps the culmination of these daily challenges was
the reason that someone described Van Deman as looking "old and terribly
tired," but in this particular instance, Van Deman could turn to Yardley to
provide the answer. In response to the problem, Yardley brought on board a
former member of the State Department's code room—Altus E. Prince—and
provided him with 10 clerks. The subsection quickly set out to prepare codes,
ciphers, and tables for use in safeguarding communications between the War
Department and the American Expeditionary Forces in France. It would take
almost a year before Prince could actually produce altogether new codebooks,
but in the interim, his staff created replacement tables every two weeks for the
existing Telegraph Code of 1915 to secure the sending of secret messages.
One of the unexpected consequences of the American Cryptographic Bureau
assuming this mission was that at least on the home front, the Signal Corps
had relinquished its traditional role of making and breaking codes.[33]

Security concerns led Yardley to establish a separate communications
center for sensitive mail instead of using the facilities of the adjutant general.

Open 24 hours, the center transmitted nearly 100 messages over the course of an average day, and the center possessed the capacity of dispatching messages to Paris within 30 minutes. More importantly, this process ensured the careful handling of all classified information; during one nine-month stretch, 25,000 messages were sent and received, half plain and half code. Special emphasis was placed on highly sensitive communiqués prepared by the Department of Ordnance and transmittals directed to bureaus overseas, to 40 military attachés worldwide, and to hundreds of intelligence officers scattered across the continental United States.[34]

Although Riverbank failed to become the great code-breaking agency originally anticipated, its resources and facilities did provide the Army with an immediate answer for training cryptologic officers. As a first step, Riverbank dispatched Powell to the Signal Corps School to learn what was presently being taught on the subject. By October, Riverbank had created a curriculum for a two-month course. Besides offering instruction, Riverbank began to prepare professional pamphlets on various aspects of cryptology; the studies reflected a scholarly approach to the subject. Publications, such as *A Method of Reconstructing the Primary Alphabet from a Single One of the Series of Secondary Alphabets*, did not impress Yardley, who was quick to point out that his staff had already exceeded such work. Yardley even commented that he believed one of the documents was a deliberate steal. These types of remarks reflected a growing tension behind the scenes between Yardley, who desired complete control of the cryptologic mission, and Fabyan, who continued to demand a visible role.[35]

Yardley soon became a court of last resort; mysteries that defied solution elsewhere within the MIS made their way to his desk. Perhaps the most bizarre case involved a dead carrier pigeon delivered by a member of the Department of Justice who wanted to know if its perforated feathers carried a hidden message; but it did not take Yardley long to determine that lice, not enemy agents, were the real culprits. A second more credible challenge came from the Department of Justice with an attached note that concerned a message intercepted from a German prisoner at an Army base. Yardley quickly recognized it for what it was—shorthand—but at the time, over a hundred different styles were being practiced throughout the world. He immediately left for the Library of Congress where he learned that the most commonly used system in Germany was the Gabelsberger; librarians also produced a 20-year-old magazine article on the subject that included testimonies from various individuals living in America who had studied the shorthand system in question. In a stroke of good fortune, several of the people listed just happened to reside in Washington, D.C., and one worked for the library itself. That same night, Yardley and the acquired expert burned the midnight oil to translate the message that revealed the prisoner's escape plan. Because the shorthand expert was himself a German American, Yardley took the added precaution of having a copy sent to another expert in New York for a second transcription.[36]

Word quickly spread to the Department of Justice and various censorship offices to send all letters in shorthand to Yardley's organization. As a result, a completely new subsection was formed along with enough experts to read over 30 different styles. Placed in charge of the operation, Franklin W. Allen, a partner in a prestigious law firm in Manhattan, freely donated his services and generously dipped into his own pocket to pay for supplies; furthermore, the shorthand operation was run out of his former law office. Besides reading messages, Allen's staff assembled a bibliography on shorthand systems as well as created a list of specialists living in America who could decipher numerous rare foreign systems. When some of the shorthand documents turned out to be simply Yiddish or Arabic, the staff turned these over to translators assigned to the MIS. When no specialist was available to solve a particular style of shorthand, Allen and his assistants attacked the problem as if it were a cryptogram. Finally, the section was responsible for training 15 shorthand specialists for the AEF, where they would be given the assignment of transcribing interrogations of high-ranking prisoners of war.

Not all cases that came Yardley's way were as easily solved as shorthand. For instance, an individual who had been a reluctant recruit by German intelligence entered the United States to spy but instead turned himself in. Having brought with him shoestrings and handkerchiefs impregnated with a secret ink, he eventually wound up in the office of the MIS and ultimately at Yardley's desk. Unfortunately, there was no one who could discover the reagent needed to expose the hidden ink, not even America's preeminent chemist and its first Nobel Prize winner in the field, Theodore W. Richards of Harvard.

A second opportunity at deciphering hidden writing soon presented itself. A search of a woman suspect who was caught while crossing the Mexican–US border revealed what appeared to be a blank piece of paper hidden in her shoe. When he received the note, Yardley immediately suspected that it contained some type of secret ink, and he surmised that given the background of the individual and the place where authorities apprehended her, a chemical reagent might not be necessary. Yardley called for a chemist from the National Research Council to supply any available equipment that could apply heat to paper. Using this makeshift laboratory set up in the basement, Yardley's people were quickly able to read the message written in Greek and intended for German agents. It also marked the beginning of another subsection—secret inks. By December, the American Cryptographic Bureau no longer seemed an appropriate designation for an element involved in such matters as shorthand and secret inks so the MIS changed the name to MI-8.[37]

Yardley used the outcome of this one secret-ink case to improve the capabilities of his new subsection. By attaching Van Deman's signature to a cable, Yardley placed a request to Great Britain for professional assistance. Stanley W. Collins, England's foremost ink expert, soon arrived in the United States for the purpose of instructing Americans in the hither-to unknown world of secret writing. Unfortunately, MI-8 was only able to acquire the services of a couple of qualified chemists and would be forced to depend mostly on motivated novices as trainees. During his first lecture, Collins made it clear that German chemists had rightly earned their reputation as the world's best, and that it was not just the secret inks themselves, but the sophisticated manner in which German intelligence used them, that would present the greater challenge.

REPORTS AND MORE REPORTS

The MIS began to publish daily and weekly intelligence summaries for the chief of staff. From the beginning, the scope of the subject matter went far beyond military subjects to include an ambitious agenda—economic, agricultural, industrial, and social—all naturally weighted to events on the home front or within Mexico. Early editions contained articles on antiwar speakers at farm cooperatives in the Midwest, the presence of IWW laborers in the oil fields, German sympathizers within the Pierce-Arrow Motor Company, and the existence of various socialist groups and their propaganda efforts. Eventually, the number of sources for articles included the AEF, Office of Naval Intelligence, and State and Justice Departments. For foreign news, the summaries were dependent on attachés but also frequently drew from newspaper clippings (foreign and domestic) as well as handouts from the Allies.

The arrival of officers with journalistic and academic backgrounds soon dramatically improved the overall tenor and substance of the documents by furnishing insights not typically found in newspapers. Commenting on antiwar literature found within the black community, the editor offered the following explanation: "The Negroes at large, even among the better educated, are beginning to doubt whether their loyalty will be repaid, or whether they should not seize the opportunity offered, when the mass of our troops are engaged in a foreign war, to strike a blow for the full recognition of their rights."[38] On other occasions, writers referred readers to professional papers on a subject if they desired more information and perspective; for instance, to understand the background on Britain's role in Ireland, the editor referred readers to the historical works of James Anthony Froude and Goldwin Smith. Finally, the summaries contained informative pieces during the early months on the ability of the German government to wage war, and in the fall, on events surrounding the Russian Revolution.

By December, Van Deman had turned the function of writing and publishing these intelligence summaries as well as other publications, such as the "Current Estimate of the Strategic Situation," over to the newly established MI-2. However, the subdividing of the collection effort among economic, political, and combat elements failed to achieve the level of efficiency originally anticipated, and there remained much duplication of effort and mission overlap. The economic subsection studied food, raw materials, manpower, transportation, communications, finance, and munitions for both belligerent and neutral nations alike. No subject seemed too insignificant—from the impact of boll weevils on the price of cotton to an assassination of a South American dictator on the cost of coffee. The combat subsection was centered on matters related to Mexico due to the possible threat of war with America's southern neighbor. The political subsection, led by Major John Foster Dulles who would later serve as President Dwight D. Eisenhower's secretary of state, prepared reports on various nations and their current power structure. To acquire the needed information, Dulles and his eight subordinates routinely remained in constant touch with over 20 US agencies.[39]

Perhaps the most carefully guarded room in Washington, D.C., was the map room of MI-2, whose walls were covered with situation maps on a variety of subjects—economic, geographic, and political as well as the various fronts where fighting occurred. The MI-2 staff also maintained maps within the War Department, House of Representatives, Army War College, and the District of Columbia Main Post Office. Finally, MI-2 responded to requests for information by creating a separate military monograph subsection, which churned out hundreds of short studies on a wide number of subjects. For instance, it prepared a monograph on aircraft facilities being used by the French Air Service that served as a helpful guide for Army planners tasked with determining future construction needs.

CENSORSHIP

The Army was already involved in censorship a year before the United States entered the war. In June 1916, while US troops fought in the Punitive Expedition in Mexico, General Scott had ordered the creation of a Bureau of Information to prevent the spread of false stories detrimental to US military interests and placed Major Douglas MacArthur as head of the agency. America's entrance into World War I would witness the rapid expansion of censorship throughout society on a scale never before envisioned. In April 1917, President Wilson signed an executive order creating the Committee on Public Information. A second order assigned the secretary of navy responsibility for monitoring all transoceanic cables and the secretary of war for all land-based telegraph and telephone lines leading outside the country. Acting on these instructions, the Army immediately established a string of telegraph control stations along the southwestern border with Mexico. Sites included Brownsville, Laredo, Eagle Pass, San Antonio, El Paso, Deming, Nogales, and San Diego, but the number of lines to be covered, lack of trained personnel, paucity of proper equipment, and absence of coordination among the eight stations doomed the effort from the start. With Canada as an ally, the United States did not feel the same necessity to monitor communications on its northern boundaries.[40]

In the beginning, censorship duties within the Army were scattered among the various staff heads and agencies, but the MIS bore the lion's share. MI-4 ensured that any pamphlet handed out to troops did not promote sedition; it also screened speeches delivered before troops by nonmilitary lecturers. In addition, the staff informed postal censors as to what subjects the War Department were interested in monitoring and then followed up with reports to the Army leadership concerning the corrective steps taken.[41] Military intelligence also assumed responsibility for censoring mail sent by prisoners of war (mostly members of the Germany navy) and internees held in the United States and subsequently attached officers to the war prison barracks at Fort Douglas, Utah, and Forts McPherson and Oglethorpe in Georgia. Army counterintelligence types assigned to the camps were credited with discovering valuable information on a group calling itself "the League of German Engineers" regarding its plans to interrupt the shipment of goods from South American countries. In another instance, intelligence learned the location of two escaped prisoners by reading their former cellmates' letters. Later, the War Department would assign the MIS responsibility for reviewing missives sent home by America's own servicemen who were held captive overseas.[42]

AN INTERIM JUDGMENT

The year 1917 had witnessed the selection of competent and dedicated leaders in key intelligence positions and the creation of a foundation for a credible counterintelligence organization. Unfortunately, the rapid expansion of negative intelligence to address the threat to America and its Army had preempted the mission to train and equip intelligence personnel destined for service overseas. There was widespread ignorance among the leadership of newly activated corps and divisions as to the proper role of intelligence. In response to reports concerning misuse of intelligence personnel, the War Department felt compelled to issue a bulletin instructing commanders not to treat their staffs as "information bureaus" or some type of public affairs element. To leave no doubt as to the mission of intelligence, the War Department issued further guidance that defined the discipline in the simplest of terms. The directive served to remind all commanders that intelligence deals almost exclusively with information of the enemy, which it collects, collates, and makes available to the operations section for use in its preparation of plans.

NOTES

1. Bruce W. Bidwell, *History of the Military Intelligence Division* (Department of Army, 1961), pt. I, chap. X, 26.

2. Diane Hamm, ed., *Military Intelligence: Its Heroes and Legends* (Arlington, VA: US Army Intelligence and Security Command, 1987), 101.

3. Ralph H. Van Deman, *The Final Memoranda* (Wilmington: Scholarly Resources, 1988), 21.

4. Joan Jensen, author of *Army Surveillance*, believed the mystery woman to have been Gertrude Atherton, who wrote some 60 books and was a regular traveler to Europe. During 1917, she wrote the book *French Women in War Time*.

5. Ann Bray, ed., *History of the Counter Intelligence Corps* (Fort Holabird: US Army Intelligence Center, 1959), Vol. III, 1.

6. John P. Finnegan, *Military Intelligence* (Washington, DC: Center of Military History, 1998), 23.

7. Bidwell, *History of the Military Intelligence Division*, pt. II, chap. XII, 5–6.

8. Samuel T. Hubbard, *Memoirs of a Staff Officer, 1917–1919* (Tuckahoe, NY: Cardinal Associates, 1959), 2.

9. Dennis E. Nolan, "A History of Military Intelligence and the AEF" chap. 1, 21.

10. Hubbard, *Memoirs of a Staff Officer, 1917–1919*, 4.

11. Jules Witcover, *Sabotage at Black Tom* (Chapel Hill, NC: Algonquin Books, 1989), 193.

12. Ralph H. Van Deman, *The Final Memoranda* (Wilmington: Scholarly Resources, 1988), 28.

13. Ibid., 25–26.

14. Bidwell, *History of the Military Intelligence Division*, pt. II, chap. XVI, 13–14.

15. Van Deman desired to have MI-3C (counterintelligence operations in the District of Columbia) designated the Army's Secret Service, but Secretary of Treasury William G. McAdoo nixed the idea, claiming sole right to the name for the president's security force.

16. Bray, *History of the Counter Intelligence Corps*, Vol. III, 66.

17. Ibid., 9, 11–12.

18. Royden Williamson, "CIP in the Early Days," 10–12.

19. War Department General Staff, War College Division, MI-3, "Provisional Counter Espionage Instructions" (February 1918), 1–2.

20. Marlborough Churchill, "The Military Intelligence Division, General Staff," *Journal of the United States Artillery* 52, no. 4 (1920): 294.

21. Bidwell, *History of the Military Intelligence Division*, pt. II, chap. XVI, 11–12.

22. Thomas M. Johnson, *Our Secret War: True American Spy Stories 1918–19* (Indianapolis: Bobbs-Merrill, 1929), 174–175.

23. Bidwell, *History of the Military Intelligence Division*, pt. II, chap. XVI, 33.

24. Thomas J. Tunney, *Throttled!* (Boston: Small, Maynard, 1919), 7.

25. Ibid., 98–99.

26. Van Deman, *The Final Memoranda*, 33–34; Richard D. Challenger, ed., *United States Military Intelligence 1917–1927* (New York: Garland, 1979), Vol. 4, vii–viii.

27. James R. Chiles, "Breaking Codes Was This Couple's Lifetime Career," *Geneva Quarterly Magazine* 2 (Fall 1988): 128–137.

28. Theodore M. Hannah, "The Many Lives of Herbert O. Yardley," Center for Cryptologic History, National Security Agency, 5.

29. Herbert O. Yardley, *The American Black Chamber* (New York: Bobbs-Merrill, 1931), 34, 35, 36.

30. The American Cryptologic Bureau may have received such a pretentious title in the beginning because other agencies, including the State and Navy Departments, quickly expressed interest in obtaining its assistance.

31. Among those who served under MI-8 was Stephen Vincent Benét, who would become a well-known writer and poet, although poor eyesight would force his premature departure from the bureau.

32. Later in the war, Germany would reverse its policy and attempt to cut the oceanic links, but would be only partially successful.

33. Herbert O. Yardley, "A History of the Code and Cipher Section during the First World War" (1919), 12.

34. Ibid., 12.

35. David Kahn, *The Reader of Gentlemen's Mail* (New Haven, CT: Yale University Press, 2004), 37.

36. Yardley, *The American Black Chamber*, 56–57.

37. Yardley, "A History of the Code," 8.

38. Challenger, *United States Military Intelligence*, Vol. 8, v–vi.

39. Bidwell, *History of the Military Intelligence Division*, pt. II, chap. XV, 5–7.

40. Ibid., pt. II, chap. XVI, 55.

41. Although the requirement for the press to protect "military information of tangible value to the enemy" was voluntary, the postmaster general could and did bar the transmittal of certain publications through the mail.

42. Bidwell, *History of the Military Intelligence Division*, pt. II, ch. XVI, 54.

3

Intelligence and the AEF

"Intelligence is as essential to modern armies as ammunition."
—Brig. Gen. Joseph E. Kuhn, Chief of the War College Division

Independence Day 1917 witnessed the US Army's 16th Infantry parading through the streets of Paris, a harbinger of events to follow. Crowds greeted the soldiers with cheers of "Vive les Teddies," a tribute to former President Theodore Roosevelt, who, in the mind of the average French citizen, was the best-known symbol of America's power. In a ceremony later the same day, Colonel Charles E. Stanton stood at the gravesite of the American Revolutionary hero and announced, "Lafayette, we are here." These words were so apropos that journalists soon were attributing them to General John Pershing himself, or as one French newsman shared with Colonel Dennis Nolan his rationale for citing the American Expeditionary Forces (AEF) commander: "Yes, I know Colonel Stanton saluted Lafayette but he is General Pershing's staff officer and his remark unquestionably had been approved by the General."[1] The early headlines had overshadowed the real work that was taking place in the background. The 1st Infantry Division had arrived; the Toul–Dijon–Troyes region to the rear of the Lorraine front was designated as the future staging area for US troops; and Saint-Nazaire, Bassens, and La Pallice on the French Atlantic coast were selected as the deep water ports to handle US goods, although most troops would in the future come ashore at Brest.

Pershing's headquarters was initially located in a private house at No. 31 Rue Constantine near the Hotel des Invalides, not far from Napoleon's tomb. The facilities were so small and cramped that they fortunately kept away many curious Americans living in Paris. Still, self-appointed advisors crowded the doorways and took up much needed space. Nolan's small staff was already feeling confined in its allotted rooms due to a storage problem caused by the numerous documents and maps that were arriving daily, as previously promised by British intelligence. A further nuisance were the French themselves, who continued to beg from any available US official answers to several so-called pressing questions: What was America's position in future peace talks and what interests did the United States have in the colonies? These masked the real motives of the French who wanted the world to know that their nation deserved a great reward after the forthcoming victory. In Colonel Nolan's mind, such thinking was far from reality. "The first thing to be done to the enemy powers was to beat them; and in the fall of 1917, it seemed to us that the division of Austria–Hungary was a very remote contingency and the prospect of Germany being driven back beyond the Rhine even more remote."[2]

The original facilities assigned as the general headquarters (GHQ) were only temporary. In September 1917, Pershing and his staff left Paris for the Caserne de Damremont, a fine regimental headquarters in the town of Chaumont, a typical French provincial city 100 miles to the east on the Marne River. Secrecy demanded the substitution of the phrase "Somewhere in France" for the actual location. As far as Nolan and his growing intelligence staff were concerned, Chaumont offered more than enough office space and billets; the most sensitive areas were hidden behind large doors painted black and marked S.S. (popularly translated "Sh! Sh!"). This did not mean that all future elements found the facilities to their satisfaction. One intelligence unit reported arriving in the dead of winter and discovering their unfinished barracks without shutters, flooring, or heat.

General Henri Philippe Pétain expressed to Nolan that he hoped the Americans would adopt the French system of intelligence, being that the AEF would operate beside his army and went on to assure the new G2 that once he saw the British intelligence in action, the Americans would be certain to choose the French model. Nolan diplomatically replied that he was embarking on a study of both systems. He always found it interesting that the French had an attitude of take it or leave it when it came to a proposal, perhaps partly attributable to the language barrier. Throughout the war, Nolan considered his French interpreter to have been a great asset—someone who did not attempt to mince words or disguise the tone of what was actually said. Nolan possessed some knowledge of French, having studied the language and serving briefly as an observer of military maneuvers in France, but still had a problem speaking fluently. As the French were in the middle of changing intelligence chiefs, Nolan was unable to undertake a full review of operations at their headquarters, but he did benefit enormously from his conversations with their cryptologic officers. General Pétain also arranged for Nolan to visit the French Third Army, where Nolan was able to witness firsthand enemy prisoners being interrogated; unfortunately, a German raid against a division where Nolan was scheduled next spelled an abrupt end to the tour.

With the British, Nolan had the opportunity of seeing their intelligence system in action during the third battle of Ypres. Unlike the French, the British always took the approach of trying to urge or persuade the Americans to follow a certain course of action. During his stay, Nolan learned how intelligence officers evaluated and used such systems as aerial photos, wireless intercept, and direction finding; he also saw firsthand the use of sound and flash ranging in locating enemy artillery. Nolan remembered admitting to a fellow officer that after meeting with the Allies, it was obvious that the AEF had been extremely shortsighted to come over with such a small staff to do a job that was emerging to be more and more difficult.[3] Finally, Nolan reported that he came away from the conferences with one bit of surprising good news; the British and French intelligence chiefs both went out of their way to emphasize that German intelligence was far from being invincible, as was popularly believed.

In the end, the new G2 selected the British system as the model for AEF intelligence. His rationale was that he identified more closely with the British. Like the Americans, they were operating on foreign soil and thus faced many of the same challenges. In addition, the French operations dominated their intelligence, whereas on the British staff, intelligence enjoyed greater parity. This was probably because the French entered the war with this pattern already in place, whereas the British had begun largely from scratch. Nolan was also thankful that his recommendation was not a hard sell to General Pershing and Chief of Staff James Harbord because British General John Charteris had already taken the opportunity to brief the US leadership on how his army's intelligence system worked as well as familiarize them with many of the collection systems.

One thing that Nolan greatly appreciated about General Pershing was that he carefully read all regulations and asked questions about those items he didn't understand, but once he had given his signature of approval, there was no second-guessing or constant revisiting the subject. This approach allowed, in Nolan's thinking, for real progress to be made in a timely manner. The most important action taken by AEF G2 during the first few months was the publication of "Intelligence Regulations," dated August 31, 1917. Heavily borrowed from various Allied documents, particularly those of British Second Army, and translated into the language of the AEF, the secret "Intelligence Regulations" was the most defining discourse on the subject that the US Army had ever prepared. It covered the functions of intelligence at army, corps, and division and showed how each echelon was to interface and to report and disseminate information. The regulations spelled out in detail the type of data that intelligence was seeking on the enemy and the various collection systems used to obtain it.[4]

The publication even introduced, for the first time, two new intelligence disciplines: weather intelligence and technical intelligence. During the first mechanized war, all belligerents acknowledged the importance of weather information for the purposes of operational planning, the deployment of aircraft, movement of artillery, and use of gas attacks. Technical intelligence concerned itself with the exploitation of enemy technology by forwarding captured pieces of previously unknown equipment and weapons, along with associated documents, to higher headquarters for further analysis.

In the same month, Nolan's office published an internal mission statement that designated the following divisions: Information G2-A, Secret Service G2-B, Topographical G2-C, and Censorship G2-D. Patterned after the British, each of the elements would eventually have a series of branches to handle specific functions. The G2 differed from its French and English counterparts in several important aspects: unlike the other Allies, Nolan's staff did not enjoy the luxury of telephonic links to its War Department and thus was forced to engage in certain atypical functions, such as propaganda and espionage in neutral countries. The AEF G2 also suffered from the reality that the Military Intelligence Section back in the States was also new and was in no position to render any immediate assistance.

To lead each of his divisions, Nolan chose regular officers who had graduated from the Army Staff College at Leavenworth or from the Staff College established in Langres, France. In Nolan's mind, "Such officers could more quickly master the technique of intelligence, and their fundamental military education enabled them more quickly to properly interpret the information they received."[5] Being a former instructor at Leavenworth and personally acquainted with many of the graduates, Colonel Arthur L. Conger was most helpful to Nolan in his early selection of staff officers. When such qualified individuals were no longer available, Nolan's next choice was veteran regular Army officers. This was in keeping with the long tradition of the Army to use qualified officers to perform intelligence functions in times of war—no previous schooling or experience in the subject matter was believed necessary. Eventually, Nolan was forced more and more to turn to reserve officers over 30 years old because of the lack of junior regular officers desiring staff duty. Next, intelligence commissioned a number of enlisted personnel who were particularly knowledgeable in a certain functional area. The decision by the adjutant general to transfer to intelligence all field clerks who were proficient in foreign languages would turn out to be a fortuitous one. Because many had attended college, they also proved to be excellent candidates for officers.

Any success enjoyed by GHQ intelligence was partially attributable to the man who served as its chief. The respect that Nolan enjoyed from his fellow officers on the general staff and from Allied counterparts greatly facilitated the progress of US intelligence. Furthermore, he showed himself to be a very competent administrator. For instance, he modeled the way he wanted his staff to operate. Nolan believed in delegating authority, and he went out of his way to ensure that the next in command, Colonel Conger, was fully prepared to assume the reins if and when it was necessary to do so. Nolan often took Conger with him to high-level conferences, and on other occasions, brought along one of the division chiefs to talk with his French or British counterpart.

When first assigned to their respective positions, heads of divisions and branches were also encouraged to watch Allied intelligence in action. Colonel Nolan even directed Conger to serve as the acting G2 of the 2nd Division for an entire month in order to evaluate the various intelligence reports received from GHQ. As US troops began to enter the front lines, Nolan and his division chiefs spent as much time as possible learning what commanders needed in terms of information; no major battle occurred without Nolan himself observing firsthand how intelligence was being utilized. General Pershing later told Nolan that he had undoubtedly witnessed more engagements than any other US general.

Those who served under him, even the junior officers, thought well of Nolan. An incident took place at the intelligence officers' mess that perhaps best relates the human side of the man. At the time, Nolan was struggling with a cold. Halfway through dinner, he suddenly felt chilled; rising, he went and sat on top of one of the Dutch ovens used to heat the room. Meanwhile, all eyes of the junior officers followed the unfolding events, especially after their noses caught a whiff of what smelled like burning wool. Suddenly, Nolan leaped in the air and attempted to extinguish the fire by beating the rear of his trousers vigorously. One of those in attendance described what happened next. "By this time, we all burst out in screams of laughter because we couldn't control ourselves any longer. One of the 'Upper Brass' rebuked us, saying 'That is not a laughing matter. Why didn't you tell the general what he was getting in for?' Our reply was unanimous, 'He is the Head—He knows what he is doing. It's not our duty to interfere with his actions.' After taking his seat again at the table, Nolan himself broke out in laughter."[6]

Nolan also modeled a strong work ethic. A typical day began at 0830 hours, when Nolan would arrive at his office in order to read the intelligence documents and to mark in blue pencil those portions he thought Pershing would want to read. Next, he was off to the staff meeting where he briefly summarized the action of the German armies during the previous 24 hours; the meeting itself seldom lasted more than a half hour. Nolan then called on

Pershing to point out on a map any recent changes in the enemy's order of battle. (Because the Americans were the only ally to possess a map showing all the units on the western front, it was normally kept hidden behind wall panels as well as guarded at night.) Often Nolan furnished the general with translated German documents obtained by intelligence collection, particularly if they contained information on changed tactics or new technology or were signed by General Erich Ludendorff, one of the German army's best minds. Pershing read these during the evening hours and would occasionally comment on them the next morning. Unless called for, Nolan did not see Pershing or the chief of staff the rest of the day. If fighting was taking place, Pershing often desired periodic updates on the status of the British and French—a difficult thing to accomplish for the simple reason that Allied intelligence was frequently too busy and a complete picture was seldom available.

Following his meeting with the general staff and Pershing, Nolan returned to his office where he met with his division chiefs and brought them up to date on all that had transpired. If there was a need-to-know issue or one of the division chiefs required a private audience with Nolan, time was set aside afterward. Nolan then went over the various daily administrative tasks with his executive officer before going to lunch. In the afternoon, Nolan usually fulfilled a variety of appointments, frequently seeing French officials from Paris, diplomatic corps personnel, and other travelers who had made their way through Chaumont, mostly from outside intelligence. Between 1600 and 1830 hours, Nolan received updates on the German army and reviewed the first draft of the daily communiqué, which was being sent to the press headquarters for release. Following the dinner hour, Nolan returned to approve the data that was going into the "Summary of Information," the "Summary of Intelligence," and the daily cable to the War Department. Nolan's day finally ended at around 2130 hours, but because normally the bulk of the day's battlefield news arrived between 1800 and 2400 hours, the work of those members of the staff finishing the next day's reports did not cease until well after midnight.[7]

THE INFORMATION DIVISION

The largest of the subelements was the Information Division or G2-A, whose functions consisted of the following: keeping up with all information regarding the state of the enemy's military establishment as a whole; the location of battle units; their strength and fighting value; the development of tactics and combat methods; the histories of divisions, especially their experience in the various battles in which they had participated; and the study of the enemy's defensive organization at the front and the state of its supply system. Over the coming months, Colonel Conger busied himself organizing the division and implementing its very challenging multidiscipline mission: economic, order of battle, aviation, artillery, publications, and code and cipher.

The war's architects felt that the economic state of all combatants was playing a crucial role in their countries' ability to remain engaged in the conflict, and some analysts even believed that the economic status of Europe's neutral countries was just as significant and should also be continually monitored. Consequently, Pershing received regular updates on the political and economic climate of Europe, but the Artillery Materiel A-2 subelement that dealt with such information would fail to achieve all the goals Conger desired because there simply weren't enough experts with the necessary background and contacts to do the job. Especially at the start, the G2 depended on the French and British reports to address the larger economic issues of Europe while the Information Division would focus on Germany's access to food and general resources. For instance, the blockade had forced the German army to rely heavily on potatoes for its basic diet and to abandon trucks in favor of railroads for transportation of troops. To gain insights on the changing political situation in Germany, the intelligence staff initially utilized knowledgeable US citizens living in Paris as well as others who had recently spent time in Berlin and were now resided in Bern, Switzerland. Besides meeting the needs of Pershing, this overall approach seemed to satisfy the requirements of the War Department back home. Later, when AEF forces became heavily involved in combat, Nolan would temporarily suspend preparing the political and economic reports altogether and only forward the daily intelligence summary to Washington.

An early example of the Economic Section's work involved General Pershing's tasking the G2 to provide him with information on the French and their so-called coal problem; the report had to be on the general's desk that night for a meeting with French officials the next day. The officer who was to prepare the report was totally clueless as to where he should turn for such information; he decided to take into his confidence a veteran US correspondent living in Paris. After puzzling over the problem, the newspaperman directed that the officer should come back with a stenographer and translator and then proceeded to dash off. Soon, he reappeared out of breath but with a document he had borrowed from a secretary to the very minister with whom Pershing was to meet. Over the next few minutes, the assembled team translated and copied key points of the document. Pershing now had the information he needed to respond to the demands of the French that America provide the ships to carry the coal to fulfill the country's needs. Not only was General Pershing ready with his answer of "No" but he was also able to point out that the host nation already possessed a greater coal reserve than was publicly being acknowledged.[8]

The Battle Order Section (A-1) was established under Captain Samuel Hubbard, who until recently had served as a member of the New York Cotton Exchange. French intelligence was of immense assistance when it attached one of its veteran officers to the newly formed section; the officer brought with him numerous helpful publications and maps as well as shared in detail how his army approached the problem. The French divided all enemy divisions into one of three categories depending on their status: those involved in attacking, those used to hold the ground taken during an attack, and those consisting of soldiers 35 years and older, usually placed in reserve or along quiet sectors of the front. By following the type of division, one could forecast the enemy's plans. For instance, a holding division replaced by an attack division obviously signaled that imminent operations were in the offing.[9]

The French strongly emphasized to the Americans that all belligerents used both prisoners and documents taken during trench raids to help identify a division and its recent movements. This meant that it was especially crucial that the new US divisions be prepared to repulse such attacks by Germans, hoping to update the status of enemy forces estimates; GHQ intelligence proceeded to relay the warning on to divisions for inclusion in their stateside training. Yet it would take time and battlefield experience before the need to be constantly on the alert became the standard practice. On November 3, 1917, a party of 40 to 50 German raiders attacked a platoon of the 16th Regiment. The Americans would suffer 3 killed, 5 wounded, and 12 taken prisoner; the Germans lost 2 dead, 7 wounded, and 1 deserter. On March 1, 1918, the 18th Regiment fought off a group of 220 enemy soldiers, killing 17, taking 4 prisoners, and inflicting 62 casualties by artillery fire on the retreating raiders. During the skirmish, 20 Americans were killed and 12 were taken prisoner.

Through his contacts with the Allies, Nolan was impressed about the urgent need to establish a Code and Ciphers Section. The British informed him that they identified two-thirds of enemy divisions by means of intercepting and decoding messages. Nolan was equally impressed about the secrecy surrounding cryptology. The prevailing attitude was that the less everyone knew, the more lives could be saved; this meant not even providing details on methodology to one's own commanders. Nolan immediately cabled the War Department for a qualified officer to take charge of the Code and Ciphers Section (A-6). The response was the dispatching of a Signal Corps officer by the name of Major Frank Moorman, a 40-year-old veteran who was serving as acting director of the Signal School. In the past, he had been assigned to the Military Information Division in the Philippines and briefly teamed with Parker Hitt to evaluate suggested changes to the Army's codes.

On paper, the signals intelligence mission of the AEF divided itself between the G2-A-6 and the Radio Intelligence Section (later changed to simply the Radio Section), which fell under the Radio Division of the chief signal officer of the AEF. The Radio Section, commanded by Major Louis R. Krumm, intercepted enemy communications and handed all recorded messages to local intelligence officers; transmissions requiring further analysis went up the chain of command to Army and GHQ. Here, the cryptanalysts under Moorman went to work. Despite the division of command, there was close coordination from the beginning, and soon intercept was placed under the operational control of Moorman and G2-A-6. This was reflected by the change of its name from Code and Ciphers to Radio Intelligence.

Although the Signal Corps lacked a sufficient number of trained intercept operators, it still was able to take the initial steps in America's war in the ether when the Second Field Signal Battalion contributed a sergeant and eight enlisted men to the effort. Besides acquiring the necessary equipment from the French, the corps had the accompanying instructional manuals translated into English. By late October, the Americans formed an agreement with the French to establish an intercept station at Gondrecourt so that its operators could practice copying enemy radio traffic. Unfortunately, Gondrecourt was located too far from the front lines, and the only intercept copied consisted of practice messages being broadcast from the American Signal School at Langres. The radio intelligence personnel jokingly wondered if German intercept operators were listening in on the same transmissions and were equally confused.[10]

When the Radio Section relocated its intercept site at Gondrecourt to Souilly, much closer to the battle lines, the move resulted in a dramatic reversal of fortune. Beginning on November 12 and working around the clock, the small cadre soon copied 393 messages as well as recorded their time, wavelengths, etc. To help identify enemy stations, signals intelligence required the creation of a vast databank. Most importantly, these early intercepts contained information unavailable through any other source, and the French Second Army asked for copies. This soon led to the publication of weekly reports and preparation of maps that showed the location of the German Fifth Army's radio stations. In December, the Radio Section established a second post at GHQ to transcribe all press communiqués along with commercial messages belonging to the Central Powers and nearby neutral countries. The copying of commercial traffic was invariably not an easy task. Most such transmissions were in code that tested the ability of the intercept operators to type them accurately before handing the reports off to intelligence analysts. Although the station at general headquarters was initially assigned only two operators, it still managed to intercept an average of 15 messages and 7 press reports using only the daylight hours.

The Radio Section received 54 additional men by December—most capable of understanding German. The chief signal officer's final report acknowledged that because of the necessity for absolute accuracy required for transcription, radio intelligence "required the most expert of radio operators to be used in intercept and goniometric stations and capable German speakers (and knowledgeable of German military organization) for the listening stations."[11] Operators who already knew manual Morse code had to be able to copy 25 words a minute, and those proficient in German only 15 words per minute. Following a 5-week course at the Signal School at Langres, where they received instruction from French officers, the graduates departed for Souilly to begin their on-the-job training. Prior to the war, most Americans were only familiar with simple tuners and crystal detectors. Learning to use the more complicated French equipment and gaining an understanding of special German characters and service abbreviations were major challenges that would require time. Eventually, an advance school was set up at Toul, southeast of St. Mihiel, where all new operators practiced under real combat conditions, such as working from a dugout.

To analyze the incoming raw intercept, Nolan cabled the Military Intelligence Section to send as many qualified specialists as quickly as possible to fill the Radio Intelligence Section, which was located at Chaumont. Arriving cryptanalysts would work out of a nondescript single-story former barracks known as the "Glass House" because of its concrete and glass composition. Absent immediate assistance from the War Department, the few US code breakers on hand benefited immensely from having contact with several top Allied cryptologists, especially Captain George Jean Painvin of the French Cipher Office, who was recognized as the Allies' foremost cryptologist. After the war, Nolan acknowledged just how crucial the effort was, and in retrospect, how he regretted not having done everything possible to seek out the best brains of the country. Moorman echoed the challenge of finding the necessary records and staff qualified to do the job. "Officers and clerks were obtained from all available sources—detailed from divisions, replacement depots, Washington, and those reclassified at Blois . . . who knew German and could think. The difficulty experienced in finding men who could actually think without a guardian was surprising."[12]

An early example attesting to the potential impact of signals intelligence occurred in the early morning hours of Christmas Day 1917. The Radio Intelligence Section had intercepted a German transmission that was quickly decoded, warning that German artillery was set to deliver a barrage somewhere along the St. Mihiel salient. With 20 minutes to spare, G2 notified US divisions to be alert for possible trench raids and to pass the warning on to the nearby French corps. Together, the French and Americans unleashed a counter-battery attack that kept the enemy in their trenches. The whole experience proved to be an early incentive to the GHQ intelligence staff that by timely exploiting information in their possession, they could play an important role in supporting the front lines.

The Air Intelligence Section (A-7) lagged behind the other functions within the Information Division because the mission itself was slow evolving. Soon after arriving in France, General Pershing separated his Air Service from under the control of the Signal Corps. The action was almost inevitable given aviation's rise as a combat arm; on a professional level, it also satisfied the long-standing grievance of pilots having to serve under nonfliers. In September, the 1st Aero Squadron deployed to France; it was followed 3 months later by the 8th Aero Squadron, which had been organized at Kelly Field, San Antonio, Texas. The new American Air Service also benefited immediately from the transfer of a number of Americans who had flown with the various Allied Air Services.

Aerial observers were first trained at Fort Sill, Oklahoma—an artillery post. Much of their instruction was only classroom theory that covered artillery, infantry, and cavalry contact; before graduating from the flight portion of their training, all future observers had to demonstrate their ability to receive and send by radio eight words a minute, to locate enemy batteries, and to direct friendly fire against them. Despite these early efforts at schooling, most US observers were not recruited; rather, they were veteran artillery observers who had volunteered for the assignment. When volunteers finally ran out in the summer of 1918, infantry and artillery officers were simply appointed.

The first US school for aerial photography was located at Langley Field, Virginia, which in October 1917 possessed only one foreign-made camera. George Eastman of Eastman Kodak opened his facilities in Rochester, New York, to begin training soldiers in developing and printing. Finally, the Signal Corps started the School of Military Aeronautics at Cornell University in Ithaca, New York. Here, as well as at Langley, French and British instructors, who had learned their skills at the front, taught future photographers, interpreters, and map compilers to take, process, and analyze images; every two weeks, the schools each received a large shipment of photos from the front for studying and posting of situation maps. Regardless of the hours spent stateside, all squadrons and their crews still faced months of hands-on training under French tutelage before they were capable of producing usable intelligence.[13]

A handful of US and Allied officers were central to AEF's future photo intelligence effort. Major James Barnes, whose claim to fame was having filmed a big game safari, was placed in charge of aerial photography. The elevation of Barnes had not taken into account the arrival of Captain Edward Jean Steichen, who would quickly be acknowledged as the rising star in the field. A first-generation American, Steichen had studied painting in Europe where he fell under the influence of Alfred Stieflitz, who had promoted the acceptance of photography as art; later British Major C. D. M. Campbell introduced Steichen to the potential of aerial photography. Barnes soon recognized his future role would be back in the States where he could continue to promote the importance of aerial intelligence in helping to win the war; meanwhile, Steichen would remain with the AEF as its resident expert. Photo interpretation also received an unexpected bonus when French General Philippe Pétain decided to reassign Captain Eugene Pépin to Pershing to serve as his personal advisor. A leader in international law relating to aviation during the prewar years, Pépin had quickly emerged as one of the giants in photographic interpretation.[14]

Major Richard Williams, the former attaché, had recently returned to Europe to assume the lead in the Dissemination and Filing Section (A-8). One of its first tasks was to provide general background information to the new AEF. After removing superfluous material, the staff had its translators copy portions of French government publications that dealt with geography, railroads, canals, political divisions, and other related subjects. Frequently, the documents required updating to reflect any recent changes; the only area not covered in the reports was Alsace-Lorraine, which was being occupied by the Germans.

In civilian life, Lieutenant Thomas H. Thomas had been a frequent visitor to France and Italy; this background would prove most useful in his new position as editor of the *Press Review*. Thomas was also aided by a US journalist who had resided in France for some time, and as a result of his extensive experience, he was able to offer invaluable insights on the political leanings of the various local newspapers. It was essential that the *Press Review* team remain in Paris following the GHQ's move to Chaumont so they could obtain the latest news articles in a timely fashion and prepare a summary of those they deemed most important. To supplement the daily dosage of news articles, the *Press Review* staff included information taken from interviews of key personnel and from research conducted at various French government libraries. All matter of subjects were open for study—political, economic, military, and social—anything that might touch directly or indirectly on national policy. Despite the inconvenience, Nolan required a half-hour conference each afternoon with Lieutenant Thomas, who made the trip from Paris to go over the day's news. Eventually, this routine ceased, and Thomas began to correspond from Paris in the form of notes. The *Press Review* proved so popular that members of Thomas's element began searching British, German, and Austro-Hungarian publications for newsworthy articles until the summary covered all of Europe. Because the staff at the GHQ did not receive US-based newspapers on a regular basis, the *Press Review* eventually carried summaries of these as well.

By the end of 1917, the Dissemination Branch was daily running off about 50 copies of the *Press Review* on a small printer in the basement of the GHQ and distributing them to the headquarters staff; each issue averaged 4,000 words and contained three to four articles. Over time, the number of press reviewers grew to comprise 20 officers, most of whom were proficient in a second language; they also benefited enormously from the 30 sergeants assigned as translators. The *Press Review* was a success because it was not merely a clipping service but provided real analysis "reduced to the briefest form compatible with a comprehensive treatment of the subject in hand."[15] The editors proved impartial and did not hesitate to criticize anyone, including the Allies; because of these critiques, Nolan ordered that the Allies not receive copies of the review and that the document be marked "SECRET." The independent nature of the *Press Review* was attributable to the number of officers who had a journalistic or academic background, such as Professor Bell of Bowdoin College and Professor Dobier of the University of Virginia who served as editors. One officer mused that simply putting a uniform on a college professor did not automatically make a disciplined soldier out of him and that he most often remained in war as he was in peacetime—an original thinker. Although much of the news contained in the major papers was outright propaganda, General Pershing used the reviews to understand better the outlook of his fellow Allies as well as the enemy. Interestingly, German authorities were very good at censoring any information regarding military matters, but not matters concerning the state of their economic and political affairs. As the size of the review expanded, the demands on the general's time also increased, so Nolan began marking the most important extracts for Pershing's attention. Despite any shortcomings, Nolan always considered the *Press Review* to have been one of the most helpful of all publications.[16]

In late October, the G2 published its first "Summary of Information," consisting initially of translated enemy documents, current enemy order of battle on the western front, and various communiqués. At first, these publications relied heavily on the intelligence reports shared by the Allies. Liaison officers with the French and British daily telephoned or telegraphed their communiqués, and US intercept stations were regularly able to copy the German and Italian versions. Editors made sure to label all information obtained from intercepted messages as simply a captured document. Because the Americans lacked the battlefield experience of their fellow Allies, the summaries often attached translated French and German documents that dealt with tactics.

A helpful source for the Information Division was Major W. P. Cresson, who held a PhD and was best known before the war for having written a book on czarist Russia. Cresson was serving as the first secretary to the US legation to St. Petersburg when Colonel Nolan persuaded him to leave the post and accept a commission with the G2. Unfortunately, Nolan's plans for the major to serve as the resident expert on Russia proved to be premature because a need arose within the AEF for someone who was knowledgeable on European royalty. Subsequently, Chief of Staff Harbord directed that Cresson be reassigned to the Belgian general headquarters; upon learning of the reassignment, Nolan encouraged Cresson to play the role of diplomat, not soldier, and to communicate America's ongoing support to Belgium's leaders and their people. While in his new assignment, Cresson still continued to provide US intelligence with valuable insights concerning recent developments in Belgium.

Another useful party who furnished crucial, hard-to-obtain information was Morton Fullerton, a correspondent with the *London Times* who had lived in various European capitals and had written a foreign affairs book, *Problems of Power*, on the eve of the Great War. The handsome American, whose signature was his mustache, just happened to be the secret lover of Edith Wharton, the novelist. He informed Nolan of his desire to be of service, but Nolan, knowing Fullerton to be an individualist, wisely thought it better not to offer him a commission. Instead, Fullerton continued to work on his own using his various contacts with national leaders and members of the French cabinet.

Throughout the war, Fullerton would periodically drop by to pay the G2 a visit or send him a personal note. Although Fullerton found Nolan totally ignorant of the map of Europe, he never felt a need to speak down to the US officer; this was evidenced by Fullerton freely sharing his strongly held views on a wide variety of conversational subjects that ranged from dismembering Germany at the end of the war, to purging Europe of bolshevism, to expressing his strongly held belief that President Woodrow Wilson was totally naïve in his approach to the postwar world. Perhaps the most practical information he shared with Nolan came in the form of a heads-up when the Allies on several occasions planned to promote the amalgamation of US forces with theirs. Forewarned, Pershing was always prepared to counter such proposals.[17]

A DOWNED AIRSHIP

An event occurred in October 1917 involving staff members of the Information Division that illustrated the potential role AEF intelligence could play in the larger war. The Germans had just launched their greatest Zeppelin raid to date, dispatching 13 airships to bomb various British ports and industrial centers. On their return trip, they ran into a violent storm that blew five of the dirigibles over France, quickly becoming easy prey for Allied planes. Two of the Zeppelins came down 40 miles west of Chaumont. Local French citizens had captured one by keeping the German crew from destroying it. The other's control car from which the pilot steered the ship bounced up and down on the ground until finally entangling itself in a tree. Eventually, the airship freed itself and, along with its crew, continued on to the Mediterranean Sea where all members would be lost.

Most of the AEF officers at the GHQ had vacated Chaumont to observe the French launching an attack on Chemin des Dames; one of the few left behind was Major Richard Williams. Hearing of the crippled airships nearby, he immediately commandeered a staff car and, along with a British general attached to the GHQ, headed to where the Zeppelins had touched down. Upon learning from the French that no papers were found on the captured craft, Williams and his companion followed the visible trail of the second ship until they arrived at a marsh. Unwilling to abandon the search, Williams waded into the water with his characteristic doggedness; the first piece of evidence recovered was a fragment of a German map, giving Williams hope that he was on the right trail. He continued to explore the area, gathering more and more pieces of varying sizes—totaling 40 bags—with some coming from the control car itself that remained lodged in the tree.[18]

Back at Chaumont, Williams and another officer from the Information Division, Captain Hubbard, worked into the night piecing together the pieces until they formed a coded map that covered the North Sea, the Irish Sea, Skagerrak (an arm of the North Sea between Norway and Denmark), and Kattegat (a strait between southwest Sweden and Denmark); only the English Channel was missing. The next morning, the pair was surprised to find the second half of the puzzle delivered to their doorstep in the most unexpected manner. A young US officer at the GHQ was telling all who would listen about the most amazing souvenir he and a fellow officer had acquired. Unknown to Williams, the two officers had actually been first on the scene and had taken from the captured Zeppelin an album with photographs and information on all types of German naval vessels, aircraft, and lighter-than-air ships. It did not take Williams and Hubbard long to realize what they held in their hands—documents that contained the key to unlocking the entire German U-boat campaign.

Playing the role of courier, Captain Hubbard immediately set out for British GHQ to obtain the necessary clearance stamp. From there he received a five-member guard force to accompany him the rest of the way to London where he proceeded to deliver the documents to an aide of Vice Admiral

William S. Sims, the commander of US naval forces in the European theater. When the chief of British Naval Intelligence saw the documents, he immediately wrote to General Nolan praising the American find and characterized it as being of the greatest value. During the following week, while the Germans remained unaware that their codes had been compromised, the British were able for the first time to read the enemy's naval radio orders. Almost every night German U-boats surfaced to communicate with German naval authorities, and by using the captured map, the British Navy successfully surprised a large number of U-boats at their appointed places of rendezvous. Based on hearsay evidence, US intelligence received feedback that the breaking of the codes had cut shipping losses from 50 to 60 a week down to 12.[19]

SECRET SERVICE DIVISION

Colonel Nolan divided the Secret Service Division (G2-B) between the Positive (B-2) and the Counterespionage (B-3) Sections, both performing roles indicative of their titles, but the former would never match in terms of resources those assigned to counterintelligence. In early talks with the British and French, Nolan came away with several important insights. The French revealed that an astounding 20 percent of their meaningful intelligence came from spies. Intercept, prisoners, aerial reconnaissance, and captured documents accounted for the other primary sources. In Nolan's thinking, the high percentage served as a real revelation. For instance, French intelligence informed him that it had a well-placed noncommissioned officer in the German army, and by using links that passed through Switzerland, the spy routinely provided warnings of upcoming attacks. The French agent had recently delivered a two-day alert, but Nolan would also learn that on another occasion, the same spy's message had arrived two days late. This served as a reminder to Nolan to not become too dependent on any single source.

Both the French and the British were quick to express their opposition to the prospect of having their new ally collect information behind enemy lines, fearing that the presence of US spies might compromise existing Allied agents by drawing unwanted attention. The French did offer to share any reports on enemy troop movements in the region of the city of Metz on the Moselle River in northeast France, and both the British and French had already provided Americans with copies of their intelligence summaries that often contained information from agents without identifying specific sources. Should Pershing remain determined to have his own spies, the Allies believed that all new agents should then be under their umbrella and control. Nolan rejected outright such thinking because he did not foresee the AEF ever being absorbed into the French and British armies, and should US troops suffer a tactical setback, he did not want it to be because of failure to utilize all intelligence-collection systems at his disposal.[20]

At this junction in the talks, the Allies suggested that if the Americans remained determined to proceed, then they should attempt to insert agents into Sweden, Denmark, and Russia, all places where their efforts, the British confessed, had been a complete failure. Switzerland was suggested as an excellent place to obtain information on military, political, and economic affairs through contact with travelers and deserters. The British also cited the possibility of utilizing business firms such as those connected with John D. Rockefeller, who had offices in Bern, Switzerland. If these proposals still did not present enough opportunity, then any place east of the Rhine was open for exploitation. The British were quick to point out that the United States, being a nation of immigrants, must possess a large pool of qualified recruits necessary to pull off such operations. Following these discussions, Nolan shared his findings with General Pershing, who responded by ordering the establishment of an independent espionage service that covered America's front lines so that there would be no dependence on others for information; at the same time, Pershing reemphasized continued cooperation with Allied intelligence.

Nolan first attempted to obtain from the War Department the services of individuals who were familiar with Germany and who could work in Switzerland, Denmark, Holland, Norway, and Sweden. When Washington showed no willingness to recruit such US businessmen with long-term ties to Europe, Nolan fell back on the next best approach that involved the military attachés assigned to the countries bordering Germany. He proposed the dispatching of a team of four or five trained officers to each country where they would work alongside the regular attaché. To obtain the necessary approval, Nolan attended a conference of US ambassadors who were convening in Bern. Not only did he gain their endorsement, but they also were quick to share useful insights obtained from firsthand knowledge of potential contacts. Because military attachés fell under the control of the War Department, Nolan also had to gain the approval of Colonel Ralph Van Deman, whose endorsement was quickly forthcoming.[21]

Given his recent experience with dispatching agents during the Punitive Expedition in Mexico, newly arrived Major Nicholas W. Campanole assumed responsibility for implementing the espionage mission. He proceeded to select reserve officers who had either been educated abroad or at onetime resided in Europe. Upon receiving training from the British and French, the officers departed to their assigned countries. From the beginning, great emphasis was placed on security. The US officers were instructed not to maintain lists of those recruited as foreign agents, to deal with no more than two individuals at a time, and to ensure that all recruited sources remained anonymous and unknown to one another. Following the suggestions of the French and British, Campanole implemented the policy that the GHQ would publish no report from any of the teams prior to the staff first analyzing it to ensure that the information collected was not merely propaganda being fed by German plants. Reports of a new type of long-range gun or a new form of deadly gasses or a dramatic increase in German divisions were typical of bogus information that the enemy routinely released. For instance, Germany had recently fed Allied intelligence news that it had secretly organized several dozen unrecorded divisions.

The G2 staff at Chaumont could obtain crucial updates from Switzerland in a matter of hours by motorcycle, and if the situation warranted it, the AEF GHQ could also receive messages by coded telegrams from those countries that bordered France. After the war, the chief of German intelligence acknowledged that he had erroneously dismissed all efforts by Allied intelligence to exploit sources in places like Switzerland simply on the basis that there was no way of getting information to the western front in a timely manner. But teams in Holland, Denmark, and the Scandinavian countries were only able to transmit initially through written dispatch by boat to Britain, taking days in the process.

One area differed from the French and British. US intelligence did not actively recruit women agents. Nolan believed that to do so would have put the United States into a bidding competition with its Allies for limited sources. Furthermore, few officers in the AEF Espionage Service possessed the background required to recruit the type of woman needed for such an assignment. Nolan recalled that he took some criticism for enacting such a policy and cited a conversation that he had in the corridors at Chaumont with a lady who was serving as a secretary to one of the generals. She confronted him with the following question, "How will you justify yourself in history for not permitting American women to serve as secret agents for our army?" To this, Nolan replied that he had too many troubles to worry about what might happen after the war ended. Nolan added that she departed more indignant than when she first stopped him.[22]

Nolan felt vindicated in his ban of recruiting women when, on one occasion, he relented and approved the enlistment of a foreign female as a source. The result proved disastrous; while drunk and on assignment, the US intelligence officer in the story crashed his car in Switzerland. Fortunately, his traveling companion, the lady agent involved, escaped unharmed, and the incident itself was covered up. In his book *Our Secret War*, Thomas Johnson estimated that the AEF would still employ some 25 women agents, but noted that most volunteered and were not hired and that the majority assisted in helping to counter the threat from enemy spies, not to play the role of spy.[23]

American espionage experienced a great breakthrough when it decided to buy the professional services of the czar's former spies, who had recently lost their employer as a result of the Russian Revolution. Trained and already in place in key locations throughout Europe, they were prepared to make an immediate impact. One of their first major contributions was the acquisition of information about Germany's plans to build a gun that could shell Paris. Disguised as workers, two agents surveyed the Krupp works at Essen. There they learned that the well-kept German secret was not an invisible airship, as Allied intelligence was conjecturing, but a "gun within a gun" and from the railroad junctions at St. Pol and Hazebrouck, its shells could reach behind enemy lines. When Major Campanole first reported the news of the long-range artillery to his fellow intelligence officers at Chaumont, everyone laughed until the rounds started falling. In recognition of Campanole's triumph, his fellow officers hosted a special dinner with champagne—all in his honor. This was somewhat out of character for Campanole, who was known for being quite tightlipped and who normally never talked about operational matters at the intelligence officers' mess.[24]

Although the Allies initially opposed the AEF becoming engaged in the spy business, their attitude toward counterintelligence was just the opposite. Seeing America as a large pot full of different nationalities, Allied intelligence automatically considered the US Army as riddled with potential German spies and individuals sympathetic to the enemy's cause. The French were paranoid at the thought of AEF soldiers wandering about their country, so they demanded that all should carry photo identifications—an inconvenient proposal that took six months before the suggestion was finally put to rest. Ironically, the French themselves were somewhat passive in their overall approach to security matters and left many aspects of enforcement in the hands of local officials. For instance, should a counterintelligence threat emerge, the French would probably take the position of observing rather than taking immediate action. In stark contrast, the British were quite strict, advocating the isolation of suspected individuals and, if merited, the execution of spies.

Six months had passed since Nolan had first sent a message requesting the creation of a Corps of Intelligence Police (CIP), but Lieutenant Williamson and his 50 sergeants would not arrive in the country until early December, at which time their début was anything but auspicious. While the lieutenant was away at Chaumont checking out his orders, CIP personnel wandered off their ship, and nearby US Marines promptly placed them under arrest. Fortunately, Williamson was eventually able to clarify his unit's status and destination.

Seeing them for the first time, one US officer could understand why they had come under suspicion; he described them as "a delegation of Cajuns from Louisiana, a sprinkling of French Canadians, a number of Europeans [Englishmen, French, Swiss, Belgians, Spaniards, Yugoslavs, and Turks], a coterie of Harvard men, and their professional antecedents ran the gamut of occupations."[25] A shakedown of the group by French officers further revealed a number of undesirables, including a former train robber and a deserter from the French army. Those who passed final muster quickly departed for Le Havre to receive schooling at the hands of veteran Allied counterintelligence officers, but the British refused to begin the instruction until each agent had obtained his civilian clothes allotment, so a onetime payment of $40 plus a $5 maintenance stipend was issued. Despite the unpromising beginnings, Nolan and Major Aristides Moreno, head of the Counterespionage Section, saw enough potential in the CIP to ask for 750 more soldiers; General Pershing immediately approved their request to the War Department.

TOPOGRAPHY DIVISION

In the beginning, the greatest demands were placed upon the Topography Division (G2-C). Prior to leaving for France, Nolan had personally requested the assignment of only one officer by name—Colonel Roger G. Alexander, a former engineering instructor at West Point, who was involved in various river and harbor projects in the State of New York. Fortunately, War Department officials approved Nolan's request in time for Alexander to sail on the S.S. *Baltic*. His mission was to create, reproduce, and supply the AEF with all the maps it required; this meant both creation of new maps and replacement of those damaged by usage or weather. If this Herculean task were not enough, the Topography Division would eventually oversee copying of aerial photos for use in intelligence reports and provide administrative oversight to the Sound and Flash Ranging Service. At the peak of the war, there would be over 2,500 soldiers committed to performing these tasks, but in the beginning, Alexander would have to make do with 10 enlisted soldiers.

In England, Alexander viewed firsthand the type of mapping organization with its printing presses at the Royal Engineer School that he would ultimately duplicate. He also received copies of several maps—enough to fit in a box, but far from enough to satisfy the insatiable demand that soon fell on his staff in France. Officers inspecting future supply bases and ports called for road maps to direct them to their destinations; the operations section of the staff wanted large-scale maps of the front and of possible training areas; the supply section wanted railroad maps of the rear areas; the surgeon wanted to know hospital locations—everyone in Pershing's headquarters demanded maps and more maps.[26] The general ignorance of European geography by AEF soldiers did not help matters; more than one American confessed to believing that Alsace-Lorraine was actually two lakes.

Over the next several months, Alexander's team worked day and night, seven days a week, in "begging, borrowing, and perhaps stealing maps on everything from Dieppe to Damascus."[27] Sources for charts of the rear areas included purchased automotive maps, the French *Geographique*, and British GHQ. However, the front zone proved a more difficult challenge; the French maps were in meters, not yards, the standard by which American infantry and artillery had trained. Because of the prospective use of French artillery by the AEF, this led to the adoption of the French method of coordinates—distances from superimposed vertical and horizontal grid lines. This decision would prove most fortuitous later when circumstances threw US troops into the French front, thus allowing Allied troops to communicate with one another.

Site surveys also became an important function that fell under Colonel Alexander's purview, beginning with artillery and machine-gun ranges under construction, planned airfields and hospitals, and any area not having a map with sufficient details. On September 1, 1917, four former members of the US Coast and Geodetic Survey performed the first mission—a proposed ordnance depot. Over the course of the war, future teams would conduct 74 such survey projects that covered 1,860 square kilometers of territory.

Priority number one was the construction of a large printing plant to supplement the mapping functions that would eventually be run by the Army, to meet the immediate needs of GHQ, and to support the rear areas. Location was crucial—near enough both to the future front and the GHQ, yet on line with base ports. Then were the necessary electrical and water requirements, plus barracks to house the troops. Langres, 25 miles away from Chaumont, seemed the perfect choice at the time; the future US front was expected to be between the city of Verdun and the Swiss border. The effort would be greatly aided by an officer on the home front who possessed the foresight to collect the necessary machinery and to have it shipped to France with priority status.

Organizationally, the 29th Topographical Engineers was labeled a "bizarrely structured regiment without a headquarters." Regardless, in December, Company A arrived to build the plant and install eight gasoline generators; over the next five months, they were joined by Companies B and H. The end result of the 29th Engineers' efforts was quite remarkable: a facility covering 60,000 square feet that allowed for type and lithographic printing, wet and dry plate photography, zinc cuts and half tones, and binding—52 presses in all. The structure also contained a large drafting room, map storage, space to build relief models, and room for instructing new arrivals.

From his initial meetings with British intelligence, Colonel Nolan recalled that their officers warned him anything that other staff elements
knew nothing about would ultimately find its way to the G2. Case in point
was sound- and flash-ranging systems—acoustic and optical devices used
to help pinpoint enemy artillery. It was when Colonel Alexander was in
London that he first learned he would have the privilege of overseeing the
effort. Fortunately, Alexander would make the acquaintance of a US graduate student in England by the name of C. B. Bazzoni, a former instructor at
the University of Pennsylvania. After convincing Bazzoni to accept a commission, Alexander immediately dispatched the new lieutenant to France in
order to obtain firsthand knowledge of the workings of the Allied acoustic
and optic devices.

Meanwhile, unbeknown to Alexander, French and British representatives had already visited the United States to inform their new ally about
the sound- and flash-ranging systems they had invented. Because the Signal
Corps was responsible for such emerging technologies as the aircraft and radio, it seemed logical to the War Department that they should also handle the
sound- and flash-ranging mission. Major Augustus Trowbridge and his assistant, Captain Theodore Lyman, both professors of physics in their civilian
lives, assumed the lead in the new project. With the help of members of the
Bureau of Standards in Washington, D.C., and the Department of Physics at
Princeton University, they conducted a number of experiments at the artillery
proving grounds at Sandy Hook, New Jersey. Dissatisfied with the results, the
two officers set sail for France to observe the Allied sound- and flash-ranging
service firsthand. On his way over, Major Trowbridge's professorial bearing
showed through because he amusingly remembered overhearing a veteran infantry sergeant commenting, "Good God, look at the kind of officers they're
sending over here to beat the Boche."[28]

To Colonel Alexander's surprise, Major Trowbridge and Captain Lyman
arrived in September and announced that they too had been assigned the
task of developing the apparatus. Despite the initial confusion, the two soon
linked up with Lieutenant Bazzoni, and within a month's time, the officers
had agreed on a strategy that called for the Americans to adopt the British
system for sound and the French for flash ranging. In November, Colonel
Alexander dispatched a special courier with the necessary designs to begin
construction of the necessary equipment, but he would not reach Washington, D.C., until the middle of January. In the interim, Major Trowbridge
would assume overall responsibility for the program and soon managed to
acquire enough systems from the Allies for Captain Lyman to begin training new arrivals.[29]

CENSORSHIP DIVISION

World War I witnessed an ever expanding effort to protect information and later to exploit the same for propaganda. In the beginning, the focus of the AEF G2 remained almost entirely on stopping the flow of sensitive information into the wrong hands. One of the first issues to be settled was whether to allow intelligence to possess its own separate communications center. Pershing initially ruled that intelligence must use the established lines until Nolan was able to convince him that secret communications necessitated extra vigilance and precautions be observed.

An early rift between the Allies and the AEF occurred over the subject of censorship. French newspapers reported the arrival of the first troops on June 26, naming the units involved, their strength, and port of embarkation without prior coordination with the Americans. They justified the stories as much-needed propaganda to bolster the morale of the French people. Pershing protested vigorously that such an act had possibly placed future troop transports in greater danger from U-boats. At the same time, he complained about the Allied press publishing exaggerated claims of AEF personnel strength and numbers of aircraft. If the Americans should have concerns, the French responded that it was all the more reason for the AEF to leave censorship matters in the hands of the host nation.

These events mandated that Nolan give personal attention to the subject, particularly as it concerned the US press. Fortunately, Nolan was not without experience in dealing with news organizations. During the Spanish-American War, he had witnessed numerous times how poor relationships between the military and the press had led to disastrous results. Nolan had participated in the first engagement of the war involving US forces trying to ship guns and horses to Cuban guerrillas. The problem was that the press had leaked the plans, and the operation ended in complete failure. Another important lesson that Nolan had taken from the war was that the Army had made a crucial mistake by allowing the press to look to General William Shafter, who commanded the expedition, as its principal source of official communications. Nolan recalled one such incident to illustrate the point. At the surrender ceremonies at Santiago, a *New York World* correspondent by the name of Scoville had gotten into an argument with General Shafter that resulted in a shoving incident. Shafter subsequently ordered Scoville to be placed in Nolan's custody for deportation, and Nolan proceeded to have the following receipt signed by the transport officer: "Received from Lieutenant D.E. Nolan, Aide-de-camp, one newspaper correspondent named Scoville."[30] Although Nolan looked back on this incident with a smile, he was quite serious in his determination to avoid similar rifts between the AEF and the US press.

Nolan took a series of steps to build a strong relationship with the accredited war correspondents representing 34 different newspaper and press associations. He began by extolling their work and reminding everyone that their jobs were as dangerous and almost as arduous as that of the soldier in the trenches. Nolan also stressed openness. "I learned before the war that if the military man was frank with the press, if he did not try with mistaken zeal to mislead it, but frankly and in confidence gave information with the understanding that his confidence be respected, that never was that confidence violated."[31] There was early discussion about commissioning all accredited writers, but across the board, newspaper men would have nothing of it, believing that such a move would undercut the freedom of the press. Still, each correspondent would be required to wear a uniform with a green armband and the letter C.

Nolan tapped Frederick Palmer as the chief press censor, who was himself a respected war correspondent having served during the Spanish-American War, Philippine insurrection, and Russo-Japanese War. On the eve of the Great War, Palmer had also prophetically written a novel, *The Last Shot*, about Europe going to war. When war did break out, Palmer headed for France, where he worked as a writer of magazine articles; in his assignment, he would become extremely knowledgeable about the local situation and what was expected of him as the chief press censor. Still Nolan had to secure a physical waiver for Palmer, who would not otherwise have passed the physical examination, given his age of 44 and his health status. Palmer once candidly described his assignment in the following manner: "A propagandist, is a professional 'yes' man, and a censor, conversely, a professional 'no' man."[32] In the coming months, it would be Nolan who would have to say "No" to Palmer's numerous attempts to resign his commission, brought about by having to suffer through the badgering at the hands of younger professionals and former associates.

To the chagrin of the US newsmen, Nolan announced that until the AEF became a reality, they still had to file their stories through a French censorship system. From the beginning, however, their overall freedom of access to the AEF and its soldiers contrasted sharply with other Allied news organizations, and this openness immediately created tensions with the French Censorship Bureau, which feared what effect their writing might have on the French morale. The AEF even furnished the correspondents with chauffeurs and transportation and allowed them to eat at local officers' messes. Upon his departure, one correspondent of the *Chicago Daily News* told Nolan, "Your policy to allow the maximum of safe publicity instead of limiting it to the easier minimum justified itself. Personally, correspondents always found you ready to hear their requests regardless of how trivial."[33] Nevertheless, during the course of the war, three US correspondents were expelled for having circumvented the censorship guidelines or for having traveled to restricted areas without prior authorization. For instance, Wythe Williams, who would go on to become a well-known news broadcaster on the Mutual radio network, faced suspension for having sent an uncensored article to *Colliers Weekly*.

In the early days of US involvement, there was little news for correspondents to report home. Many of the writers who had already been in Paris for some time were anxiously awaiting any stories on the AEF and its upcoming plans. Remarkably, most had bought into French propaganda that the United States was somehow going to furnish aircraft on a scale and size previously unheard of and that these aircraft would bring about a swift end to the war by bombing German cities into submission and forcing the German Air Service out of the battle. Instead of talking about aviation, Nolan encouraged stories to be written on subjects that addressed the real needs of America's fighting forces—infantry, artillery, engineers, communications, tanks, and machine guns—so that the nation and its people would have a clear picture of the true challenges that lay ahead.

Nolan soon placed the Censorship Division (G2-D) into the capable hands of Major Marlborough Churchill, who had been attached to the US military mission in Paris prior to America's entrance into the war. Only after consulting with the Allies to gain a better understanding from their experiences of what really worked did Churchill set about to create the regulations covering censorship. The Americans chose to be somewhat less restrictive, by using rules that had the widest possible application and that allowed the greatest amount of protection. Areas covered by regulations involved the mail, photographs, official and private papers, and telephone. Any mention of units (their locations or capabilities), aircraft, supplies, lines of communications (railroads or roads), and morale was prohibited; and this applied to both rear and front areas.

The censorship of a soldier's personal mail was the responsibility of an officer in his unit; for a sense of greater privacy, a soldier could send letters in a specially marked blue envelope that allowed for a censor who did not know him personally to review the correspondence. US soldiers were encouraged to write home frequently; thus their letters were handled as expeditiously as possible. Due to the prompt movement of the mail, US soldiers were that much less tempted to violate guidelines and to use the French civilian postal system. The French were the direct opposite, holding up their soldiers' mail for weeks before forwarding it. A prohibition existed against corresponding with strangers or even advertisers as well as sending any mail to a private address back in the United States that did not exist prior to August 1914. Because individual censors could interpret the guidelines differently, the system ensured that a base censor periodically double checked a regiment's mail. The system passed correspondence containing any foreign terms through the base censor in Paris, which could manage up to 50 languages. Only Chinese and Japanese required civilian assistance. Although understaffed, the base censor was still able to process more than 30 million letters, of which 6 million were examined. Beginning in July 1918, the base censor became equipped with a chemical laboratory that scanned over 50,000 letters for hidden messages. There were a few instances involving soldiers using different forms of secret writing, ranging from saliva and urine to lemon juice and milk. The messages mostly described conditions in the soldier's unit or attempted to communicate with relatives residing in Germany.[34]

What soldiers were forbidden to write or talk about they were also forbidden from carrying on their persons. This meant no official or unofficial documents that might betray order of battle to the enemy. Unfortunately, many US Doughboys, such as America's greatest hero of the war Sergeant Alvin York of Tennessee, reasoned otherwise. In his diary, he recorded the following conversation: "I told him [the company commander] I was not admitting whether I did or didn't and he told me it would betray a lot of valuable information to the Germans if I was captured. And I told him that I didn't come to the war to be captured, and I wasn't going to be captured, and if the Germans ever got any information out of me they would have to get it out of my dead body." Of course, it was exactly off dead bodies that enemy intelligence obtained letters, diaries, and other papers that helped to identify units and their state of preparedness.

During World War I, propaganda was viewed for the first time as a vital function that extended far beyond the immediate battlefield. Like many of America's leaders back home, the AEF intelligence officers tended to exaggerate the role played by German propaganda in the war, citing recent disasters in Italy, the present crisis in Russia, and the hostile attitude of certain neutrals. Consequently, it was natural that staff members of G2-D were eager to launch their own propaganda efforts. An early attempt at getting the American message out was a December article that appeared in French newspapers titled "An Hour with General Pershing." After having provided helpful insights on the political bent of various French news organizations, the same reporter shared how to take advantage of the papers for publishing America's own views.

NEW YEAR'S EVE

Although nine months had passed, America's test still lay in the future. Upon reviewing the situation firsthand, Colonel Charles P. Summerall reported to

Secretary Newton Baker that in his estimation, the Allies could not possibly win the war before the summer of 1919. On the other hand, America's forces in France had already achieved a number of important milestones. They suffered their first four casualties on September 4 when a German bomb struck a hospital at Dannes-Camiers. US troops entered the front lines on October 20 near a town named Lunéville, or "Looneyville" as the soldiers called it. Three days later, Sergeant Alex Arch pulled the lanyard and fired the first round of artillery. In late November, members of the 11th, 12th, and 14th Engineer Regiments participated with the British in the Cambrai campaign, and the US soldiers now went by the name of Yanks or Doughboys. More importantly, by New Year's Eve 1918, the AEF had 175,000 officers and men and five US divisions: 1st Division, 26th Division, 2nd Division (both Army and Marines), 42nd or the so-called Rainbow Division, and 41st Division.

The contributions of the Allies in helping make AEF intelligence a reality cannot be overstated; they furnished the Americans with an organizational blueprint, many of the early instructors, and much of the startup pieces of equipment. The G2 staff at the GHQ also benefited immensely from having a cadre of officers who were both competent and motivated. Regardless, 1917 ended with a sobering reminder of just how much more work remained in terms of providing the Army's combat forces with a functional intelligence arm. Nine months into the war, and the expanding AEF had neither a viable intelligence system nor a token counterintelligence organization in place.

NOTES

1. Dennis E. Nolan, "A History of Military Intelligence and the AEF: A Working Draft," chap. 4, 9.
2. Ibid., chap. 3, 2.
3. Nolan, "A History of Military Intelligence and the AEF," chap. "2-12-35," 9.
4. American Expeditionary Forces, "Intelligence Regulations" (August 31, 1917).
5. Nolan, "A History of Military Intelligence and the AEF," chap. 4, 3.
6. Samuel T. Hubbard, *Memoirs of a Staff Officer, 1917–1919* (Tuckahoe, NY: Cardinal Associates, 1959), 52–53.
7. Nolan, "A History of Military Intelligence and the AEF," chap. "3-4-36," 3–4.
8. Hubbard, *Memoirs of a Staff Officer*, 16–18.
9. Ibid., 28–29.
10. War Department, Office of the Chief Signal Officer, *Final Report of the Radio Intelligence Section, General Staff, General Headquarters, American Expeditionary Forces* (Washington, DC: Office of the Chief Signal Officer, 1935), 15.
11. War Department, *Report of the Chief Signal Officer* (Washington, DC: Government Printing Office, 1919), 305.

12. War Department, Office of the Chief Signal Officer, *Final Report*, 15.

13. Terrence J. Finnegan, *Shooting the Front* (Washington, DC: NDIC Press, 2006), 422–426.

14. Ibid., 198–199, 232–234, 461.

15. Nolan, "A History of Military Intelligence and the AEF," chap. "Pub. Dict.," 3.

16. Ibid.

17. Marion Mainwaring, *Mysteries of Paris* (Hanover and London: University Press of New England, 2001), 222–223, 219.

18. Diane Hamm, ed., *Military Intelligence: Its Heroes and Legends* (Arlington, VA: US Army Intelligence and Security Command, 1987), 103–107.

19. Hubbard, *Memoirs of a Staff Officer*, 120–127.

20. Nolan, "A History of Military Intelligence and the AEF," chap. 4, 17.

21. Ibid., chap. "Espionage & Counter-Espionage," 5.

22. Nolan, "A History of Military Intelligence and the AEF," chap. "1-25-35," 6.

23. Thomas M. Johnson, *Our Secret War* (Indianapolis: Bobbs-Merrill, 1929), 299.

24. Ibid., 210.

25. Ann Bray, ed., *History of the Counter Intelligence Corps* (Fort Holabird: US Army Intelligence Center, 1959), Vol. III, 12.

26. Nolan, "A History of Military Intelligence and the AEF," chap. "Topography," 3–4.

27. Ibid., 4.

28. Nolan, "A History of Military Intelligence and the AEF," 18.

29. Ibid.

30. Nolan, "A History of Military Intelligence and the AEF," chap. "Press," 4.

31. Ibid., 6.

32. Nolan, "A History of Military Intelligence and the AEF," chap. 4, 7–8.

33. Junius B. Wood, Letter to BG Dennis E. Nolan, AEF, G2 (July 6, 1919).

34. Nolan, "A History of Military Intelligence and the AEF," chap. "Base Censor in Paris," 6.

4

Securing the Home Front

"Don't talk. Stop and think. Ask yourself if what you were about to say
might help the enemy. Spies are listening."

—Poster issued by the Intelligence Officer, Northeastern Department

During the first six months of 1918, Colonel Ralph Van Deman witnessed
the transformation of his Military Intelligence Section (MIS) from a skeleton
organization to one with sufficient personnel to begin tackling the larger
security challenges facing the Army; the numbers rose steadily until they
reached nearly 70 percent of the final total. In February, the War Department
leadership formally acknowledged the emerging importance of the intelligence mission by upgrading its status to that of a branch, removing MIS from
under the administrative control of the War College and reassigning it to the
Executive Division of the General Staff, which was reflected in the changing
of its name to the Military Intelligence Branch (MIB).

The growth in size and stature would necessitate a series of relocations. In
March, with files in hand, Van Deman and his staff moved out of the cramped
space within the War College to an apartment building, Monroe Courts, located at the corner of 15th and M Streets, NW, just west of Thomas Circle and
much closer to the agencies with whom intelligence regularly interfaced, but
the stay at Monroe Courts lasted only three short months. Again, MIB found
itself on the move before settling into the upper floors of the Hooe Building
at 1330 F Street, NW, two blocks east of the White House. Here, for the first
time, the staff element enjoyed sufficient space to expand, and here for the
duration of the war it would remain. Regardless of the location, Major Herbert Yardley and his cryptologists always occupied the top floor due to the
sensitive nature of their work.

One major factor in its dramatic growth was that the MIB had assumed a series of new missions. The creation of MI-6 and MI-7 represented a logical transfer of functions to military intelligence that was long overdue. The nucleus of the MI-7 (Graphics) Section came from the War College, which had been responsible for acquiring and maintaining an ever-expanding map collection. While a part of the MIB, MI-7 would further enlarge its capability of reproducing maps and eventually acquired an up-to-date laboratory to copy photographs. The MI-6 (Translation) was similar to MI-7 in that it supported all elements within MIB as well as the entire War Department, but instead of maps, it provided translators and, on occasion, interpreters. The number of languages within MI-6's inventory steadily rose from 4 to more than 20, but by utilizing non-Army civilians, the Translation Section had at its disposal 48 different languages and major dialects. The workload of MI-6 increased as it began to assist other government agencies and various Allied military missions situated in Washington, D.C. Among their other day-to-day duties, MI-6 members routinely scanned a large number of foreign periodicals and publications for matters of military interest; one use of the information was to create a huge database containing foreign technical terms and abbreviations.

On the other hand, during the course of World War I, military intelligence acquired several functions that had little to do with its primary mission, and no single explanation exists as to why Van Deman and the MIB agreed to take them on. In some instances, it was simply a matter of saluting and doing what was necessary for the larger war effort; on other occasions, it represented the typical bureaucratic tendency to acquire greater prominence through added missions and their accompanying resources.

Military morale was undoubtedly the function least connected to military intelligence. Going as far back as early 1917, Army officials were made aware of an article titled "The Soul of an Army" by General E. L. Munson, who argued forcefully for greater participation by the War Department in the matter of troop morale. Initially, the Army's leadership opted to leave esprit-de-corps where it had always rested—with the commander in the field. In May 1918, this changed when the Training and Instruction Branch of the War Plans Division was made responsible for the "psychological stimulation of American troops." Reports from counterintelligence agents had first alerted the Army to the issue of troop morale, so the MIB was naturally among the various elements designated to provide input on how to tackle the subject. At an early conference, MIB representatives pointed out to those present that intelligence alone possessed both the money and machinery needed to carry out day-to-day operations. So in June, the War Department reassigned the mission to the MIB's new Military Morale Section.[1]

One major flaw of the induction system had been its failure to determine whether resident aliens drawn into the draft even possessed sufficient language skills to understand basic military commands in English. Typical of the type of situations that arose was the case of a recent emigrant from Russia who, after having spent six months in the stockade, was finally able to explain through an interpreter that he had been inducted into the Army without ever having received a draft notice.

In early 1918, D. Chauncey Brewer, former president of the North American Civil League for Immigrants, became head of the newly created MI-3F (Foreign Speaking Soldiers). He immediately went to work establishing contacts with each of the Army's major training camps as well as authorities in the key metropolitan centers. Brewer and his small staff labored to ensure that aliens in the Army received fair treatment by alerting authorities to potential problems as well as recommending changes to existing policy. For instance, arrangements were made for certain cultural groups to have their own religious services. Another experiment that worked well took place at Camps Gordon and Devens, where soldiers were organized by their backgrounds (Greeks, Armenians, etc.) into companies and provided with officers who spoke both their language and English. Almost overnight, morale increased 100-fold; this was evidenced by the dramatic drop in disciplinary cases.[2]

ORGANIZING COUNTERINTELLIGENCE

As chief of the MIB, Van Deman made sure that the primary focus remained on counterintelligence. The largest of MI-3's subsections had responsibility for issuing daily and weekly reports on its activities to Van Deman and to the chief of staff as well as dispatching weekly bulletins to the intelligence staffs assigned to the Army departments, divisions, and other major US agencies. These documents covered a wide range of subjects from security alerts to instructions on how better to counter emerging threats. Equally important was the MIB's preparation and distribution of a manual for intelligence officers on interpreting military rules and civilian laws that pertained to counterintelligence. In response to the requests by commanders and staffs in the field, the MIB also issued manuals to provide them with a better understanding of the Army's overall counterintelligence mission as well as what part they were expected to play in it.

In January, the MIB assumed a major new function when the Signal Corps relinquished all responsibilities for providing its own security along with personnel assigned to its Security Service; simultaneously, the War Department would transfer the security mission formerly assigned to the Aircraft Production Bureau. Together these missions would fall under the Air Service and Signal Troops Subsection (MI-3E), to be overseen by newly commissioned Wesley Brown, formerly of the Department of Justice. The Signal Corps' retreat from the security business had come on the heels of an investigation of its Photographic Division that had uncovered major shortcomings. When the MIB assumed the reins, it promptly separated from service four Signal Corps officers who had either engaged in pro-German activities or worked for German-owned businesses prior to the start of the war.

In February, MI-3O was created to cover all special staffs and their auxiliary elements: Motor Transport, Medical, Dental, and Veterinary Corps. The Chemical Warfare Service received special attention because of the sensitive nature of the information and materiel handled; consequently, all of its military and civilian personnel underwent background checks. The same strict security guidelines would also cover the 98 members of the very secret Radio Intelligence Service. Over the course of the war, MI-3E and MI-3O handled more than 4,500 investigations, resulting in the Army court-martialing or discharging 100 soldiers, transferring another 100 to nonsensitive branches, and interning 12 enemy aliens.

Various civilian organizations were soon on their way overseas to help support the troops in the rear areas, although some labored fairly close to the combat zone. MI-3I (Auxiliary) was established in May to ensure that the workforce was a loyal one, beginning with seven organizations that were initially recognized by the War Department—YMCA, YWCA, National Catholic War Council, American Library Association, Salvation Army, Jewish Welfare Board, and War Community Service. Because of the nature of how the American Red Cross funded its organization, MI-3I approached the agency differently. Many of the organizations, such as the Red Cross and the YMCA, had taken independent steps to screen the backgrounds of those going overseas, and it was largely a matter of coordination with MIB officials. As America's war effort reached full stride, myriad other relief organizations were added to the list; among them the Armenian and Syrian Relief Committee and the Women's Overseas Hospital Unit. A little over 8,000 of the workers required thorough investigations, but only 257 of the cases raised serious concerns. For some inexplicable reason, most involved YMCA workers.[3]

There was a constant need to check counterintelligence files for names. Subsection MI-3H (Investigation of Personnel) managed a small office specifically created to respond to other agencies. For instance, Congress passed a law in May allowing for the expeditious naturalization of aliens within the military if they could produce satisfactory evidence of loyalty. Each applicant submitted a personal history that in turn was coordinated with other government and private agencies to ensure accuracy. As a result of its work, the staff of MI-3H favorably closed 4,830 investigations; only 325 failed to gain approval because of character issues.

In the civilian sector, MI-4H (Special Cases) handled the coordination of cases involving so-called obnoxious persons—many of them foreign nationals who had made themselves a constant distraction to the war effort and, in the process, became targets for deportation. Typical was Jechalski Farroway, a former Irish policeman, who often found his name in the local papers for brawling with New York City Police following a night on the town. Later, it would be aliens who openly embraced anarchy, militant socialism, and bolshevism. The *Washington Post* was among those who were more than happy to witness such individuals being shipped back to their homeland: "The sight of 54 bewhiskered, ranting, howling, mentally warped, law-defying aliens, in the custody of Federal officials, locked in railroad coaches and journeying to an Atlantic port for deportation to foreign shores, is sufficient to cheer the soul of every loyal American."

MI-4 continuously expanded its web of contacts with other governmental and nongovernmental sources for the purpose of collecting information that might have an impact on the security of the war effort. For instance, in January a letter went out to the chief of police in each municipality with a population of more than 10,000 in order to solicit assistance in identifying potential enemy agents. Yet missions belonging to MI-4 were always in a constant state of flux. Typical was MI-4C (Enemy Finance and Trade), a two-person office whose purpose was to expose business and commercial establishments used for enemy causes, including espionage. MI-4C's existence was short lived because it soon discovered that other agencies (the War Trade Board, Federal Reserve Board, and Alien Property Custodian) were already performing the same function.

Needing to ensure that its counterintelligence operations were within the law, the MIB created subsection MI-4G (Legal Matters) and placed Captain George S. Hornblower, a prominent New York attorney in civil law, in charge. Not only did Hornblower alert the MIB and the Army as to the latest legal rulings, but he also testified on numerous occasions in front of congressional committees, spoke at various conferences, and studied proposed legislation. In early 1918, Congress debated a law that would have created "war zones" around certain sensitive industrial areas and turned their security over to the War Department, thus greatly expanding the powers of the MIB. The Justice Department, however, would have none of it and successfully lobbied against such a proposal.[4]

In April 1918, MIB created MI-4I (Labor and Sabotage) for the purposes of addressing labor matters, industrial sabotage, and disloyalty among

Catholic priests. Its chief mission was to learn of planned strikes before they began; sources of such information included the Plant Protection Service, intelligence staffs within the various geographic departments, and local law enforcement authorities. In the process, the chief of MI-4I, Major Eugene F. Kinkead, maintained close liaison with Samuel Gompers, president of the American Federation of Labor. If MI-4I anticipated a strike, then the federal government could serve papers on the labor leaders reminding them of their obligations to support the war effort. Averted strikes included labor disputes at the following companies: Albany Car Wheels, Mendelson Potash of New York, Detroit-Cleveland Navigation, Rice and Hutchins (military shoes), and the Springfield Aircraft Corporation.

Major Kinkead also provided support to Colonel Brice P. Disque of the Army Signal Corps whose mission was to oversee the harvesting of trees in the Pacific Northwest for use in building airplanes destined for the air war in France. His efforts were being hindered by loggers who belonged to the Industrial Workers of the World, which regarded the Great War as nothing more than a capitalist conflict. The union's newspaper announced that "Capitalists of America we will fight against you not for you!"[5] The Industrial Workers of the World (IWW), or "Wobblies" as they were often called, claimed a membership of 60,000 and were among America's poorest-paid and least-skilled industrial and agrarian laborers. The IWW was the only union whose ranks were open to one and all—including women and recent immigrants of whom many harbored bias against one of the Allies.

In his *Final Memoranda*, Van Deman wrote, "There were many other incidents . . . in the United States which the leaders of the various Irish organizations hoped would make trouble for Great Britain."[6] One such case began when postal censors intercepted a letter written in secret ink and then turned it over to the MIB for exploitation. The message contained plans to destroy a large copper mine in the western United States and named the mastermind of the plot as the current head of an Irish-fraternal organization. Subsequently, authorities arrested the would-be saboteur as he boarded a westbound train leaving Buffalo, New York. Other investigations revealed that a handful of priests had known contacts with Irish Americans involved in sabotage. To sever these connections, Major Kinkead arranged an understanding with James Cardinal Gibbons of Baltimore; the agreement allowed the MIB to request that a US attorney alert the appropriate bishop who, in turn, would counsel the priest in question.

Although he was under no pressure to do so, Van Deman occasionally went out of his way to embrace new functions. The most visible of these was an association with the American Protective League (APL). With the encouragement of Attorney General Thomas W. Gregory, the APL had been created two weeks prior to America's entrance into the war; this followed the pattern set by both France and Great Britain, which had similar organizations. The US government's relationship with the APL was to utilize citizen groups to help enforce various war measures, including the apprehension of draft dodgers and identification of those whose actions undermined America's war efforts. The APL was an amalgam of various patriotic organizations and maintained almost 600 local branches throughout the country, totaling 60,000 to 100,000 members. Each member possessed credentials in the form of a card and a badge, and the various offices used stationery indicating an association with the Department of Justice, which oversaw the APL's National Board of Directors. Attorney General Gregory went on record to say that the APL was tremendously helpful in the work of the Bureau of Investigation within the Department of Justice.[7]

From the beginning, the APL had its opponents who cited instances when members exceeded their authority. Some of the critics even came from within the government itself. Secretary of Treasury William G. McAdoo, who oversaw the Secret Service, complained directly to President Woodrow Wilson and compared the APL to the Sons of Liberty of the American Revolution, which was well known for having perpetrated abuses against nonpatriots. There were serious examples of violations of civil liberties, if not by the APL, then by other local vigilante groups. In Collinsville, Illinois, a mob of 500 townspeople accused a man of being a German spy and then dragged him through the streets before murdering him. A crowd broke into a school in Nebraska and destroyed all books written in German, including Bibles. On a nonviolent level, the US public temporarily rechristened German-sounding foods, such as hamburgers, sauerkraut, and frankfurters, with more patriotic terms ("freedom sandwich" and "freedom cabbage"). Elsewhere, Lutheran and Mennonite churches felt compelled to accelerate their transition to English-only services.

Van Deman also shared his concern over the independent nature of the APL as well as some of the actions taken by its membership: "This sort of thing was extremely dangerous and it was evident that these must be stopped at once."[8] To bring the APL under stricter supervision, Van Deman ordered the commissioning of its leadership and their relocation to Washington, D.C., and the MIB prepared a primer for members of the APL so they might better understand their function and legal parameters. Although there were bumps along the way, Van Deman expressed his overall satisfaction with the new arrangement forged during late 1917: "In the beginning, there was a little trouble in getting some of the members to understand exactly what orders meant and some of the smaller groups did make more or less trouble in questioning the loyalty of persons in their communities. However, that was dealt with a pretty strong hand and within a short time such activities ceased."[9]

By establishing a liaison office with the APL, the MIB was able to make better use of the organization's resources, especially as it impacted the Army's counterintelligence mission. For instance, the APL helped to locate many of the 300,000 members of the armed services who deserted over the course of the war. The APL also provided assistance to the general war effort; the membership assumed responsibility for gathering maps, books, magazines, and reports to provide US fighting forces with an orientation of French geography and culture. After screening the printed material, the MIB had tons of the documents shipped off to the American Expeditionary Forces (AEF).

A second civilian-based mission that Van Deman saw as being essential to the security of the nation's war effort was the protection of various industries and their workforce against arson or sabotage as well as the safe shipment of finished goods to ports of embarkation. Edmund Leigh, who had held a similar position with the Baltimore and Ohio Railroad prior to the war, was placed in charge of the Plant Production Service. Because the scope of the new Plant Protection Service, which consisted of 340 agents, touched on matters of concern to the Army, the MIB formed a separate unit within MI-4 to support Leigh and sent liaison personnel to each of his 14 district offices. The close relationship with the MIB was further facilitated by the Plant Protection Service being headquartered in a neighboring office within the Hooe Building in downtown Washington, D.C. Initially, Van Deman had proposed commissioning Leigh, in keeping with the precedent of the APL leadership, but Leigh told Van Deman that he believed he could work better as a civilian than he could as an officer in the Army.[10]

The Plant Protection Service covered 5,000 industries and provided information to 30,000 plants to aid them in upgrading their security, such as hiring guards and watchmen, implementing identification systems, and taking steps to prevent fires. The system that the Plant Protection Service adopted to ensure loyalty within the rank and file was reminiscent of the one being employed by Army counterintelligence. At each facility, a pyramid of trusted workers watched over their fellow employees and reported any suspicious on-the-job behavior or talk; agents of the Plant Protection Service then initiated a follow-up investigation to determine whether the individuals in question were agitators or honest employees. After the war, Van Deman labeled the Plant Protection Service's effort as "excellent" for having successfully investigated over 5,000 cases that had interrupted or delayed war production.

Colonel Dennis Nolan requested permission to assign counterintelligence personnel to neutral countries. In response, the secretary of war issued a statement that outright rejected such a proposal, citing the examples of the French and British whose attachés routinely performed counterespionage duties within Holland, Switzerland, and Denmark, which bordered the enemy or enemy-controlled nations. In early 1918, the policy was modified, again to imitate the Allies. In the future, US attachés worldwide were to assist in identifying and arresting all persons who attempted to evade passport controls. Besides passengers traveling to and from the United States, crew members on ships faced special scrutiny because of their ability to carry contraband materials and secret messages. Military attachés were on particularly high alert in Cuba, Spain, Sweden, Norway, Mexico, and Argentina. Several nations within the group had a sizable segment of the population sympathetic to the German cause; others were anti-American and still bore bitter memories of the Spanish-American War or past US interventions in their country's affairs.[11]

One of the most notable counterintelligence cases handled by military attachés involved Walter Scheele, German saboteur extraordinaire. Following America's entry into the war, a major manhunt was unleashed for the person or persons responsible for the incendiary devices being placed aboard US cargo ships carrying goods and munitions to the Allies. Upon learning that several of his compatriots had been arrested, Scheele, who was described as being by nature a nervous person, fled to Cuba, where he immediately came under suspicion of local authorities; in turn, they alerted Captain Thomas F. Van Natta. The US military attaché subsequently arranged for the arrest of the German chemist and his transfer back to Washington, D.C. Fortunately, Scheele became a most cooperative prisoner by providing important data on German gases and chemicals. Agents also used information obtained from Scheele to notify the Corps of Intelligence Police serving within the AEF's rear zone so they could direct searches of incoming cargos for incendiary devices. While demonstrating how one of his bombs worked in a secret US laboratory near West Point, New York, Scheele suffered severe wounds from an explosion; he would never fully recover and, a short time later, succumbed to pneumonia.[12]

The neutral nation of Switzerland was full of spies and counterspies from all the belligerents. Upon visiting the country, one senior US officer reported that he found it so "loaded with German, Austro-Hungarian and Turkish spies it was thought best that I keep quiet as possible."[13] But as long as they did not threaten the country's neutrality, local authorities tended to allow them to ply their trade. One German agent in particular would become a great menace to the Allies—his identity was unknown other than "the Master." He used contacts in the various banks to understand how Allied intelligence was spending their money and had members of his spy ring infiltrate local police departments. Elsewhere, the German ringleader used agents to pose as hotel chambermaids and railroad conductors and paid off customs inspectors who monitored the borders and telegraph operators who copied down important cables. The Master often used disguises and occasionally donned the uniform of Swiss officials to extract important information directly from members of Allied delegations. Over time, the Master was credited with the compromise of more than 200 agents, among them 21 French spies living in Germany in the spring of 1918. In the words of one French intelligence officer, the Master did more harm than "half of their German generals."

The US Army officer in Thomas Johnson's book *Our Secret War* was not named, but he would play an important role in exposing the identity of the German spy chief. It all began in the city of Bern, where by chance the officer, most likely assigned to the US military mission, ran into a foreigner whose family he had befriended before the war. "Zero," as he would become known, was actually a German officer who was working as a spy for the Master. He also confessed to his US friend that his brother, also an officer, had been accidentally shot by a prominent German official and his death covered up. The American would use this personal tragedy and Zero's displeasure with the course that the German Empire was taking as the means to win his support in unmasking the Master.[14]

As it turned out the Master was none other than Captain Karl von Einem, who frequently traveled between Germany and Switzerland to care for interned soldiers and was well known by many local officials. Although von Einem was caught, he had over the months compromised many prominent Swiss officials and would find his way into an asylum instead of a prison. From there, he made an easy escape using a waiting car and motor boat. Allied intelligence would receive notice of his successful break by means of an intercepted telegram that read, "Arrived here safely last night." On the positive side, 60 members of von Einem's ring were rounded up. As far as Zero, the Americans helped him and his sister to flee to Italy to avoid retribution at the hands of German officials.

COUNTERINTELLIGENCE IN ACTION

On the eve of World War II, a military intelligence officer was busily reconstituting a counterintelligence element within the Army to meet the emerging security challenges. As he looked back to World War I for perspective, one case stood out in his mind as representing the potential impact of Army counterintelligence; the investigation was also notable because it touched on several echelons of the intelligence system as well as various disciplines. Van Deman would simply label it "a most spectacular piece of work."

Kurt Jahnke, a German-born naturalized US citizen and former Marine, was a seasoned veteran of the espionage business having teamed up with Lothar Witzke in perhaps two of the more memorable acts of sabotage against the United States. On the East Coast, the pair had pulled off the destruction of the Black Tom terminal in New York harbor, and on the West Coast, they had orchestrated a similar attack on the Navy Yard at Mare Island near Vallejo, California. Knowing that he was a suspect in the Mare Island explosion, Jahnke boldly walked into the local offices of the Federal Bureau of Investigation (FBI) where he proceeded to offer his services as a counterspy to help apprehend the culprits. His actions so caught the authorities off guard that Jahnke would gain the necessary time to disappear south of the border.

When Jahnke arrived in Mexico City in 1917, he proceeded to appoint himself chief of what remained of Germany's secret service. Soon thereafter, an informant relayed news to the MIB that Berlin had assigned one of their star agents, K. A. Jahnke of Mexico City—to promote mutiny in the US Army. This warning—coupled with the British having intercepted and decoded German communiqués that also named Jahnke and disclosed several of his plans—was enough to motivate the Allies to take preemptive action. The British employed William Graves, a black Canadian, who had once lived in the United States.

The intelligence officers of the Western Department launched a second operation on their own. At the border town of Nogales, Arizona, Captain Joel A. Lipscomb directed Special Agent Byron S. Butcher to recruit an informant who could report on the activities of potential German spies. His choice proved to be an excellent one—Paul Altendorf from Poland, who had studied medicine at the University of Krakow. After much time spent traveling throughout South America, Altendorf had taken a commission as a colonel under the Mexican military governor of the State of Sonora, which bordered Arizona. The final player was William Neunhoffer, a Texan by birth but with German parents. In real life, Neunhoffer was an attorney from San Antonio, but as a member of the Texas National Guard, he had helped to secure the border in response to Pancho Villa's raid. The Justice Department had specifically recruited Neunhoffer because of his ability to speak both German and Spanish fluently and quickly dispatched its new agent to Mexico City under the guise of a draft dodger. None of the three Allied counterspies knew the identity of the others, and it is very unlikely that the parent organizations ever bothered to coordinate their operations in advance.

In November, Jahnke received the long-awaited marching orders from the fatherland by way of a Danish sea captain. In response, Jahnke laid out a very ambitious plan that included the bombing of the Panama Canal as well as various industrial and military targets within the western United States. For the latter assignment, Jahnke chose the one man whom he could depend on to pull it off—his former partner, but Witzke would not be going alone. Three new recruits happened to show up at the Juarez Hotel in Mexico City asking by name for the one person who could put them in contact with Jahnke. Seizing upon Witzke's trip north as an opportunity to train these new soldiers in the war on terror, Jahnke selected Graves and Altendorf to go along.

On January 16, 1918, Witzke, Graves, and Altendorf set off for the port of Manzanilla, where they boarded a ship to Mazatlan and then proceeded on to Nogales. Carrying with him a Russian passport with an alias of Pablo Waberski, Witzke drank and talked on the long trip. Besides his current plans, which involved joining forces with members of the IWW for a large-scale bombing campaign, Witzke divulged to Altendorf his past deeds to include the Black Tom attack and boasted of having already killed many people. When the party arrived in Hermosillo within the state of Sonora, Altendorf introduced Witzke to General Calles, his former superior, and then excused himself from accompanying Witzke and Graves any farther. The following night, Altendorf surreptitiously boarded a freight train also bound for Nogales in order to keep track of Witzke's movements.

At the US consulate in Nogales, Altendorf (known as "Operative A-1") met with his handler Special Agent Butcher to put together a plan to trap Witzke. As long as the German agent kept his suitcases in a nearby hotel south of the border, Butcher and his men arranged with US officials to allow Witzke to come and go at will, all the while maintaining a close watch. In the meantime, Butcher proceeded to debrief Altendorf. Believing that they now possessed enough information for an arrest, Captain Lipscom ordered Butcher and another agent to apprehend Witzke. It did not take long before the intelligence officers found a slip of paper with a 424-letter cryptogram sewn inside the upper left sleeve of Witzke's jacket. Captain Lipscom and Agent Butcher then journeyed to the Sonora side of the border where they bought off some of the locals and proceeded to remove Witzke's luggage from his shabby hotel. In the suitcase, they discovered a letter written in code along with a cipher table of words and phrases for use in dispatching telegrams. The documents were quickly bundled up and dispatched to Washington, D.C., and the MIB. Meanwhile, the news of the apprehension of Witzke had quickly spread, helping neutralize six other saboteurs destined for the United States but who instead decided to retreat into Mexico.[15]

Upon receipt of the documents, Colonel Van Deman would turn them over to Yardley, who in turn would give the documents to Captain John Manly, his best cryptanalyst. Manly quickly determined that German intelligence had used a transposition cipher, but was uncertain whether it had been written in Spanish, English, or German. Upon establishing a frequency table that counted each time a particular letter was written, the MIB staff eliminated Spanish because there were 12 k's and no q's, both unusual for that language.

Subsequently, MI-8 began to focus on German due to the presence of 20 *h*'s and 15 *c*'s. Because German *c*'s are often followed by a *k* or an *h*, it was then checked to determine if a pattern existed between these letters. After some effort creating various tables, Manly and his team unraveled the secret message. The translated script contained the following damning words: "The bearer of this is a subject of the Empire who travels as a Russian under the name of Pablo Waberski. He is a German secret agent." Signed "Von Eckhardt," Germany's minister to Mexico.[16]

Although caught red handed, 22-year-old Witzke refused to divulge any information to Special Agent Butcher. "If I told you, I would be a traitor, and that I will never be." In August 1918, Witzke faced a military court at Fort Sam Houston, Texas, where in his own defense he concocted a story about having been a bandit, not a saboteur. While in jail, Witzke attempted to smuggle out a second coded message that was confiscated and again sent to the MIB for translation. Among other things, the prisoner desired more money in hopes of bribing his guards. The British also made available to investigators various communiqués that spelled out Witzke's position as well as the purpose of his travels to the United States. In spite of the fact that no evidence was ever introduced at the trial linking him to the Black Tom bombing, the spy who bragged about having killed many was found guilty and sentenced to death—the only individual during the war to receive such a verdict within the United States.[17]

Codes issued specifically for agents, such as the ones broken in the Witzke investigation, were the rarity. As a rule, German spies in the United States devised their own codes using whatever means were readily available and conditions permitted. For example, one spy periodically sent a bundle of US newspapers to Mexico; the sheet with the message had a designated tear; for some reason, the page most often chosen was the editorial section. The first column would contain the code; letters would be pricked with a small pin or a toothpick dipped in lemon juice. The holes themselves were so tiny that they frequently required a reading glass to be seen or to be displayed over a light. In another instance, how a postage stamp was positioned on an envelope was employed to indicate ship movements.[18]

The case of Maria von Kretschmann also illustrated the crucial linkage between different intelligence agencies and disciplines. Born in Argentina to a former Prussian cavalry officer, Maria claimed to have been a distant relative to an illegitimate heir of Jerome Bonaparte, Napoleon's younger brother. While still a young woman, Maria had journeyed to Germany, where she studied languages and was married briefly to José de Victorica from Chile, which provided her with a passport from a neutral country. Soon thereafter, she made the acquaintance of the chief of German intelligence Colonel

Walther Nicolai, who influenced her into joining the espionage service. When war broke out, she spent the first two years using her writing skills to encourage the Sinn Fein in Ireland to rebel openly against the British.

With diplomatic conditions with the United States deteriorating, German intelligence dispatched Victorica with a false passport to the States in hopes of preparing articles to encourage pacifists (especially among Catholics), promote pro-German policies, and fan the flames of anti-British feelings. Although stories have described her as "a stunning blonde, about 35 years of age," she had, in reality, hair that was light brown and was somewhat plump in stature. Others noted her intellect coupled with an air of social grace, but unfortunately, at some point in her life, she had acquired a serious morphine habit. Besides serving as a propagandist, she was to assist Herman Wessels, who was working undercover while posing as an official of the Hamburg-Amerika shipping line. To locate potential targets for a campaign of terror, Wessels routinely traveled to New Jersey to survey manufacturers of various munitions. Among the pair's ill-conceived ideas was one to hide explosives inside imported toy blocks, but the bombing phase of Victorica's mission would never materialize beyond recruiting additional Irish dockworkers to plant explosives aboard freighters.

British intelligence first alerted US authorities that it suspected a certain "A.C. Fellows, 21 Sinclair Avenue, Hoboken, New Jersey" to have ties with German intelligence. Upon investigation, US counterintelligence personnel learned that the former inhabitants had long since disappeared but still decided to place the residence under watch and to monitor all mail coming to the address. Their patience paid off when in January 1918, the Bureau of Investigation turned some intercepted letters over to MI-8 for examination. At this point, MI-8's secret-ink laboratory and the iodine-vapor test were still awaiting completion. Using the reagents already known to be in use by German agents, the chemists failed initially to detect any secret writing on the first letter, but on the second, they hit pay dirt. Although the concealed message was vague, intelligence specialists could easily read between the lines. The contents appeared to be a letter of concern over a friend's illness, but in spy talk it was believed to refer to the writer being under surveillance and unable to perform his or her assigned mission. "Invest capital in the great war industries, docks, and navigation as you judge best" meant sabotage. The hidden message also revealed a name "Dear Mrs. Gerhardt" and a return address—a rooming house west of Central Park.

It was soon learned that an occupant at the boarding place—a steward aboard the S.S. *Christianiafjord*—had received two pieces of mail in Norway for delivery in the United States. After being stuffed inside his shoes, the envelopes suffered sufficient damage to cause the courier to use new envelopes.

Here he had made a crucial mistake. He inadvertently switched the letters and the one that should have gone to A. C. Fellows went to Mrs. Gerhardt and vice versa. By now, the US and British officials joined forces. The unraveling began when investigators discovered a residence for the mysterious Mrs. Gerhardt. From her, they learned that she had received a number of letters not addressed to her personally, and that she remembered some of the earlier ones contained the name Victorica. Sometimes spies used an innocent person's address as a cover for mail that they would later claim. Authorities passed this latter piece of information on to members of British intelligence who searched their old cable files. Soon the British found one with the name Victorica. By using the code found in secret ink on one of the original letters, MI-8 was able to decipher the cable message, and for the first time link Madame Maria de Victorica with German intelligence.

Following the disclosure and arrest of several contacts, authorities began to close in on the German spy. On April 16, 1918, US agents observed an associate of Victorica's entering St. Patrick's Cathedral in midtown Manhattan, where he sat down in a pew and began reading a newspaper left behind by a young girl. Between the pages were 21 thousand-dollar bank notes sent by German Minister von Eckhardt in Mexico. The courier next hailed a taxi for the upscale Hotel Nassau, which overlooked the ocean at Long Beach, Long Island. Here, he placed the money into the hands of Victorica, who was currently registered under the name of Marie de Vussiere. Eleven days later, US authorities would order her arrest.[19]

Although condemned by letters and secret ink found in her possession, Victorica, the would-be spymaster, never faced prison, probably due to the war's end and poor health brought on by her drug addiction. She would die of pneumonia two years later while still out on bond, her last month spent alternating between a convent where she received care from Catholic sisters and a private sanatorium.[20] Victorica's case would serve as a revelation of how the war in the shadows was progressing. The Central Powers were still focused, at this late date, on delivering bombs to hinder America's ability to ship goods and men to the front. It also revealed that German intelligence was in disarray in America; its leadership frantically wanted to initiate other cells apart from the one headed by Victorica. Finally, America's counterintelligence agencies were developing into an effective spy-catching web that, at least for the moment, seemed to put many foreign agents on the run.

Unfortunately, not all investigations were handled so smoothly as the Victorica and Witzke cases. There was a French double agent by the name of Jamie Soto, a Spanish physician by profession, whom the Germans trusted to collect information on US troop transports arriving in France. Consequently, his French handler proposed to Major John W. Lang, the American military attaché in Spain, that he should make the arrangement for Soto to journey to America so that the spy could interface with local German intelligence operatives and feed them false information concerning shipping routes, while at the same time learn about planned points of attack by their submarines. Major Lang quickly orchestrated a plan for Soto to travel incognito from Spain to Cuba and from there to New York City.

Within the New York City MI office, a lieutenant, whose last name was Villa, was appointed as Soto's handler; unfortunately, working with a double agent was something altogether new for most US counterintelligence officers. Soon, Soto made the contacts with German agents as planned and subsequently arranged for Villa to monitor his conversations. Soto, like many of his fellow spies, associated with a variety of disreputable characters in his daily comings and goings. In the minds of Villa and his boss, Major Nicholas Biddle, who in his former life was a well-known member of high society, this was not only shocking but it meant that Soto could not be trusted. One veteran intelligence officer would label Biddle's handling of the whole affair as "puerile." In time, Soto fell under the suspicion of the FBI and was picked up for questioning by the Justice Department. At this crucial moment, Biddle should have intervened but declined. The results proved disastrous. Soto faced detention on Ellis Island, thus effectively ending his mission in the United States. French intelligence was livid that the case had been so bungled. Simultaneously, in Spain, Major Lang lost almost all credibility in his future dealings with local members of Allied intelligence. The Spanish government protested vigorously, and even Soto's family publicly demanded his immediate release.[21]

Eventually, US authorities dispatched Soto to France along with a warning from Biddle that Allied intelligence services should continue to watch him carefully. Despite what had happened, the story would have an unexpected ending. At a Franco-Spanish border checkpoint while awaiting his return to his native country, Soto poured out his feelings of anger to the local intelligence officer Lieutenant Leo J. Careaga and told of his plans to let the Spanish public know of his version of events. No record exists as to exactly what Careaga said to Soto to console him, but in some manner, he was still able to convince Soto to remain with AEF counterintelligence. Soto would honor his word and serve as a valuable source in several successful cases that helped to protect US troops within the rear areas.

Finally, not all of the Army's counterintelligence successes occurred in Europe or the States. Operating out of the old Fort Santiago in the city of Manila in the Philippines, Army intelligence ran a small but effective effort to counter the threats of pro-German groups and sympathizers, as well as help blunt the designs of the Japanese, who hoped to exploit the situation while America remained focused on Europe. When war broke out, German owners of vessels docked in the port of Manila attempted to scuttle their ships, lest they fall into the hands of the US government. Lorenzo Alvarado, who worked undercover for the Army, was able to warn officials in time to save more than 20 ships from destruction. Other highlights included the identification and arrest of a number of individuals in possession of classified documents. Alvarado and fellow agents were also involved in helping to spy out Japanese elements on the large island of Mindanao where they planned to stir up anti-American feelings as well as to foment attacks against government officials.[22]

INTELLIGENCE GATHERING

The MIB was involved in more than counterintelligence. By the early months of 1918, Yardley and MI-8 had taken important steps in becoming the principal cryptologic agency in the government, having assumed all the training and any residual code-breaking activity remaining at Riverbank. Yardley was able to effect the changes by commissioning two of Riverbanks' instructors (William Friedman and J. A. Powell) and having them reassigned to MI-8 and eventually overseas. The last cryptologic class held at Riverbank comprised 87 officers who, for their class photo, stood facing either to the front or looking off to the side in order to spell out the coded message, "Knowledge Is Power." Over time, MI-8 would train more than just cryptologists bound for service with the AEF; attachés and their assistants along with a number of other intelligence types, underwent a basic course in codes and ciphers.

In time, MI-8 began systematically to address various countries' cryptosystems starting with Chile, which contained a large settlement of Germans, and was the one remaining country in South America not to have broken off diplomatic relations with Germany. A second country of high interest was naturally Mexico. The two men whom Yardley chose to take the lead were Victor Weiskopf and Claus Bogel; the former, a Bavarian by birth, had spent years in Mexico and had already had some experience within the Justice Department in solving financial messages secured by unsophisticated Mexican ciphers. For instance, the Mexican consul general in New York City used a monoalphabetic cipher, not dissimilar to the cryptograms found in newspapers. Thus, when the State Department handed the War Department an enciphered message from Mexico, MI-8 was able to solve it almost immediately and furnish US officials with a clear picture of what was transpiring within the Mexican leadership.[23]

In January 1918, the Signal Corps created the Radio Intelligence Service, under the command of Major Carl Kinsley. Although the War Department did not formally recognize the organization until 2 months later, Van Deman was deeply involved in advocating its establishment. The 84 enlisted men and 16 officers belonged to the Signal Corps but were attached on special duty to the military intelligence element of the respective department in whose jurisdiction they were located. A string of 12 radio-tractor units (RTU; comprising 10 men each) ran along the New Mexico and Texas border with Mexico; in addition, there was one lone station near the town of Houlton, Maine. The chief signal officer also wrote of a final covert site in Mexico City itself but furnished no other details. Utilizing large loop antennas turned by hand, the Radio Intelligence Service conducted much the same mission as that of its sister organization for the AEF—intercepting radio communications and conducting direction finding. If asked by anyone about their mission, they were to reply that they were members of a "radio-training unit." A separate subsection within MIB coordinated the effort with the results flowing to MI-8 for analysis and exploitation.[24]

The small town of Houlton lay on the Canadian border. Here an intercept site copied diplomatic messages being transmitted from the powerful station POZ near Berlin to EGC in Madrid, Spain—a supposedly neutral nation. At the same time, a few intercept sites in France run by AEF signals intelligence were also copying diplomatic messages from Berlin and routinely transmitting copies back to MIB. Captain Charles J. Mendelsohn, who in the civilian world had excelled both in the classics and mathematics, served as the head of MI-8's German Code Solving Unit. Mendelsohn's team initially received some assistance when British cryptologists decided to share a partial reconstruction of the infamous Arthur Zimmermann telegram and a sample of other decoded intercepts. Taking full advantage of the large number of clerk-typists within MIB, MI-8 was able to prepare frequency tables of the various letters to achieve perhaps its greatest triumph—the breaking of the German diplomatic system. The cryptanalysts confirmed their success by deciphering Germany's 1,500-word prewar message to America's secretary of state and then compared it with the actual memorandum on file. While attacking the code, Mendelsohn and his staff mused that German officials probably no more heeded the advice of their cryptologists on how to protect their communiqués than US signal personnel did theirs.[25]

In late January, Berlin began to broadcast messages without an address or signature, repeating one message over 60 times during a 10-day period. The manner in which German operators were sending the messages led US intelligence to believe that the transmissions were intended for agents in a distant country. At the same time, the Radio Intelligence Service along the southern border began to intercept daily radiograms coming from an unknown station in Mexico. The high-power broadcasts were sent at certain times during the

day, and the sender repeated each code word twice, meaning that he was trying to communicate to a station a long distance away. By tuning their radio
direction finders to the signal, the tractor units soon pinpointed the location
of the transmitter—Chapultepee, the site of the Mexican government's most
powerful station with a callsign of XDA. It soon became apparent that Mexico was allowing German officials to talk, but about what? US cryptanalysts
went to work to find out.

One of the messages offered to provide Mexico with machinery and tech-
nicians to build aircraft; the same message also told of purchasing rifles in
Japan for Mexico. A second transmission authorized the German minister to
give Mexico 10 million Spanish pesetas for the purpose of remaining neutral
during the war. The same minister had also been urging Germany to pay
20 times that amount to Mexico to launch an open war against its northern
neighbor. Among those in Washington who were in receipt of the translated
messages, there was real excitement over the insights into the intentions of
Germany, Mexico, and Japan; as far back as the Zimmermann telegram, Germany had encouraged Mexico to ask Japan to join them in the war against the
United States. On the other hand, this gold mine of information would not last
long because Berlin suddenly stopped transmitting for some unknown reason,
and when it began again, the code was different.[26]

Not all success of cryptologists came from employing brainpower. A compromised cipher or a captured codebook on the battlefield often provided the
key to cracking the enemy's secrets. Besides these chance findings, all sides
actively engaged in efforts to steal the information needed by their cryptanalysts. When secret correspondence was intercepted and information extracted,
the documents still had to be sent on in such a manner as not to arouse suspicion. This brought MIB staff personnel in touch with the world of opening
and resealing letters, forgery of diplomatic seals, photography, duplication
of paper and envelopes if damaged, duplication of postmarks, replacing or
duplicating seals, etc. As an example, while involved in a series of counterintelligence investigations, MI-8 gained access to encrypted messages of high
Mexican officials by opening their correspondence. To reseal the documents,
specialists made a new wax impression by using an old Mexican centavo.[27]

SECRET INKS

To combat the enemy's secret inks, Allied chemists began on a regular basis
to share information. Consequently, the team effort soon produced a general
reagent—iodine vapor—that put them a step ahead of the Germans. Yardley
described the process: "Insert a secret-ink letter in a glass case and shoot in a

thin vapor of iodine. This vapor gradually settles into all the tiny crevices of the paper, all the tissues that had been disturbed by pen and water. Even to the naked eye there forms a clear outline of writing." No longer was it necessary to test one known reagent after another. Subsequently, MIB set up two laboratories—one within its Washington office to handle input from across the United States. Upon receiving his commission, Aloysius J. McGrail, a 27-year-old PhD in chemistry from nearby Catholic University, took charge of the effort.[28] The Army established its second secret-ink laboratory at the postal censorship office in Manhattan, where Emmett K. Carver, who possessed a PhD in chemistry from Harvard, was given oversight authority. Four women at the Manhattan office weekly treated an average of 2,000 suspicious letters with chemicals, but they would discover only 50 missives that contained possible secret writings. Among the group's successes was a letter signed "Maud" that possessed a number of cover addresses in several neutral countries along with instructions to target docks, war industries, and mercury mines. This resulted in the War Industries Board implementing tighter security measures within America's mercury industry.

The triumph of iodine vapor was short-lived; the German scientists once again assumed the lead by developing a means to trump the test. Finally, after hundreds of experiments, US chemists discovered the new method of concealment: "if a letter is written in secret ink, dried, dampened lightly by a brush dipped in distilled water, then dried again and pressed with an iron—secret ink cannot be developed by an iodine-vapor bath . . . because the dampening process disturbs all the fibers of the papers."[29] With this revelation, it appeared that a standoff had been reached; the Allies could not read German secret inks and vice versa. Somewhat by chance, scientists then discovered that by brushing strips of two different chemicals on a suspected letter, they would run together if secret ink were present. It was now only a matter of time before a second general reagent became available that could reveal all secrets. When it happened, Allied intelligence immediately put new safeguards into place.

MORE REPORTS

Elsewhere, the MI-2 staff began to forward their daily and weekly summaries to the president and secretary of state. A new feature was the current order of battle and updating of events on the western front, especially as it pertained to the US sector. The summaries also contained developments in the evolving situation in Russia—a matter of upmost interest to the Wilson administration. In his documentary history, Richard Challenger cites various examples of the types of insights provided: "Transportation is the key to supplying economic aid to Serbia. The railroads are fast becoming useless under the present inefficient Russian management. If present conditions continue it will soon be impossible to send materials to the interior in sufficient quantity and congestion will ensue at the ports of debarkation if freight is shipped from America in large quantities." A report from the military attaché in Russia argued that involvement in a civil war would be counter to US and Allied interests. "It is important to understand Trotsky's point of view. He was never under German direction" and "Negotiations for peace are inevitable and further attempts to interfere with the same will only serve to embitter the Russian people." On the subject of rising concerns that Germany itself might turn to bolshevism, a summary contained the following assurances: "A reliable and experienced observer who has returned from Berlin states that Bolshevism will never prevail in Germany and that most Germans are afraid of it."[30]

On the other hand, there were other reports that were simply inaccurate. In the early months of 1918, the weekly intelligence summaries frequently contained updates on the location and timing of the anticipated German offensive based more on rumors than solid intelligence. There was often the tendency for new intelligence officers to want to play the role of prophet rather than objective analyst. An example of serious misjudgment was repeating the fears frequently voiced by Allied analysts that Germany's real strategy was the creation of a "Teutonic corridor," which would supposedly stretch to China and India. This meant that the German leadership would withdraw some or all of their forces on the western front in order to shift them to Asia. The basis of such thinking was attributable to Germany's role in fomenting revolution within Russia.

Marlborough Churchill lamented the fact that few in the AEF actually read the weekly report regarding the activities of the MIB, because they were often too busy. Churchill also acknowledged that merely reading a report was not enough; greater personal contact between G2 and MIB was essential. The lack of communications and coordination could be attributed in part to MIB not becoming a separate division until August; at the same time, the buildup of line units prevented Nolan from sending more officers back to speak directly with members of the War Department staff.[31]

FINISHING THE COURSE

During the summer of 1918, military intelligence achieved an organizational and operational status at home that would not be surpassed until World War II. The appointment of Major General Peyton C. March as the chief of staff was responsible for this elevated position. Fresh from the battlefields of France, where he had served as chief of artillery for the AEF, March reorganized the General Staff into four functional divisions, designating intelligence as one of them. This was just one of many actions taken by March in his drive for greater efficiency. Consequently, on August 26, MIB changed its title to the Military Intelligence Division (MID), but it was more than just a mere redesignation. The director of military intelligence could now organize, direct, and coordinate the intelligence service, and for the first time, he gained, at least on paper, a piece of the intelligence training mission. Nevertheless, when MID attempted to exercise control over intelligence training in the field, the War Plans Division resisted, resulting in an agreement that left the director of military intelligence with only a small voice in policy matters, particularly as they pertained to the recruitment and training of positive intelligence personnel.

The new MID also brought with it new leadership. Ironically, Colonel Van Deman, who had worked so hard to make this day a reality, was not on hand at the inauguration of MID but had departed several days earlier for France. As a regular officer who desired a future in the Army, Van Deman knew that it was imperative for him to seek wartime service overseas. Future intelligence professionals would never forget Van Deman's contributions and sacrifice, and in time, would bestow on him the honorary title of "Father of Military Intelligence."

Recently arrived from France, where he had held a leadership post within the G2 staff at the GHQ, Marlborough Churchill was a logical choice to replace Van Deman as the new director of military intelligence. An officer who served under both men said that Churchill had the bearing of "a fine line officer" but still managed to relate to his subordinates in an informal manner; the same officer went on to state that he considered Churchill to have been an outstanding executive. The MID benefited from Churchill's close personal ties to Chief of Staff General March, something that Van Deman never enjoyed during his tenure. The 40-year-old Churchill would also have the distinction of being one of two US intelligence officers who, for the first time, acquired the rank of brigadier general. (Nolan, the AEF G2 received a simultaneous promotion in August.)

The MID was now large enough for General Churchill to bifurcate it into two major branches in keeping with the British. The Negative and Positive Branches further divided the various sections between them. It was logical that MI-3 (Counterespionage Military Service) and MI-4 (Counterespionage Civilian Sector) should fall under the Negative Branch and that MI-2 (Foreign Intelligence) should be under the Positive Branch. But it was not so obvious that MI-8, which touched on both intelligence collection and security of communications, belonged solely to the Positive Branch, and other sections, such as MI-6 (Translation), were meant to support all of MID. This created a lack of balance in the new organization. Between July and September, the last four sections were established: MI-9 (Field Intelligence), MI-10 (Censorship), MI-11 (Passports) and MI-12 (Graft and Fraud)—all but MI-9 falling under the Negative Branch. In a final analysis, 42 of the 57 sections and subsections belonged to the Negative Branch, and of those few assigned to the Positive Branch, at least half of them had a hand in counterintelligence-related missions.

PROPAGANDA

The War Department handed intelligence a number of missions simply because the discipline of military intelligence was so undefined as to invite new initiatives. Back in September 1917, President Wilson had tasked his close personal advisor and confidant Colonel Edward M. House to supervise an initiative that insiders dubbed "the Inquiry." Working out of the home of the American Geographical Society in New York City, the group busied itself assembling the necessary data needed should a Peace Conference ever take place. Walter Lippmann, a prominent writer for the New York *Herald Tribune*, served as the first secretary, but it would not be until July 1918 that Colonel Van Deman would exchange liaison officers with the conference.[32]

George Creel, a former journalist and progressive reformer from Colorado, served as the nation's chief propagandist and defined his mission in the following manner: "What was needed, and what we installed, was official machinery for the preparation and release of all news bearing upon America's war effort—not opinion nor conjecture, but facts—a running record of each day's progress in order that the fathers and mothers of the United States might gain a certain sense of partnership." Creel went on to name those given the job of meeting these goals: "Newspapermen of standing and ability were sworn into the government service and placed at the very heart of the endeavor in the War and Navy departments, in the War Trade Board, the War Industries Board, the Department of Justice, and the Department of Labor." Although the military had no say in policymaking, MI-2 maintained close liaison with Creel's organization—the Committee on Public Information—in order to align the Army's activities with the national effort. More precisely, the mission of MI-2's new psychological subsection was "to study enemy propaganda and to see that suitable counter-propaganda was initiated, and also that positive propaganda of our own was introduced into enemy armies and enemy countries."[33]

To fulfill these functions overseas, Captain Herbert Blankenhorn, a former city editor of the *New York Evening Sun*, busily set about training personnel who would accompany him to France, where they planned to assemble the necessary resources to unleash a propaganda campaign across enemy lines. Blankenhorn proposed following up the fall 1918 campaign with a second initiative directed against Austria-Hungary. Of course, Blankenhorn's plans would have to first be coordinated with his French, British, and Italian counterparts, but for the immediate, only one thing remained before Blankenhorn could depart for France—a delimitation agreement had to be prepared between the War Department and the Committee on Public Information. The signed document gave the military authority over all propaganda efforts against enemy countries but not regarding neutral or Allied nations. Blankenhorn immediately departed carrying a letter to General John Pershing from Secretary Newton Baker, a strong advocate for the use of propaganda. Blankenhorn no sooner arrived in France when he received word that the Committee on Public Information had reneged on its earlier agreement. Upon further reflection, the committee members felt strongly that they and they alone possessed authority over all propaganda efforts; the military was to serve only in an advisory capacity.

Retrospectively, too many military and civilian players wanted a piece of the action because they had come to believe falsely that propaganda was a major factor in the conduct of the war. In the meantime, President Wilson had, at the request of the State Department and his advisor Colonel House, commissioned Lippmann, who was known as a capable spokesman and an original thinker, to assist the War Department in its propaganda effort. When Captain Lippmann arrived in France, he had with him additional instructions from Secretary Baker regarding the use of propaganda. In Baker's words, "I have assured the State Department and Colonel House that his [Lippmann's] work with us would not mean the termination of his duties with them."[34] Although assigned on paper to Blankenhorn's element inside the G2, Lippmann thought of himself as separate and continued to communicate directly with Secretary Baker and Colonel House.

Believing that Lippmann's actions could have potentially embarrassing consequences, military leaders in the War Department felt it necessary to send a reminder to Secretary Baker. "The gathering of data for propagandist literature, the printing of it, the distributing of it, in so far as this work relates to the projection of such material over the fighting lines among the enemy troops should be carried out by the Intelligence Section of the General Staff."[35] To put an exclamation point to the whole affair, General Pershing himself complained to the War Department that members of Blankenhorn's organization (a not too subtle reference to Lippmann) were going outside prescribed channels. Nolan finally solved the problem by dispatching Lippmann and Blankenhorn to London to confer directly with James Keeley, a former US newspaperman who represented Creel's Committee on Public Information on the Inter-Allied Propaganda Board. From the meeting, the three arrived at an agreement that called for the AEF to place into Keeley's hands the information he requested. Subsequently, he and his staff would write, translate, and print the final products and then have them returned to the AEF for distribution across enemy lines.

ATTACHÉS

World War I witnessed a dramatic increase in the number of assigned attachés (more than 100) overseas at some 26 different posts. In the spring of 1918, Van Deman approved the consolidation of all functions related to military attachés into a separate section (MI-5). As the War Department received added resources, it could for the first time provide attachés with much-needed support, especially in Europe, where they had taken on myriad new missions: propaganda-related activities, interrogation of escaped Allied prisoners of war and enemy deserters, detection of major smuggling operations, and location of hostile communications facilities.

Being an attaché was not a soft job. As Colonel Marlborough Churchill explained it, "these men performed a task that was at once difficult, delicate, and sometimes vital to the success of our arms."[36] Just because US officers and agents were operating in neutral countries did not mean that they were totally out of harm's way; even in Switzerland, they received their share of bumps and bruises. One officer reported that upon departing the US legation late one night, a burly figure suddenly appeared from the shadows. His blackjack rendered the victim semiconscious, but the military attaché was still able to keep the assailant from obtaining his sought-after prize—the keys to the building. On another occasion, a US case officer was ambushed while driving his car on a mission-related trip near the Italian frontier. This time a bit of luck allowed him to escape unscathed.

As far back as the summer of 1917, the British government had first proposed that Allied attachés within London, Paris, and Washington, D.C., take the lead in creating intermilitary intelligence groups. Ten months would elapse before the Allies in Washington finally established an official foreign liaison service so there could be "one channel through which all information of a military nature, imparted to the foreign military representatives, will be supervised and controlled."[37] Lieutenant Colonel Constant Cordier was the military intelligence officer selected to head the new organization and subsequently reported directly to the chief of staff.

In the summer of 1918, Major Royall Taylor, chief of the military mission in France, began participating with other Allied military personnel attached to the Second (Intelligence) Bureau of the French War Ministry. Having spent his early career in the diplomatic corps, 32-year-old Taylor was a perfect fit for the assignment. The so-called Inter-Allied Bureau regularly exchanged information on trade, political, economic, and industrial conditions in enemy and neutral countries and activity of enemy agents in Allied and neutral countries. Bruce W. Bidwell in his *History of the Military Intelligence Division* comments that there was "no evidence that the departmental military intelligence agency [MID] ever received any helpful information" from this group, but the greater sharing of intelligence did contribute to the war effort overseas, especially in the gathering of economic news from across Europe.[38] The staff of Major Taylor also routinely relayed to US counterintelligence any information obtained from the Allies regarding the names and identification of known enemy spies as well as their methodology; the names and descriptions of various criminals and undesirables; and any relevant data intercepted by French postal and telegraph controls. In turn, Taylor made available to his fellow allies similar information obtained by the Americans.

After abandoning their counterespionage role altogether, military attachés refocused the last four months of the war on collecting positive intelligence, but MI-5's original idea of establishing a coordinated "spy-net" abroad was for the most part too little and too late. Still, MI-5 could point to examples of successes by individual attachés. In Italy, Colonel M. C. Buckey reported a week in advance that the Russians were planning to conclude a separate peace with Germany and to take part in Allied negotiations with Bulgaria. The US attaché to Norway enjoyed a close relationship with local authorities who passed on information concerning Germany's involvement in the Russian Revolution. In Denmark, Colonel Oscar N. Solbert prepared a report indicating that the Danes were not starving but were, in reality, supplying Germany with a large amount of food and goods. He also learned from a German that his country was shipping arms and ammunition via U-boat to the Sinn Fein in Ireland. Ultimately, this would aid the British in foiling a plan to land a revolutionary leader in Ireland. Late in the war, Solbert alerted the Allies to mutinies taking place in several of Germany's port cities. In Holland, Colonel Edward Davis ran one of the most successful US spy rings of the war. His informants included an individual who was close to an officer on the German General Staff and another who maintained a friendly relationship with the chief of engineers. And sometimes it was the innocuous that proved important. The attaché in Switzerland reported seeing an amusing story in a German paper about a man who rented his boots; digging further, he found that exorbitant prices were being paid for used shoes, meaning only one thing—there was a scarcity of leather.[39]

Throughout the Bolshevik Revolution, the War Department had an officer in Russia who served both as liaison and military attaché. In February 1918, Colonel James A. Ruggles succeeded General William V. Judson and continued to work the intelligence mission out of the US embassy as it relocated from Moscow to Petrograd, Vologda, and finally Archangel in northern Russia. Ruggles and his staff would prove particularly adept in advancing the evolving US policy. In March, Colonel Ruggles and Major E. F. Riggs served as the representatives of Ambassador David Francis in a meeting with Leon Trotsky, who was commissar of war under Premier Nikolai Lenin; the topics of discussion involved the issue of US military support against the threat of a possible German invasion and the status of the Russian army. In September, Ruggles communicated his findings in person to members of the Supreme War Council in Paris.[40]

CODE MAKING

As far as MI-8's own code making went, it took until June 1918 before Army cryptographers finally produced a substitute for the 1915 Telegraph Code; the so-called Code No. 5, which had two parts, used super-encipherment tables to further enhance its security. Unfortunately, it took only a matter of days for various non-MI Army organizations to compromise MI-8's masterpiece, and its replacement would not be ready until after the war was over. Chief of Staff General Tasker Bliss had also ordered that a special code be prepared for place names, but by the time code books were printed and distributed in October, the battle lines had been so redrawn as to make the documents no longer applicable. Cryptographers also went to work on a second specialty code to deal with casualty lists, but because no one staff element within the War Department could provide a complete list of all organizations and units overseas, there would be an intolerable delay before the code was finally finished. On the plus side, there were lessons learned in the production and distribution phase so that after the Armistice, when military intelligence issued a new code for attachés, it was in their hands within two weeks.[41]

In July, the Navy got out of the cryptanalytic business altogether when it fired its employees, turned its secret-ink equipment over to MI-8, and attached a liaison officer full time to MI-8. Apparently, from the start, personnel within the Navy office responsible for code breaking had remained quite secretive for a good reason—they were doing no work. The Navy Signal Office continued to maintain responsibility for creating its own codes, although

Yardley's cursory analysis of the finished products revealed that they were all quite easily breakable. Although numerous cryptograms were arriving daily from the State Department, the Navy, and various censorship offices, MI-8 did not possess a sufficient number of cryptanalysts to make a sizable dent in the workload until August 1918.

In the same month, Yardley departed MI-8, leaving it in the capable hands of his assistant, Major John Manly. The chief of MI-8 had become so exhausted from the constant strain he faced that he sought reassignment; consequently, his superiors suggested that he begin to make plans to lead a cipher bureau that would accompany the expeditionary force departing for Siberia. Fortunately, for Yardley, fate conveniently intervened in the form of a telegram from the AEF that requested his services as a liaison officer with the Allied cryptologic bureaus. Yardley was probably not the only one glad for his departure orders; a few of his fellow code breakers were finding him increasingly disagreeable.

While in Europe, Yardley busied himself by visiting his British and French counterparts to gain new insights into the ever-changing world of cryptology, but when he called on them, Yardley quickly discovered that he was not welcomed with the same open arms. Although high French officials had given their assurances to Yardley that he could have access to diplomatic cables moving between Berlin and Madrid, not even one was provided. The Allies had gladly cooperated when it came to military codes and ciphers; they were not about to do the same with their diplomatic communications.

NEGATIVE BRANCH

The growth of the Negative Branch throughout 1918 continued to exceed its sister organization—the Positive Branch. The MI-3 alone grew from 6 officers, 7 civilian agents, and 14 intelligence police in January to 279 military and civilian persons by November. The single section divided itself into 12 subsections, a veritable alphabetical soup consisting of small offices, each with a very thin slice of the counterintelligence pie. Unlike the Positive Branch, counterintelligence enjoyed supervisory powers over their officers in the field because of its ability to implement policy on how investigations were to be conducted. MI-3 often sent out officers to various camps and posts to assist intelligence officers as well as to make local authorities better aware of the Army's counterintelligence program. In October, MI-3 arranged for a number of intelligence officers to travel to Washington, D.C., where they received the latest information on security matters, but only two such conferences would be held prior to the cessation of hostilities.

When the former War Department representative to the National Censorship Board stepped down in August, General Churchill, chief of MID, assumed the title of chief censor for the Army and all the responsibilities that went with it. This led to the establishment of MI-10, which oversaw a wide range of subjects within the Army's purview: mail, publications, telegraph, radio, and photographs. Most of the missions were not actually new, but in fact, had been previously performed by various sections within MID. For instance, MI-4 gave up censorship of mail and publications. The new chief of MI-10 was 45-year-old Rupert Hughes, who was a noted author and future film producer and composer, as well as the uncle to future business magnate Howard Hughes.

By Armistice, MI-10B had representatives in each of the 12 postal censorship stations located across the country and eventually would assign 12 officers to military attachés in Europe to help with censorship duties. MI-10G initiated a review of 1,400 newspapers printed in some 33 different languages by various foreign-language presses across the United States; the survey discovered that a number of the publications were consistently printing stories that screeners labeled anti-American. Another element of MI-10 perused mainstream US newspapers for editorial comment on leading war issues; these were published semiweekly and forwarded to the secretary of war and the GHQ of the AEF. The same office worked closely with the Committee on Public Information regarding voluntary censorship of the press, but MID struggled when it came to banning books from military libraries and the US mail. Determining what subject matter fell within the category of actually being detrimental to the war effort was the main problem, although by the war's end, MID had succeeded in identifying 124 documents for removal from circulation.[42]

As US forces went into combat, the need to censure news photos and motion picture film grew exponentially. The MID attached personnel to the Executive Committee on Public Information in New York to help review commercial photographs and motion pictures destined for both domestic and foreign consumption. Besides security concerns, any photos that reflected negatively on servicemen were banned for fear that Germany could insert a different caption and use the image for propaganda purposes. Pictures that depicted soldiers suffering from illness were typical of those that found the censor mark.

Given its wide range of responsibilities, MI-10 quickly became a major player within MID. The staff of MI-10 consisted of 30 officers and 60 civilian employees; if personnel involved in postal and radio censorship across the country were included, the full organization amounted to nearly 300 persons. Because it focused on many matters that seemed on the surface to be secondary and not directly relevant to the security of the Army, MI-10 constantly faced criticism by others within MID for having drawn away too many personnel and monetary resources that could have been put to better use elsewhere.[43]

In May 1918, President Wilson signed off on the Passport Act; the numerous regulations that followed led MI-3 and MI-4 to divest themselves of passport control responsibilities and for MID to create in September a separate MI-11 (Passport and Port Control). Because there were six other major players (State, Justice, Treasury, Labor, Commerce, and Navy), the War Department had to speak with one voice, and MI-11 would become that voice. Under the US system, MI-11 primarily served to assist and advise. This consisted of opening up MID's investigative files to the State Department on those who desired to travel overseas; providing personnel to assist port authorities in examining incoming and outgoing travelers; and using the military attaché offices to screen those who desired visas to the United States. Situated across the country, the offices of the American Protective League also lent a hand to the State Department by confirming information on passport applicants. During the last three months of 1918 alone, MI-11 became increasingly busy responding to names submitted for travel permits to Europe; altogether, the numbers reached over 30,000 applications for US passports and alien departure permits.

Late in the war, MID, against its own stated policy, assumed responsibility for weeding out graft or fraud committed by Army civilians. Various members of the War Department staff expressed dissatisfaction concerning how the quartermaster general investigators had been performing their duties; the same signed memo also contained a recommendation that the function be transferred to military intelligence. The chief of staff signed off on August 16, and MI-12 came into being, eventually handling 1,128 cases that resulted in 517 arrests and 206 convictions in civilian or military courts. Besides bringing wrongdoers to justice, MI-12 earned credit for recovering some $495,582 in stolen government property. In one high-profile case, agents placed a sales representative from a large steel company under surveillance upon the suspicion that his sudden, extravagant lifestyle was the result of his having bribed officials within Army ordnance. During the course of its investigation, MI-12 employed skilled Corps of Intelligence Police agents to plant hidden microphones to gather the necessary evidence.[44]

THE FINAL REPORT

From the beginning, several conditions hindered the development of the intelligence effort on the home front. For starters, the commanders of America's fighting forces entered the war without any inkling as to what role intelligence or counterintelligence should play, and most would continue to remain ignorant until they reached France and experienced combat firsthand. Second, the intelligence element within the War Department remained a junior partner, even after it had become a member of the General Staff late in the war. The director of military intelligence never controlled the selection process of intelligence personnel or even defined their qualifications, except in the broadest of terms. More important, MID had no control over training of intelligence officers and specialists assigned to combat units, so the AEF would be forced to assume much of the task by default. Because it would take almost a year before reaching a sufficient level of personnel, MID could not begin to adequately support the intelligence efforts of the AEF until very late in the war. By this time, AEF had taken on a number of the responsibilities—such as espionage in nearby neutral countries—that normally should have been the purview of the War Department.

Without doubt, MID's greatest contribution lay in the area of counterintelligence, although the internal threat to the Army proved highly exaggerated. In 1919, Colonel Walther Nicolai, former chief of German intelligence, wrote, "England and America were all but completely protected by the sea against the penetration of our espionage. . . . So much the greater sensation did the few spies make who succeeded in getting in."[45] Besides enemy agents being few in number and largely ineffective, hyphenated Americans, with only a few exceptions, also remained loyal. Units drawn from German-settled areas such as Chicago, Milwaukee, or central Texas may have done more than their share of grumbling, but once fighting started, they proved just as American as the next. There were even attempts in German-run prison camps late in the war to turn alien American soldiers into enemy agents, but there is no evidence that any of the efforts met with success.

Regardless, Van Deman and his staff would create an effective counterespionage system starting from scratch and without the benefit of precedent. MID wrote the doctrine and put into place basic security procedures, such as photo identification cards, that would remain in effect long after the war had ended. Military intelligence also labored to ensure that certain high-risk functions of the Army, such as aviation, signal, and chemical, received special attention. In the end, Army counterintelligence delivered a loyal fighting unit overseas that greatly helped to allay the fears of America's allies. Likewise, military intelligence guaranteed the same degree of loyalty for the civilian volunteers who accompanied the soldiers. A major key to MID's success in weeding out sedition was the generous amount of time allotted in fulfilling its mission; more than half of the 2 million soldiers assigned to the AEF did not actually arrive until the last four months of the war.

The efforts of MID also touched on the larger war effort involving the US populace and worked alongside civilian authorities to help root out would-be saboteurs and to protect vital wartime industries. Because a focus on civil liberties had not yet reached national consciousness, MID did not face modern-day oversight. Still, military intelligence demonstrated self-imposed restraints as illustrated by its establishment of its own legal counsel. Also Van Deman's action to bring the American Protective League leadership under his control and to prepare written guidance for its membership helped ensure that abuses were minimized.

Another important contributor on the home front was Yardley's MI-8, which for the first time placed US cryptology on par with other major powers—just at a time when the science of code breaking was changing. David Kahn, who wrote *The Codebreakers*, noted that for 400 years, analysis had been characterized by a sole individual wrestling with a single cryptogram in an isolated chamber, but World War I witnessed greater use of communications, more sophisticated codes, and increased specialization in cryptanalysis, thus ushering in a new era.[46] In his biography of Yardley, Kahn concluded that the legacy of the first chief of MI-8 was not as a cryptologist but as an administrator and visionary—someone who had skillfully introduced a new discipline by giving his staff the tools and direction they needed to succeed. In total MI-8 read over 10,000 messages and solved 50 codes and ciphers of 8 different nations.[47] With the assistance of the Radio Intelligence Service, Yardley and his staff had furnished the United States' leadership with crucial insights as to the intentions of various foreign leaders and worked alongside counterintelligence in successfully bringing to conclusion a number of its most high-profile cases. Riverbank and MI-8 also successfully trained the Army's cryptologists, one of the few bright spots in intelligence schooling on the home front; on the other hand, its attention to training officers for work overseas delayed MI-8's own ability to acquire all the personnel needed to tackle its ever-expanding workload, which included both secret inks and shorthand.

The publication of intelligence summaries, which critically analyzed a wide range of subjects related to the conduct of the war, was as good an indicator as any in demonstrating how far military intelligence had progressed in such a short time. Important sources of the summaries and foreign intelligence in general were the military attachés. Unfortunately, those stationed throughout Europe were encumbered by an array of secondary missions that greatly undermined their effectiveness. Despite these distractions, they still achieved a number of remarkable intelligence coups by taking advantage of their foreign contacts that alerted authorities in Washington to shifting political events in the host countries.

In retrospect, the rapid expansion of military intelligence on the home front became a challenge in itself. The seemly unlimited number of resources had made portions of the mission inefficient, causing too many personnel and monies to be directed toward marginal and irrelevant functions, such as censorship, and in the process encouraged a lack of vision. While addressing secondary problems, no expenditure of effort was made to laying a foundation for military intelligence in the war's aftermath, such as creating a small foreign studies program, indentifying a means to meet future language requirements, and establishing an office to monitor emerging doctrines and technologies—any of which would have gone a long way in helping military intelligence to take its next step.

NOTES

1. Bruce W. Bidwell, *History of the Military Intelligence Division* (Department of Army, 1961), pt. II, chap. XVI, 73.
2. Camps E. Alexander Powell, *The Army behind the Army* (New York: Scribner's, 1919), 379.
3. Bidwell, *History of the Military Intelligence Division*, pt. II, chap. XVI, 21–23.
4. Ibid., 38–39.
5. Peter Carlson, *Roughneck* (Toronto: McLeod Limited, 1983), 242–244.
6. Ralph H. Van Deman, *The Final Memoranda* (Wilmington: Scholarly Resources, 1988), 35.
7. Bidwell, *History of the Military Intelligence Division*, pt. II, chap. XVI, 31.
8. Van Deman, *Final Memoranda*, 31.
9. Ibid., 31–32.
10. Bidwell, *History of the Military Intelligence Division*, pt. II, chap. XV, 26.
11. Ann Bray, ed., *History of the Counter Intelligence Corps* (Fort Holabird: US Army Intelligence Center, 1959), Vol. III, 33–34.
12. James Gilbert, with John P. Finnegan and Ann Bray, *In the Shadow of the Sphinx* (Fort Belvoir, VA: US Army Intelligence and Security Command, 2003), 14.
13. Van Deman, *Final Memoranda*, 60.
14. Thomas M. Johnson, *Our Secret War* (Indianapolis: Bobbs-Merrill, 1929), 142–149.
15. Herbert O. Yardley, *The American Black Chamber* (New York: Bobbs-Merrill, 1931), chap. VII.
16. David Kahn, *The Reader of Gentlemen's Mail* (New Haven, CT: Yale University Press, 2004), 43–44.
17. While in prison, Witzke would risk his life during a fire to save fellow inmates, and in 1923, upon Germany's request, Naval Lieutenant Witzke would see his sentence commuted after which he would return home with an Iron Cross First and Second Class as well as a hero's welcome.

18. "German Cryptographic Systems during the First World War," paper of unknown origin probably prepared by the Army Signal Security Agency, 26.

19. A. A. Hoehling, *Women Who Spied* (Lanham, MD: Madison Books, 1993), 95.

20. Victorica's final resting place would be the Gate of Heaven Cemetery, Hawthorne, New York, under a marker that read innocuously, "Grave 8, Plot B."

21. Bray, *History of the Counter Intelligence Corps*, Vol. III, 40–42.

22. After World War I, Alvarado would go on to a distinguished career as a noncommissioned officer in the Corps of Intelligence Police.

23. Theodore M. Hannah, "The Many Lives of Herbert O. Yardley" (Center for Cryptologic History, National Security Agency), 6; Richard D. Challenger, ed., *United States Military Intelligence 1917–1927* (New York: Garland, 1979), Vol. 1, ix.

24. Bidwell, *History of the Military Intelligence Division*, pt. II, chap. XVI, 57; War Department, *Report of the Chief Signal Officer* (Washington, DC: Government Printing Office, 1919), 337–338.

25. Yardley, *American Black Chamber*, 173.

26. Ibid., 138–139.

27. Kahn, *The Reader of Gentlemen's Mail*, 117.

28. Lieutenant McGrail would have the distinction of leading the army's secret-ink effort in both World War I and II.

29. Yardley, *American Black Chamber*, 81.

30. Challenger, *United States Military Intelligence 1917–1927*, Vol. 1, v–xvi.

31. Bidwell, *History of the Military Intelligence Division*, pt. II, chap. XVIII, 9.

32. Ibid., 12–13.

33. Bidwell, *History of the Military Intelligence Division*, 10.

34. Ibid., 17.

35. Bidwell, *History of the Military Intelligence Division*, 18.

36. Marlborough Churchill, "The Military Intelligence Division, General Staff," *Journal of the United States Artillery* 52, no. 4 (1920): 301.

37. Bidwell, *History of the Military Intelligence Division*, pt. II, chap. XIV, 9.

38. Ibid., 19.

39. Ibid., chap. XV, 30–32.

40. Ibid., chap. XVII, 43.

41. Herbert O. Yardley, "A History of the Code and Cipher Section during the First World War" (War Department, 1919), 9.

42. Nationwide, President Wilson's postmaster general, Albert S. Burleson, took the lead in the suppression of various publications deemed distracting from the war effort.

43. Bidwell, *History of the Military Intelligence Division*, pt. II, chap. XVI, 67.

44. Ibid., 27.

45. Dennis E. Nolan, "A History of Military Intelligence and the AEF: A Working Draft," chap. IV, 18.

46. David Kahn, *The Codebreakers* (New York: Macmillan, 1967), 348.

47. Kahn, *Reader of Gentlemen's Mail*, 50.

During the Civil War, signal towers served as platforms to watch for enemy movements. National Archives Records Agency (NARA)

Colonel Arthur Wagner was an early advocate for the Army's use of intelligence. National Archives Records Agency (NARA)

An Army balloon at Fort My-
ers, Virginia, in 1908. National
Archives Records Agency (NARA)

In 1914, the Signal Corps
acquired three radio trac-
tors. National Archives
Records Agency (NARA)

German Ambassador von Bernstorff (on right)
financed acts of sabotage on US soil. Library of
Congress

Secretary of War Newton
Baker (left) overruled Chief
of Staff General Hugh Scott
(right) by establishing MIS.
Library of Congress

The War College would serve as the first home for the Military Intelligence Service.
National Archives Records Agency (NARA)

Badge worn by counterintelligence agents. Intelligence and Security Command (INSCOM)

Eccentric millionaire George Fabyan would help solve the Army's cryptologic problems. National Security Agency

Colonel Dennis E. Nolan became the Army's first G2. National Archives Records Agency (NARA)

While French instructors observe, AEF intercept operators practice their skills. National Archives Records Agency (NARA)

A French officer demonstrates an aerial camera to American trainees. National Archives Records Agency (NARA)

The 29th Engineers tackled the herculean job of preparing tons of maps. National Archives Records Agency (NARA)

A parabolic was the more mobile of the two types of sound ranging devices. National Archives Records Agency (NARA)

Colonel Van Deman would receive the title of "Father of Military Intelligence." National Archives Records Agency (NARA)

In 1918, MID moved into the Hooe Building at 1330 F Street, NW, Washington, DC. Library of Congress

Against the war, members of the IWW union slowed down production. Library of Congress

Lothar Witzke was one of the most deadly saboteurs to target the United States. Copyright Brown Brothers

Members of MI-8 made a lasting contribution to Army cryptology. Intelligence and Security Command (INSCOM)

General Marlborough Churchill would be the first chief of MID. National Archives Records Agency (NARA)

Soldiers assigned to a Type R observation balloon struggle against the wind. National Archives Records Agency (NARA)

Aerial photographer sights his camera from the rear cockpit. National Archives Records Agency (NARA)

A CIP detachment along with officers and stenographers. Back row, far left is SGT Peter de Pasqua, first decorated agent. Intelligence and Security Command (INSCOM)

In Paris, counterintelligence officers examine documents for secret inks. National Archives Records Agency (NARA)

The Army's first cryptologist, Colonel Parker Hitt studies a code. National Archives Records Agency (NARA)

Monitoring Station No. 2 listens for AEF secrets being passed in the clear. National Archives Records Agency (NARA)

AEF intelligence prepared guidelines for the handling of the mail. National Archives Records Agency (NARA)

Observer of the 2nd Balloon Company receives last-minute briefing. National Archives Records Agency (NARA)

Officials watch an interrogation of enemy soldier in progress. National Archives Records Agency (NARA)

Belgian and US counterintelligence officers question a suspected enemy agent. National Archives Records Agency (NARA)

When necessary, reconnaissance aircraft used dropped messages as a backup. National Archives Records Agency (NARA)

Mobile intercept operations in Germany helped to track defeated forces. National Archives Records Agency (NARA)

CPT J. Rives Childs (left) and MAJ Herbert O. Yardley (right) handled codes during Peace Conference. National Archives Records Agency (NARA)

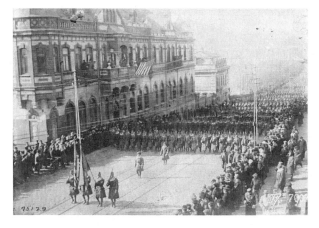

American troops march past their headquarters in Vladivostok. Library of Congress

A bombing at Wall Street in 1920 was symbolic of the unrest following WWI. Library of Congress

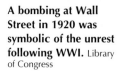

5

Tested under Fire

"Faulty plans are generally the result in war of insufficient knowledge of the state of affairs on the enemy's side, more particularly as regards his strength, his morale, his positions, and his plans."

—Colonel Walter C. Sweeney

In 1918, the challenge for intelligence was the same as for the larger US Army—fielding a trained force in sufficient numbers. Unlike the first months overseas, there was a shift in emphasis from the G2 staff at general headquarters (GHQ) to the line units, but training combat intelligence officers had been handicapped from the beginning by the lack of any type of realistic instruction being conducted on the home front. The exception were those officers and enlisted personnel involved in technical fields, such as air or signal intelligence; they had come through separate schools and were thus better equipped to continue their next step—on-the-job training.

The first class given to division intelligence officers had occurred in November 1917 when the War Department ordered all such personnel to the War College for a two-week course, but the brevity of training coupled with a cursory review of nonrelevant subjects would undermine any real progress. Other obstacles were the lack of instructors with the necessary background and the absence of study manuals. The one and only piece of literature available was something innocuously titled *Instructions on the Research and Study of Information*. During these early courses, research problems were often assigned to the students; on one occasion, they were directed as a group to find what information the various governmental agencies had on the subject of economic resources of the Central Powers; not surprisingly, the answer was none.

In December, General Pershing signed off on a cable to the War Department indicating that all future instruction of intelligence officers should take place in France. Subsequently, it was arranged that they would deploy three months in advance of their divisions. Initially, this training consisted only of a brief visit to the front lines followed by attendance at the American Expeditionary Forces (AEF) General Staff College in Langres, France. One problem with the new arrangement was that an intelligence officer often found himself separated from his division just when it was beginning to meld as a unit.

Not all intelligence officers received formal training. The intelligence staffs at corps and below benefited immensely from Colonel Dennis Nolan's liberal policy of allowing staff officers, with the exception of his four principal division chiefs, to seek reassignment. Most regular officers desired a position at or near the front, and when they obtained it, they often took with them others who had served under them at the GHQ. Although sometimes criticized for letting go of a key person, Nolan normally had more personnel on hand than were actually required. One advantage from this approach was ensuring the placement of officers who understood just how the intelligence system actually worked. They knew what type of information each echelon required as well as what its collection responsibilities were; they also grasped the larger picture, such as what reports were being exchanged with fellow allies. After the war, a number of the officers acknowledged to Nolan just how much they had learned at Chaumont even beyond their daily assignments; for instance, while dining at one of the messes for members of the intelligence staff, they often talked shop and took the opportunity to pose questions to the various division chiefs and resident experts.[1]

In July 1918, the AEF finally obtained its own separate American Intelligence School at Langres. The school was unique in that enlisted specialists went to classes alongside officers. Major Thomas Carton served as the first director, and a handful of Allied officers assisted the US staff. The school focused on giving its students an overview of combat intelligence along with an introduction to the various disciplines. The curriculum always began with a lecture on the recent history and organization of the German army, and the classes lasted either eight weeks or two six-week periods with a break in between. There were even opportunities for hands-on instruction; for example, the class on human intelligence ended with an opportunity to participate in interrogating real enemy prisoners.[2]

The average class size was 46; this allowed school officials to become acquainted with the individual student and thus better able to place him within the system where he often faced additional specialty instruction and on-the-job training. Many of the new arrivals thought they were going to perform one type of assignment and would wind up being transferred to a totally different discipline or, as one officer explained the situation, "We took these fellows, however, and told them to forget what they were told back in the United States and we straightened them out."[3]

Despite the new Intelligence School at Langres, the prospects of organizing two army headquarters within the next five months would force the AEF to try and solve once and for all the problem of inadequately trained intelligence officers arriving overseas. In the summer of 1918, Nolan dispatched Colonel F. L. Dengler to the War Department. Besides assuming a position within the Training and Instruction Branch of the War Plans Division, Dengler also became head of the new MI-9 (Field Intelligence) Section—a small office devoted to policy matters. Despite Colonel Dengler's elevated status within the Military Intelligence Division (MID), his numerous visits to training camps, and his ongoing recommendations for major changes, the chief of the Training and Instruction Branch met all efforts to alter the status quo with strenuous opposition, and in the end, Dengler failed to achieve any meaningful progress.

INTELLIGENCE IN THE FIELD

Intelligence answered a number of basic questions for combat commanders: Where were their own forces and where were the enemy's forces? For the latter, maps were obviously invaluable; updates relied heavily on topographical surveys and aerial photographs. Other forms of collection that were helpful in identifying the location of German units included observation posts, balloons, and direction-finding sites. During actual periods of combat, flash and sound ranging devices targeted the enemy's guns in order to deliver more effective counter-fire; the same for air intercept, which copied communications between spotting aircraft and enemy batteries. Because World War I was mostly fought along a stalemated front, artillery was truly the king of the battle given its accuracy and ability to reach behind enemy lines. It was natural that there would be resources within the intelligence arsenal that were devoted solely to locating the placement of the enemy's concealed guns.

The next question was to discern who were the opposing forces? And what were their plans? This came from knowing the makeup and objective of the opposing divisions. Information used in the creation of such an order of battle was derived from many sources: scouts, train watchers, radio intercept, direction finding, photo intelligence, interrogation of prisoners, and captured documents. Finally, field commanders required early warning. Here, both radio and telephone intercepts were especially useful. At night, acoustic devices were deployed to alert platoons of the 56th Engineers, who manned searchlights for antiaircraft that enemy aircraft were approaching, and when nighttime conditions were ideal, the Air Service was able to perform reconnaissance missions.

During the winter and spring of 1918, the US Army busily deployed arriving units along a quiet sector where a series of trenches radiated outward from the no-man's land. At each echelon, intelligence had an area of responsibility for which it was accountable. At regiment and below, those involved in observation, scouting, and trench raids underwent training. Some learned how to use maps, others practiced with field glasses, and all underwent lessons in what was called woodcraft—the study of one's natural surroundings and how to listen and see at night. Those who showed no enthusiasm or aptitude for this type of work were immediately dispatched back to their parent unit. During the final stage of instruction, trainees attended a Center of Resistance where they practiced their new skills in a setting simulating combat conditions.[4]

During those periods when codes were not being routinely broken, greater reliance was placed on raids to reconfirm the identification of opposing forces through captured prisoners and documents. Often it was the G2 at division or corps who recommended to his commander when a raid into an entrenched position should be ordered; a brigade or regiment might direct a raid when there were no trenches. Over time, forays became more and more dangerous as all belligerents moved out of their forward trenches, requiring patrols to travel deeper into enemy-held territory.

In keeping with British doctrine, all US battalions possessed a small scout detachment of 15 enlisted men from which the local commander drew no more than two soldiers to accompany each raiding party. Because the battalion commander was responsible for knowing everything going on within his small piece of the front, he was motivated to select some of his best soldiers as scouts. Another indicator of their value was that when the battalion suffered casualties, its leadership always made sure that the scout positions were among the first filled. This led Nolan to express concern as to whether the scouts might be suffering disproportional losses. A closer study revealed that this was not the case and that the casualty rate of scouts was in keeping with the rest of the infantry.

Although trained to use the trench knife to silently kill an opponent, the scouts' primary assignment was to search dead bodies for official and personal documents, cut off identification markings from uniforms, and survey the dugouts for items of interest. Without soldiers specifically trained to collect the sought-after items, raids seldom produced meaningful information, or as one officer lamented, "They haven't searched the dead, they didn't cut off in the excitement the markings on the uniforms to show the division that was opposite and you had a perfectly futile loss of men because nobody was charged with this particular activity."[5]

Besides participating in raids, scouts also engaged in more traditional types of missions. On the night of May 18, the 166th Infantry Regiment dispatched a four-man team led by Lieutenant John Leslie to cross the no-man's land and reconnoiter the town of Hau de Ancerviller. From a clump of trees just outside the village, the concealed soldiers were able to see three machine gun positions, an artillery battery, and the path being used by sentries. The Americans could even identify in the distance the sound of three passing supply trains and witnessed firsthand the arrival of a wagon caravan. Given the news of increased activities, higher headquarters subsequently directed more raids into the area to determine more clearly the exact intentions of the Germans.

At the regimental level, an intelligence officer, or S2, was normally appointed from among staff members. Lieutenant Shipley Thomas recalled standing before his commander and hearing these words, "Young man, you are the Regimental Intelligence Officer, whatever the hell that is."[6] According to regulations, regimental intelligence was to forward to the next echelon items of interest collected from the battlefield or during a raid. If the local geography allowed for an elevated position with a good view of the area and adequate concealment, the regiment could then designate an eight-person crew to man an observation post; an experienced infantryman proved to be the ideal observer. Manual Morse code, by either telegraph or a lighted blinker, was used to transmit reports to the rear where a draftsman recorded all new items of interest on a situation map and prepared a report for division intelligence.

Regimental intelligence was told "to live with the enemy." Captain C. S. Coulter, Intelligence Officer with the 18th Infantry Regiment, wrote that this meant "every move of the enemy, every light and flare; every shot fired by his field pieces, trench mortars, machine guns and rifles, must be recorded and interpreted."[7] Sometimes even the most trivial reporting could denote something of importance. One regimental observation post recalled seeing a few Germans in light gray uniforms with green insignia. The news was transmitted up the chain without any action being taken. At the GHQ, a member of the intelligence staff was finally able to identify the unknown officers as being assigned to the Jaeger Division, a first-class assault unit that had been long missing from the front. Because such a unit would normally lead an offensive, intelligence immediately posted an alert to nearby Allied troops.

Although not part of the regiment's chain of command, the Radio Intelligence Section had listening stations close to the frontlines. During the first years of the war, all belligerents used telegraph and telephone lines for communications, but because they ran throughout the front zone, the lines were subject to wiretapping. Over time, combatants adopted a form of ground relay, such as the French *telegraphie par sol*, known simply as TSP. Using this method, signal personnel drove iron poles into the ground for transmissions at low frequency at a distance up to 4 or 5 kilometers. Because TSP and ground telephone required no wires or antennas, such systems also left communications less vulnerable to enemy artillery.

Despite the use of ground relay, low-level communications were still susceptible to interception by using an apparatus that employed the principle of electromagnetic induction; the right type of soil and the amount of dampness were also crucial factors in determining conductivity. "By constructing loops of wire paralleling the enemy's lines of communication and magnifying by means of an amplifier the tiny electric currents induced in them, it was possible to intercept the messages. . . . In addition, copper-mesh mats or metallic rods were buried as near the enemy's wires as possible, and from here, wires led to the amplifier."[8] (The new US SCR-72 amplifier would eventually prove superior to the French model.)[9] By means of these grounds, stray currents and leaks from enemy wires were magnified into audibility. Interception was also possible against a single wire that used a ground return and the two-wire systems where the lines were separated by at least 12 inches. Within wooded areas, loop antennas used for intercept were often attached to tree tops near but out of sight of enemy forces.

In February 1918, the 1st Division assumed a position on the southern flank of the St. Mihiel Salient, where the first two US listening stations became replacements for the French sites. An eyewitness described the difference between the first two US stations in the following manner: "the station at Marvoisin was a hole in the ground, and one at Seicheprey a hole above the ground."[10] The operators at the former site lived in quarters inside a dugout the size of a packing crate filled with the smell of earth mixed with other unpleasant odors. Here, the four men assigned to the site ate, slept, and worked; their only companions being foot-long rodents. Colonel Frank Moorman wrote:

> The requirements for an ideal listening-station operator are very severe. He must be thoroughly familiar with the German language, including the special military terms. He must be able to read accurately buzzer messages in continental code through all kinds of jamming and static. . . . Most important of all, he must be able to exercise judgment in order to give information of immediate value to the local commander and to prepare the daily report, giving the probable location of enemy ground-telegraph stations and other data which might be useful in determining the time of enemy reliefs and the disposition of hostile forces.[11]

Of the various assignments performed by radio intelligence, none was more hazardous and replete with challenges than serving at a listening station, which was always no more than a kilometer from the front lines. The point of intercept had to take place within at least 3 to 4 kilometers of the base line being used, and if the signals originated from wires, then the distance fell to 2 or 3 kilometers. At least on one occasion, the close proximity to the enemy was almost disastrous. During a German attack, the area where a listening station was located was temporarily overrun, but the operators stayed hunkered down and kept copying until a US counterattack recaptured the loss ground.

From time to time, German communications went silent, requiring the listening station to extend its intercept lines. An AEF operator described one such occasion:

[L]eading the patrol meant crawling for 3 hours to cover a distance of a few hundred yards. But every 5 minutes or less a star shell from their lines would suddenly leap into the sky to illuminate a square mile of territory. Then we were forced to flatten out into immobility so that the color of our clothes might blend with that of the earth. Thus, we struggled and toiled, first through our own barbed-wire entanglements and then into the ditches and shell craters and across the dangerous ground swells until we reached the creek. The operator sought about until he discovered a clump of bushes and gentle hummock shielding him from the enemy's vision. He then hurriedly scooped out a hole in the creek mud, buried the mat, to which he attached a double line, and hastily covered up his operations.[12]

The return trip posed even greater risks. Although alerted that a patrol would be coming in at 0100 hours, some trigger-happy sentry fired shots in their direction, thinking them to be the enemy. "The automatic rifles and machine guns began firing. . . . And the shrapnel curtain swept us with a gentle spray of steel fragments and earth clods. We scooted for cover, dived into shell holes, squirmed between shielding undulations." This was followed by the enemy letting go a few artillery rounds of its own, but eventually, the patrol was able to find its way back through an opening in the lines.

Later when the enemy adopted the strategy of expanding the depth of the no man's land, it meant that listening operators had to venture into patrolled areas in order to install a new antenna. During one such mission, operators spent several days hidden inside the ruins of a farmhouse that lay in clear sight of German soldiers and used the cover of darkness to shield their efforts to repair the lines. It was equally important that all return lines were continuously checked so that the enemy didn't wiretap into them to hear stray TSP signals emanating from nearby friendly stations.

Often it wasn't what was said on the telephone, but what could be inferred from the conversation. For instance, if the party on line asked for the location of various types of facilities, such as dressing stations, it meant that they were new arrivals. Intercept operators also alerted higher headquarters when any mention was made of a specific time or date, as well as the manner in which the transmission was received—all possible indicators of a forthcoming attack. Changes in the accents or tone of operators or a different type of greeting could also reflect the arrival of a replacement unit. For instance, even how everyday terms such as *bitte* for please or *guten morgen* for good morning were used could betray a new operator. Other indicators were decreases or increases in the volume of a transmission or adoption of new procedures often associated with pending enemy attacks. By hearing the loudness of a signal, listening stations could even estimate, with some degree of accuracy, the transmitter's distance, and by drawing lines between the communications links, operators could re-create a chain of command within a division.

Each day at 0600 hours, the listening stations prepared reports for the corps G2 on everything heard over the previous 24 hours; two more copies went to the intelligence officer at division. The reports, however, were often at least 48 hours old before arriving at their final destination. Operators were directed to hand over all urgent messages to the nearest officer for him either to take necessary action or to forward the reports up the chain of command, but infantry officers who had no prior experience in dealing with such intelligence sometimes failed to appreciate the requirement to act on the information in a timely manner.

The telephone would remain the enemy's primary means of communications from infantry battalion to the rear; a captured document acknowledged the damage done by careless talk: "The most serious harm yet to the German front has without doubt been through imprudent telephone conversations."[13] On one occasion, German operators passed news of having intercepted plans over the telephone for an Allied gas attack; this alert was in turn copied by US intercept stations, which were able to warn the French to change the time and place of the attack.

By the summer of 1918, the Germans would undertake a number of steps to improve their communications security. One was to use electrical generators to mask any possible ground intercept. By the same token, the reverse was equally true; when the generator was operating, the Americans could talk on their own phones without any fear that the Germans were overhearing them. Still, for a few hours a day, perhaps for maintenance purposes, the electronic screen was shut down, and a signal went out for the Americans to cease their conversations and for listening stations to resume their copying.

INTELLIGENCE WITHIN DIVISION

Originally, the brigade was not considered a link in the intelligence system. Experience changed this, making the adjutant responsible for appointing an intelligence officer to collect and maintain information on the immediate area so that the data could be transferred to his replacement. The brigade's area of interest was defined as 1 mile to the rear of the enemy's front lines, and its primary means of obtaining information was simple observation. Items of special interest included machine-gun and trench-mortar emplacements, improved trenches, dumps, trench railways, reserve dugouts, observation posts, and command posts. After making a close study of the enemy's artillery fire, a sergeant who was serving as an observer reported that enemy gunners had a tendency to "walk" their artillery fire diagonally across to the right. To minimize casualties, advancing US troops began to walk left at an oblique angle to avoid the incoming shells. The brigade intelligence officer was also assigned the task of transferring all captured documents and prisoners to division unless there was some bit of information that had an immediate impact on his unit's security.

Most divisions were assigned a trained intelligence officer; those without one appointed an individual from within their staff. At division, intelligence was responsible for a collection zone 2 miles behind enemy lines. During periods of fighting, intelligence conducted a brief examination of prisoners in order to determine if they possessed information of immediate interest, particularly as it pertained to order of battle. Experience showed that a cup of coffee and a cigarette were useful tools in winning the cooperation of new prisoners. Division intelligence also examined captured enemy projectiles, bombs, and grenades along with related equipment, such as trench mortars. For items of high interest, such as aerial bombs, fuses, and howitzer shells, the local intelligence officer would prepare a description of the captured ordnance and forward it to incoming divisions undergoing training; a second copy went to corps G2. If a new or unique item was recovered, then intelligence forwarded the actual device. In one instance, a US scout crawled unnoticed into an enemy's unattended trench and successfully exited with a new type of machine gun; he had enough time to scribble a receipt for the borrowed weapon. The intelligence officers were also responsible for the distribution of maps and reports within their division and the preparation of a summary of intelligence that covered all locally collected information. When all was relatively quiet and stable, the division routinely produced informative summaries that focused on order of battle, but once fighting began, the division's reporting dropped off significantly in terms of regularity and content. As far as collection systems, most were either on the front lines or at corps, which directed the artillery; divisions would have only balloons.

Despite the Signal Corps' earlier history with balloons, the US Army's school for ballooning had been active at Fort Leavenworth for less than five months when America entered the war. Colonel Frank P. Lahm, chief of the Air Service, Second Army, indicated that the Balloon Service's greatest challenges were in persuading the General Staff that it was required and in securing the necessary personnel and materiel on a timely basis. The effort owed a great debt to the foresight of Major East of the Balloon Service. The major placed an early order with the French for equipment components, such as cabling and baskets, and requisitioned Fiat trucks and cars from the Italians. For its supply of hydrogen and the balloons themselves, the Balloon Service was dependent on the home front. The high-grade cloth, which consisted of 140 threads per square inch, was a challenge, but US industry was up to the test, delivering 1,025 balloons of all sorts and shapes to the US Army. Finally, Major East dispatched a cable to the States requesting necessary soldiers to fill the companies, along with a note urging their immediate deployment.[14]

Colonel Lahm credited the French for helping to get the Balloon Service off the ground. In October 1917, a conference of US and French officers agreed to build the US balloon facility at Vadenay, north of Chalons-sur-Marne and near the French Balloon School. America's ally also supplied a cadre of specialists to begin teaching arriving artillery on how to operate the balloons. By March, the AEF's own school for balloonists was finally finished at Camp Souge, where the French quickly made good on their promise to train up to 100 US officers as observers. All totaled, 199 officers and 623 enlisted men received training on how to handle the winches, to perform observation duties, to fire machine guns, and to operate radios. A full company consisted of 182 soldiers, but most were used to man the ropes that controlled and moved the large, unwieldy 92-foot balloons on or near the ground. Winches were utilized to raise and lower the balloons—hence, the popular nickname of kite-balloon. Under the best of conditions, a stationary gasoline-driven windlass was able to pull down at a rate of 1,600 feet a minute, surpassing the descent speed of a typical elevator; while moving an airborne balloon to a new location, a mobile winch could travel at 5 miles an hour or better.[15]

By the end of the war, the Balloon Service had a total of 35 companies serving throughout France: the companies were almost evenly divided by whom they supported—intelligence or artillery—despite the similarity in the skills of the observers. Artillery received a higher priority so that when the first four balloon companies arrived in France in late 1917, the Balloon Service immediately dispatched them to one of the firing ranges. The 2nd Balloon Company was the first on the frontlines, where it relieved a French unit near Royaumeix in late February 1918. Two more companies came on board in April—also taking the place of French units.

Along the stabilized front, balloons more than adequately performed their spotting duties for the artillery and provided general surveillance for the G2; on a clear day with a good pair of field glasses, an observer at an altitude of 1,000 meters could see large objects up to 10 miles away. Over the course of the war, US observers made 1,642 ascents in the Zone of Advance, which translated into over 3,000 hours, and reported enemy battalions 400 times, enemy traffic (both roads and railroads) 1,113 times, and enemy infantry movements 22 times. Balloons also supported the infantry by taking photos of the horizon that were used in preparing panoramic mosaics.[16]

Because the life expectancy of a balloon was only 15 minutes, US observers, unlike airplane crews, wore parachutes that they used some 116 times, minimizing the number of casualties to a single officer who died when debris from a burning balloon fell on his chute. Two other observers were captured after their balloons were blown by strong winds into enemy territory. When one officer jumped five times in a single day, his commander thought well enough to recommend him for the Distinguished Service Cross. A major shortcoming was that when an observer jumped, he most often left his records and instruments behind. Toward the end of the war, a basket chute was developed in which an observer simply pulled a chord and down came basket and all; Americans made 30 such successful landings.

The most hazardous duty in the Balloon Service was on the ground, where approximately 125 were killed or wounded from small-arms fire, gas, and artillery. Day-to-day life was generally rough for those in a balloon company; one soldier who spent 250 continuous days in action reported that conditions were "on the front . . . very poor—dysentery, poison gas [phosgene and chlorine], no sanitation, very poor food."[17] An especially arduous task was the ongoing requirement to conceal balloons. This usually meant preparing a suitable hiding place among trees by cutting both trees and limbs and digging up stumps that might puncture a balloon being moved. In the morning hours while still dark, a balloon was relocated at least a mile away from its bed in order to set up for its ascent.

For much of his life, Colonel Lahm had been a balloon enthusiast to the point of participating in the sport of racing, and at beginning of the war, he had served as the commandant at the Fort Leavenworth Balloon School. So it was not surprising that Colonel Lahm should speak in glowing terms regarding the overall performance of balloon platforms during the course of the war, claiming that the US Balloon Service was the most successful part of the Air Service mission.[18] The Germans themselves saw balloons as a greater threat than Allied planes, crediting their aviators with 1.5 planes shot down for every Allied balloon destroyed. Any success balloons enjoyed over aircraft was attributable to the telephonic links that allowed for instantaneous communication between the observer and the ground. Ironically, the Balloon Service's greatest failure was its inability to improve coordination with the fixed-wing half of the Air Service, but all attempts at establishing greater cooperation never went beyond informal talks.

THE CORPS

By late winter, the AEF had grown to the point that corps began to appear along America's front. The area assigned to corps intelligence extended 5 miles from the enemy's front, and data and maps, along with dates, were to be maintained on everything from buried cables to supply dumps to roads. Six of the officers who served as G2 at corps benefited significantly from having been assigned initially to GHQ intelligence; because of their experience, they understood that the corps echelon was crucial to the collection process. The regulations specifically emphasized that the staff should not see themselves as a mere post office moving information to Army headquarters; rather, they were assigned the responsibility of noting the reliability of all sources. For instance, corps personnel held the key to captured documents and prisoners by differentiating which were more important and required immediate exploitation.

The G2 at corps used reports from divisions, captured documents, observation, and prisoners in preparing his own report and then proceeded to forward it along with attached photos. Should the information be considered time sensitive, the G2 staff could transmit it via telegraph; likewise, captured documents of interest and knowledgeable prisoners were dispatched as quickly as possible back to Army G2. The corps was also responsible for publishing an intelligence summary. Information came from the various reports being produced by corps staff elements as well as from divisions and higher headquarters, but the contents were restricted to the immediate area of operations because the summary was often distributed down to regiments, making it subject to capture.

Along with the G2 at Army, corps intelligence possessed the authority to prepare orders for the Air Service to conduct daily photo and reconnaissance missions. Accompanying the request was a map that laid out the zone to be covered, the urgency of the mission, and the desired altitude or resolution of the final product. A sector of interest might be passed over for observation every day and every three to five days photographed; these types of aerial missions were used in creating mosaics for maps and supplementing various intelligence reports.

Darkness could mask the movement of forces from their billets to the front, and soon night marches became the norm for all belligerents; units often ended their marches by hiding in a wooded area. On the other hand, a clear night with a full moon could offer sufficient light for an observer to see when flying beneath 2,000 feet; the dropping of parachute flares that burned for 4 minutes also provided enough exposure for an observer to ascertain troop movements. Besides the cover of darkness, fog and rain placed limits on aerial photography, but following rain, the presence of tracks that betrayed the concealment of troops in wooded areas could often be photographed. There was one distinct advantage in working during less than favorable weather—the threat from enemy pursuit planes was decidedly lessened.

Both army and corps appointed intelligence officers and attached them to air observation groups. Their principal responsibility was to receive and interpret photographs and observation reports and pass the information on to the appropriate element. Often, air intelligence officers personally debriefed observers following a mission. This was why observers really had to possess the background to aid in identification of the terrain and targets and the ability to communicate that knowledge, but final interpretation remained solely with the intelligence officer.

Another important mission performed by aerial observers was to "find the line"—orders given to locate advancing friendly infantry or patrols. It was a particularly dangerous assignment because of the low altitude, sometimes only a few hundred meters, and within range of both artillery and machine guns. Once a unit was located, the plane was to fire rockets, and the infantry was to acknowledge in kind, because it was frequently difficult for observers to distinguish between friend and foe. But infantry elements most often chose not to respond with rockets for fear of giving away their position to the enemy and subjecting themselves to increased shelling. As a substitute, infantry could lay out panels to signify that they were friendly. On October 2, after several days of searching, Second Lieutenant W. J. Rogers, observer with the 50th Aero Squadron, finally spotted the panels belonging to the so-called Lost Battalion, which was surrounded by enemy forces. To let the beleaguered US troops know that help was on the way, the 50th Squadron dispatched a second plane to drop all the candy bars and cigarettes that its members could scrounge.

By April, the I Corps Observation Group, consisting of the 1st, 12th, and 18th Squadrons, was finally in place. Most of the group's personnel had not previously seen action, with the exception of observers who had already flown missions as members of French crews. The quiet Toul sector would serve as a useful bridge for the Air Service between training and actual combat conditions; the drawback being that conditions were less than realistic.

The air crews faced antiaircraft fire that at times could be heavy but seldom were engaged by enemy pursuit planes. The lack of activity on the ground in the Toul sector also meant that the Air Service would not make major contributions to the sector's intelligence picture.

On 15 April, a plane from the 1st Aero Squadron took off on its first official reconnaissance mission. Lieutenant Fred E. D'Amour, a photographer on one of the early flights, described the experience.

> Started for the front. Low clouds blocked our flight path and we lost our fighter protection. Went ahead anyway to get the assigned pictures. The photographs depicted strong points in the rear of the German lines. The first film magazine was taken of the target area without incident, but after five pictures behind enemy lines, we decided to make a reconnaissance of the enemy rear in an effort to locate pillboxes in the area and any new construction. After noting the position of these installations, we started home at an altitude of 600 meters with average ground fire being fired at us. . . . When we were still 12 kilometers inside the German lines an antiaircraft shell exploded directly under the motor, tearing a large piece off the end of the propeller blade and stopping the motor. We started down; emptied our machine guns on the way down because we had incendiary bullets in them. The German guns increased their barrage and our plane took more hits. Just as Lieutenant Wold was leveling off preparatory to landing, the motor started again . . . and we flew the rest of the way which was about 10 kilometers at from 10 to 40 meters altitude.[19]

While laboratory buildings were still undergoing construction, early photographs were developed, washed, and printed in photo cars parked along the side of the road. This was possible because there were few useful photos to print—10 plates over one two-week period—but there were exceptions. Lieutenant D'Amour indicated that following his flight, "the chief of the army corps visited the field and stated that the photographs taken that day had given them information of valuable importance and that dugouts sheltering an entire regiment of enemy troops had been located and destroyed by our artillery after being detected on one of our pictures."[20]

The number of aircraft had become so widespread that by the last year of the war, it was virtually impossible to launch a major surprise attack. The presence of new ammunition dumps, extension of roads, and deployment of new narrow gauge railroads for the purpose of transporting ammunition were all easily seen from the air and could signal an upcoming offensive. The year 1918 was also an important milestone in aviation intelligence because it was then that commanders began relying much more on air photography than observation. The advantages were obvious: the ability to compare and contrast past and present photos and to search and examine the ground in greater detail—the eye of the camera was simply superior to the onetime scan of the human eye. Vertical photos were most commonly taken and were useful in the creation of mosaics for maps. An oblique photo presented a distorted view but allowed a commander to comprehend better what lay before him; on the eve of an attack or in anticipation of a counterattack, oblique photos were taken to discover the locations of enemy shelters with reinforcements. To discover what the enemy knew about one's own area of operations, intelligence could also order oblique photos of its own positions.

The greatest handicap for photo interpreters was not having seen firsthand the type of terrain or items that they were expected to identify. This is why Captain Edward Steichen strongly recommended that all interpreters undergo some flight time. A photo interpreter required several important skills; foremost was to comprehend the length and shape of shadows from known objects. Without shadows, it was difficult to distinguish a haystack from a gun emplacement, a trench from an embankment. An interpreter also had to understand that photos represented the amount of light reflected; this was important in identifying such diverse items as dense vegetation or smooth road surfaces. To make the best use of sun angles, which accentuated the shadows, as well as to surprise the enemy, priority was given to missions flown during the early morning hours.

All belligerents made a major investment in camouflaging. Cover for the US sector alone required 4.328 million square yards of burlap; 200,000 gallons of paint; 7,700 fishnets; 50,000 pounds of wire; and 2.160 million square yards of poultry netting. In his book *Shooting the Front*, Colonel Terrence Finnegan indicates that both negative and positive forms of camouflage were employed. The positive form was utilized to suggest that a certain course of action was being planned when just the opposite was true; for example, to show the presence of a phantom division. The negative approach was far more common and was deployed to conceal the size and location of a combat unit along with its weapons. As the war wore on, the art of deception became more and more sophisticated, especially since airplanes were being forced to fly at such high altitudes. For example, the Germans utilized smoke-emitting autos on railroad tracks to simulate trains and instructed their commanders to make concealing troops from air observers their number one consideration when deciding where troops encamped. The British painted one of their corps headquarters to look like ruins, and fishnets were often used to hide the extent of recent bomb damage.[21]

Besides the familiar box-style camera, the British introduced the machine gun camera that was much like firing a Marlin gun—point and press the trigger; the Americans would later improve upon it. When the Americans first entered the war, all cameras were nonautomatic and used a variety of plates; the 4-by-5-inch plate was the most popular and the one finally adopted by the

Air Service. In January 1918, the Air Service also began utilizing film that could take up to 100 successive exposures; air suction was employed to hold the film absolutely flat. An electric motor changed the film and automatically set the shutter; the operator only had to start the machinery and regulate the camera speed to that of the aircraft. Regardless of the camera, all were worthless without quality lenses; unfortunately, a major shortcoming of the Allied photo effort was a failure to standardize the lenses so that they could have been produced on a larger scale.[22]

As important as the camera was, radios that permitted communications between air and ground and between pilot and observer were equally crucial. The creation of a special headset that allowed an aircrew to receive messages and the invention of a transmitter that was sensitive to the human voice but shut out other sounds were both considered major breakthroughs. Radios were especially effective when used by corps squadrons, as army squadrons often flew deeper missions that were beyond receiving range.

The G2 at corps repeatedly published orders reminding soldiers that everything from enemy helmets to personal correspondence collected off the enemy dead belonged to the US Army and was to be immediately turned in. Regardless, US troops still engaged in their share of souvenir collecting—an activity that would continue to plague Army intelligence during future wars. Although hard to come by, captured official and personal documents were considered one of the most reliable intelligence sources; code books, in particular, proved a veritable gold mine that could continue to unlock secrets as to the enemy's future plans. Coming upon a burial detail, an inspector general discovered to his horror that all the German soldiers had their pockets turned out and promptly filed a report that Americans were robbing the dead. It had to be explained to him that intelligence personnel were simply following instructions by removing all documents.

Anything such as orders and casualty lists that touched on or disclosed the status of a unit's manpower was considered valuable. Early in the war, unit pay books had been a great source. Not only did they show the name and type of the unit, but also the dates when it received its call up, where it underwent training, and whether or not it had previously seen service. Later, the Germans omitted all background data and began to substitute numbers for the assigned soldiers. For instance, an infantry company possessed 250 men, each numbered consecutively from 1 to 250; replacements were numbered above 250 and dated, so regardless of the enemy's feeble attempt to mask the status of a unit, losses suffered during a certain period could still be easily calculated. Besides using the information for order of battle purposes, intelligence also provided background data to interrogators to help verify information disclosed by prisoners.

Among personal documents, letters from time to time contained insights on the status of the enemy's war efforts and manpower shortages; for instance, a letter might divulge that a former factory worker back home had been drafted into the Army or that someone previously rejected for service had been reexamined and accepted—all clues as to how far the manpower pool had dropped. On one occasion, a postcard of a German soldier fell into the hands of British analysts who determined from the writing the previously unknown location of a certain German corps. This further confirmed what an American source in Switzerland had already reported, resulting in the realignment of Allied troops who stopped the advance of the Germans and reestablished a new line.[23]

During a trench raid by US troops in January 1918, scouts discovered a portion of a newspaper from Metz, located in northeastern France and occupied by the Germans. It contained the following announcement: "A [numbered] Guard Band will hold a concert in Metz on the following Sunday." The location of the division to which the band belonged had previously eluded identification. Knowing that the division was essential for launching any offensive in the St. Mihiel sector, US intelligence reasoned that no action would take place for at least one to three weeks because of the estimated travel time from Metz.

Prior to offensive operations, the corps G2 designated teams consisting of four sergeants and an officer to help handle the anticipated increase in number of prisoners. Exploitation of information from captured prisoners greatly depended on the skill of individual interrogators and their knowledge of the enemy's military terms, slang, tactics, and equipment. Because many US interrogators had either studied or lived for a time in Germany, they proved superior to the British but not the French. Lawyers in civilian life were often good interrogators because of prior experience with asking questions. Sometimes interrogators were able to exploit ethnic divisions that existed within the ranks; soldiers who were from Poland, Denmark, Alsace-Lorraine region, and southern Germany proved the most willing to give up information. It was not uncommon, especially near the end of the war, for an intelligence interrogator to walk down a line of prisoners, asking each one, "*Bist du Pole?*"

It was soon evident that information obtained from the typical German soldier during a battle was usually unreliable. A prisoner of war often felt conflicted between gaining the good graces of his captors and remaining loyal to his comrades-in-arms. Furthermore, a prisoner frequently had no idea of the larger picture of the battlefield and was only aware of what had happened to his immediate squad; and if the fighting had been intense, the prisoner tended to exaggerate the number of losses. On the other hand, the same prisoner could prove to be a great source of information regarding the status of his unit, its previous losses, and general morale. Consequently, interrogators mostly focused their interviews on the past when the prisoner joined his unit, not only to identify the unit but to trace its movements to and from the front lines. AEF analysts often used the information to help learn the overall intention of enemy strategists.

One captured German soldier with the rank of *Vice-Feldwebbers* (equivalent to a sergeant major) told his interrogating officer an amazing story. He had worked as a barber in Chicago for 15 years and had returned to his native Germany to see his aging parents. Unfortunately, when war broke out, he was drafted into the Army, despite his protests. Most of his time was spent on the eastern front, but like many of his fellow soldiers, he eventually had been sent west. All the while, he resolved to escape and return to the United States. The G2 at II Corps was Colonel "Vinegar Joe" Stilwell, who would later command US forces in the China-Burma-India theater in World War II. Stilwell immediately sensed the potential value of his new prisoner, so he promised the captive passage back to the States if he would work the prison cages to determine what, if any, valuable information could be gleaned from his fellow soldiers.[24] In the same manner, US interpreters were occasionally dressed in German uniforms and placed in compounds for the purposes of listening; following his interrogation, a prisoner would often boast to his comrades on how he had misled his captors. Finally, on rare occasions when a knowledgeable, cooperative prisoner was identified, he could be taken into the front lines to help confirm what observers were seeing.

Because all enemy divisions, brigades, and regiments possessed radios, signals intelligence focused much of its resources on exploiting the messages being transmitted through the airways. In time, the Radio Intelligence Section established eight stations to the rear; from there, they were able to intercept 72,688 messages and pick up nearly 238,000 calls. Based largely on tone alone, US intercept personnel never experienced any problems distinguishing German radio traffic being sent in code, but it did take a while before the operators acknowledged the need to copy as many wireless messages as possible due to the difficulty in differentiating between what was important and unimportant.

Following the recovery of a particularly important code, Nolan wrote admiringly of the unique abilities of the intercept operators.

When one considers that the messages copied appear to the Signal Corps operator as simply a series of letters without meaning; that such messages are the hardest to copy; that in order to be sure of getting the valuable messages it had been necessary to copy several hundred useless ones each day over long periods of time; and that the copying was done under difficult conditions and through interference which confused all but the best operators; it is possible to appreciate the fine work which was done in this intercept. In this one case, one of the messages would have made the others useless. The American operators were the only ones who copied all three messages with sufficient accuracy to permit the breaking of the new German code.[25]

Using a nearby telegraph, Signal Corps personnel, who manned the intercept sites 24 hours a day, transmitted all copied transmissions to Army headquarters where analysts waited to decode and read the messages. If the Army lacked the men or expertise to complete the task, then the intercept was forwarded on to the GHQ, where there were 60 additional cryptanalysts organized by skill and area of specialty. Once a message was read, it was immediately dispatched to the appropriate combat commander.

Radio traffic was normally conducted within its own echelon; thus boundaries of enemy units could easily be discovered. To try to mask the origin of messages, the enemy began sending pseudo messages across their divisional boundary, but German operators made a crucial mistake by sending only real messages within the same division. By assuming all messages followed this pattern, it greatly cut down on the requirement to examine all messages with the same detail. The enemy also adopted a strategy of sending fake messages so that the level of activity would remain constant, thus helping to disguise a buildup of communications surrounding an upcoming operation. On a handful of occasions, the enemy attempted the opposite—by reducing its signal activity and then launching a surprise assault.

Over time, radio intelligence possessed some 20 direction-finding sites at staggered intervals. Radio intercept would alert each station within the goniometric net to take a bearing of "the calling station by manipulating the adjusting knobs with one hand while rotating a revolving frame with the other to find the two points of silence; in the meantime noting the call letters, time, points of silence, and figuring the mean of these, the wave length and intensity of signals, and whether a message or call was sent, and in addition recording all this data."[26] The data were then taken to a "map board" that consisted of a table and a 1:80,000 scale map. "Locations of gonio stations are indicated by placing a protractor (complete circle) on the map, with its center over the exact geographical position occupied by the station in the field and with its zero degree mark pointing due north. A thread of suitable length is fastened at one end at the center of each protractor by means of a thumb tack, and at the other end to a small weight." The location of the enemy's radio transmitter would be indicated by the spot where the bearings taken by two or more direction-finding stations crossed.

On January 10, 1918, the first two of the goniometric stations were collocated with intercept sites at Froides and Landrecourt; a third station was added in February. At each station, the three assigned sergeants were soon averaging 150 bearings over a 24-hour period. On May 27, during an enemy attack, one US station alone took a bearing every two minutes, resulting in some 670 bearings in a single day—a record—and over the course of 10 months, AEF operators were credited with 176,000 bearings. Operators evaluated each of the bearings as being "certain," "probable," or "doubtful" and passed this information by telegraph to their net control station, which forwarded the locations of enemy transmitters to the G2's at Army and corps.[27]

When analysts combined direction-finding results with intercept, they often learned which enemy stations were communicating with one another and thus determining an order of battle. Because enemy transmitters were usually close to some type of headquarters, analysts could pinpoint their general locations as well as estimate the number of regiments and battalions. Signals intelligence also depicted changes in command and control. In the words of Colonel Frank Moorman, "Changing stations indicated a changing front. The grouping of stations betrayed the grouping of commands. An increased number of stations reflected an increase in the number of troops."[28]

As codes became more difficult to solve, the importance of direction-finding grew. This was especially true during the last year of the war when both sides made every effort to reduce the amount of information furnished the enemy in terms of locations and distribution of stations. Although enemy transmitters might change call names on a daily basis, the location of the stations themselves most often remained the same for the direction-finding operator. Also during this same period, the US goniometric operators were benefiting from the use of improved instruments that made it possible to help pinpoint a location with fewer attempts.

The air intercept mission provided early warnings to friendly pursuit planes by alerting them to the presence of enemy observation aircraft performing spotting duties for their artillery. Over time, some enemy pilots consistently demonstrated a greater commitment in carrying out their assignments by continuously communicating with the ground. It was especially worth the effort for Allied intelligence to keep track of them, and air intercept operators soon labeled these pilots as "Red." Other enemy pilots proved more easily distracted and were less likely to finish their mission; appropriately, these were labeled "Yellow." The bottom line was that should an operator pick up a "Red," he needed to expend extra effort. Often the enemy radio operator with whom the plane communicated was recognized by his callsign. Because his location was frequently close to the artillery in question, this added clue was used in helping to pinpoint the battery. When notified by air intercept, goniometers would also lock in on the communications link between the plane and ground, further helping to identify more precisely the location of the enemy's artillery. After pinpointing the enemy's guns, AEF intelligence notified its artillery to launch preemptive fire and also alerted nearby infantry to expect incoming rounds.[29]

Air intercept did more than just target the enemy's artillery. Zeppelins on bombing raids would occasionally broadcast a call of "Where am I?" and request that their direction-finding units provide assistance. Simultaneously, friendly direction-finding sites simultaneously took bearings, learning the approximate time that the air ships would hit London or Paris and the path they would follow. Such information was immediately delivered to the appropriate authorities. Finally, air intercept forwarded its collected information daily to the Air Section within GHQ intelligence so that staff members could chart German aerial activity. For the most part, the vast majority of air intercept activity was limited to trench warfare; once troops began major offensives in the fall of 1918, the function was no longer as useful. For one thing, the constant movement of direction-finders mounted in trucks made the use of direct telephone lines virtually impossible.

In time, five of the US corps would have flash and sound ranging troops under the staff supervision of the G2 and attached to artillery headquarters. But first, the fielding of the flash and sound ranging equipment would have to negotiate a number of hurdles. When sound ranging ran out of strings of very fine platinum wire, Major Augustus Trowbridge, chief of the Flash and Sound Ranging Service, traveled to Paris where he failed to find any; he did learn of a possible source in Lyons, where he headed next. Unfortunately, the elderly gentleman with the sought-after wire indicated that he couldn't afford to part with any. Seeing that his train did not leave until 3 o'clock and that he was in need of lunch, Trowbridge invited the owner of the platinum to accompany him. At about 2 o'clock, following a bottle of wine, Trowbridge's guest began to show a change of heart, "How much of this platinum wire did you want anyway?"[30] The US officer indicated that he needed 200 strands. As it was such a small contribution to a common cause, the Frenchman generously waived immediate payment, and promised if more was needed in the future, he would gladly provide it. Unshaven, Trowbridge reappeared two days later with his pockets full of the essential wire.

Flash ranging was dependent on line of sight and good visibility, which meant that the apparatus had to be positioned at an elevated site, and it was targeted against artillery located within 2 to 3 miles of the front line. What cannot be seen can still be heard because sound travels at 1,086 feet per second, much slower than light. When the noise of a fired round reached a particular sound ranging system, a calculation of its arc was made; the differences between the times reported by each operator in the net was used to determine both distance and direction of the artillery piece in question. Adjustments were made for atmospheric humidity, temperature, and wind, and each bearing was assigned an accuracy rating of between 50 to 200 yards. In the same manner, sound ranging was also used to help correct friendly fire.

By late spring, the Flash and Sound Ranging Service was demonstrating its ability to pinpoint the location of enemy artillery, but because it could target deeper, out-of-sight artillery and was not affected by weather, sound ranging would emerge as the more valuable of the two systems.[31] Acoustic devices were either four-horn or parabolic; the Americans having developed a paraboloid that weighed 1,300 pounds—one-sixth the weight of the French version—and thus offering greater mobility when disassembled. At night, acoustic devices were deployed to warn of approaching enemy aircraft and sometimes to help target the aircraft, but airplanes traveling at different altitudes and speeds required sophisticated calculations and thus were far more difficult to pinpoint. During such operations, sound ranging worked closely with the 56th Engineers who manned the searchlights.

ARMY HEADQUARTERS

The key word for lower echelons was collection, whereas the key word at army G2 was collation. In the words of a British officer, army headquarters was "the point of the spear." And "If the point is dull, the spear fails in its mission." Thus, on paper, the functions of an army G2 staff, which possessed its own analysts, were quite extensive, beginning with reviewing the 14 to 20 reports routinely received from lower echelons. To run off thousands of copies of its own intelligence summaries, the army G2, like his counterpart at corps, possessed several one-cylinder presses mounted in the back of trucks, but for a major campaign, the army intelligence staff still required the added assistance of presses at the GHQ.

The army G2 was also responsible for an area of operations that stretched 20 miles behind enemy lines. To fulfill its obligations, intelligence deployed deep air reconnaissance and possessed observation posts with high-powered telescopes; a principal target of the latter was to survey railroad lines in the rear areas. On several occasions, intelligence at army headquarters parachuted spies behind enemy lines for the purpose of gathering information, but never to the extent publicized in news stories. The great difficulty in such an adventure was selecting the right person for the job—someone without a foreign accent but with extensive knowledge of the local culture and geography. This is why the majority of dropped personnel were paid agents from nearby neutral countries; another reason was that the services of spies from countries like Belgium could be had for a fraction of the cost of others. These airborne spies often carried with them pigeons to transport messages because the use of winged communications was so widespread in World War I as evidenced by the thousands of birds that the AEF brought to France. One side risk was that seeing a meal in the offing, soldiers from both sides often tried to shoot down the birds. So by the end of the war, Allied scientists were busy experimenting with new means of agent communications, including the possible use of infrared rays.

GHQ: FILLING THE VOID

Due to First Army not officially coming into existence until August, elements of the GHQ G2 would continue to be principally responsible for all planning up to and including the AEF's first large-scale offensive campaign in September 1918 against the St. Mihiel salient. This meant that GHQ staff would have to pull double duty. The lack of an intermediate headquarters did not prove to be a major obstacle in Colonel Nolan's mind. For some time, he had embraced the French thinking that such missions as interrogation of key personnel, exploitation of documents, and unraveling of codes required assembling of a sufficient number of qualified analysts in a rear area. This is why he rejected the requests by commanders for small teams to be assigned to forward elements on the basis that analysis was not a one-man job and required the massing of talent in sufficient numbers. And although often hard for field commanders to appreciate, this would become the practice embraced by the military intelligence leadership for generations to come.

The Secret Service division at Chaumont routinely received information from agents situated in nearby countries. One of the great success stories came from Denmark, where under the subversion of Colonel Oscar N. Solbert, US case officers created a network of train watchers. Any movement of troops, whether it was to the front, from the front, or between sectors, was a crucial indicator of the enemy's intentions and the scope of their operations. Because of heavy use of the tracks, it took three days for trains transporting a complete division to pass over a bridge; a coded cablegram could place this information in the hands of the intelligence staff at Chaumont within six days. By early 1918, US observers were daily monitoring the movement of trains arriving from the eastern front and entering their sector; intelligence utilized watchers at the large train centers of Cologne, Coblenz, Essen, Metz, Conflans, and Magdeburg. If the trains passed through Liege and then entered Belgium, British intelligence assumed the responsibility and later shared the information. During the last months of the war, the Americans added a watching service at Treves; from here, they could determine the trains' final destination.[32]

The watcher had to be in and around the tracks, making a dishonest station employee the ideal person. A number of the train watchers hired by US intelligence were former members of the now defunct Russian spy network. Spies in enemy territory, of course, ran a risk, but as one pointed out, if you knew the routine of German counterintelligence, you could easily work around it. At Coblenz, the local German counterintelligence chief was particularly adept in keeping tabs on all strangers, so much so that being assigned to the area became a death sentence for many a spy; thus no one volunteered for the assignment without receiving double compensation. A good spy in a high-risk situation often averaged $10,000 a year, a princely sum for the times. (Of all the belligerents, Americans always paid top dollar.) Someone later estimated that the Americans lost about 5 percent of their agents during the war, which was in keeping with the overall death rate of the larger AEF.[33]

There were twists and turns when it came to the spy game. In one instance, three different intelligence services (Germany, United States, and France) employed a highly educated Polish lady. The G2 staff knew this because she repeatedly filed reports full of false data, the very type the Germans commonly fed the Allies. Although the military information she passed on was worthless, her description of the political climate in Germany proved extremely accurate, so much so that Allied intelligence maintained her as a source.

On another occasion, a French case officer was having an affair with the wife of a German military attaché assigned to Switzerland. Because he did not want French officials to know about the liaison while still taking advantage of the information she was providing, he arranged for his mistress to pass the documents directly to Colonel W. F. Godson, US military attaché in Bern. Meanwhile, the head of the French secret service let his counterparts know that he considered her a great source of information. It was very evident to anyone involved that her so-called overheard conversations at the German embassy were nothing more than fabrications, but because French egos were involved, Colonel Godson felt obligated to play the gullible intelligence officer, all the while enduring raised eyebrows from those within his own legation.

During late spring of 1918, an important organizational piece of signals intelligence fell into place. Colonel Moorman selected Lieutenant C. H. Matz, who was competent in both German and French, to command radio intercept and oversee the breaking of codes for the anticipated First Army. Matz's organization would submit reports just as if First Army existed and was fully operational. If signals intelligence was to be of any value, it had to be exploited in a timely fashion, but far enough away to avoid constant relocations. On June 12, Matz opened an office at Toul to cover the Meuse-

Moselle sector; later he moved with other First Army intelligence elements to Neufchateau but still maintained operations at Toul.

In the early months of 1918, the fledgling US code-breaking effort was dependent on assistance from the British and French. The first code that AEF cryptanalysts tackled was a trinumeral type that was changed every 10 days. Used within divisions, the code seldom contained information of great value, but with enough text, intelligence could easily break it and use the information in its identification of units. Captured German cryptologic-related documents were a godsend to US analysts. At first, linguists assigned to the G2 at Chaumont handled their translation, but because the supporting documents often proved so technical, the function was eventually turned over to A-6 itself, whose own trained transcribers would, over time, produce a library filled with documents for use by radio intelligence.

Code breakers did not enjoy the same success with the second type of code—also a three-letter code but with 2,000 groups assigned to words or phrases. Every four weeks, the code changed unless there had been some type of compromise. Following the implementation of a new code, it took a week before analysts could determine the nature of the message; they often received a break when the enemy would broadcast certain types of reports on a given schedule. By the second week, the AEF code breakers were reading some of the transmissions, and as the third week approached, they could decode all traffic. This meant that signals intelligence enjoyed approximately a week of total access to the enemy's secrets. As far as ciphers, German combat forces would, for the most part, abandon them. Those exceptions included periods of unusually heavy combat activity when they were used to communicate among the army, corps, and divisions.

Colonel Moorman had a profound appreciation for the handful of officers who tackled enemy codes and ciphers. "The real code man, the one making original solutions has a difficult task. He must fix his mind absolutely on the work in hand. If his feet are cold, if he is hungry or thirsty or ill, if the office is noisy, if the light is bad, if he is wondering what became of his bedding roll during the last move or what kind of billet he will get after the next one, his work is certain to suffer."[34] On top of this, cryptanalysts seldom received the credit that Moorman believed they were due. After achieving an important breakthrough, Moorman lamented, "We tried several ways to make ourselves known so that people would appreciate us without making too much talk, but it didn't work. We finally decided that the only thing to do was to do our work and say nothing about it."[35]

Radio intelligence also began to apply the principles of another form of analysis, long before it was formally acknowledged. Using what a later generation called traffic analysis, code breakers examined an intercepted message to determine what could be gleaned from its format and externals apart from the text itself. For example, who was the originator and what route did the message follow? Many of the first insights came by studying old German transmissions provided by British and French intelligence; in this manner, code breakers learned which intercepts to tackle first. It was determined that regiments communicated with divisions, divisions with divisions and corps, and that the grouping of stations within a division betrayed an organizational identity or boundary, something in which the Order of Battle Section placed great stock. It also helped that for a while Germans used a different key on the number code for each division.

Callsigns identified a station; thus, by following the callsigns, analysts could re-create the order of battle by drawing lines when one station routinely communicated with another. By the summer of 1918, the Germans adopted a number of tactics to shield their units' identity. One tactic was to use new call letters every day, but French analysts quickly observed that although each German army unit employed a different set of callsigns, the First and the Third army units used duplicate sets. Intelligence specialists also learned that when individual stations selected a new callsign each day from a list, they betrayed a pattern in how that selection was made. On the basis of this observation alone, Allied signals intelligence issued a warning of a major offensive being planned.

Like cryptology, intelligence from overhead would have two masters: the Air Service and the G2. Based on the British model, the Air Section within the Information Division assigned intelligence officers to all reconnaissance squadrons and groups for the purpose of transmitting collection requirements and receiving the results. How well this worked largely depended on the relationship and good standing between the intelligence officer and his squadron. In the 91st Squadron and later the First Army Observation Group, the intelligence officers proved to be up to the task. Unfortunately, they were the exception. Intelligence officers also sent copies of their reports back to the GHQ where in May 1918, the G2 began to publish the state of enemy air forces in a document known as the "Summary of Air Information," eventually adding the status of America's own Air Service, which, by June, possessed 13 squadrons, of which 6 were devoted to observation.

From the beginning, aerial intelligence was plagued by a number of serious problems—many eluding a final solution. For instance, the Air Section at the GHQ faced a constant shortage of qualified personnel made worse by frequent turnover. More important, the air intelligence mission in the field suffered from a lack of sufficient numbers of competent and trained personnel to analyze the photographs. It did not help matters that members of the Air Service's own Photographic Section were often better qualified at interpreting photos than the intelligence officers. Photo analysis was one of those technical skills where hands-on experience trumped classroom study.

There was also a fundamental disconnect between intelligence and the Air Service. This resulted in frequent confrontations with General Billy Mitchell, who commanded the Air Service, and would eventually lead to a showdown between him and General Hugh A. Drum, the chief of staff at First Army. Mitchell continually pushed for a more autonomous role for aviation in keeping with the British model. Bombing and independent air operations behind enemy lines, not photography, were Mitchell's priorities; in contrast, intelligence was just one in a series of daily tasks, not a function that demanded immediate attention at a particular moment.[36] Nolan summed up the situation as follows: "Mitchell had one excuse after another." Ultimately this would cause General Drum to resort to reminding General Mitchell in no uncertain terms that his resources were there to support the ground war in keeping with General John Pershing's wishes, but Mitchell simply proceeded to laugh off his superior's admonitions. On October 9, General Mitchell sent a personal invitation to both Drum and Nolan to observe firsthand the sendoff of 200 US and French bombers on a raid, a not-too-subtle reminder of where Mitchell thought the priorities of the Air Service should reside.[37]

The Order of Battle Section continuously updated concise histories of enemy divisions, but the Americans differed from their fellow Allies in that they wanted information on the entire front, not just along their particular sector. To process the incoming information, the Order of Battle Section maintained a separate folder on each enemy division; inside was all available information along with the name of the source, its dependability, and the date of acquisition. When infantry regiments were shifted to another division, staff personnel simply removed the relevant sheets and transferred them to the receiving division folder. To illustrate the importance of the folders, GHQ intelligence received the following intercept from the field: "the barrage will go down at 12:30 A.M." One of several divisions could be the target, so an analyst checked each of the folders. Only in one did he find what he was looking for. An observation post had sighted messenger dogs that were practicing running back and forth from the front lines. Such dogs were often used to carry messages during enemy trench raids and attacks; this information was sufficient for the analyst to notify the 26th Division to expect the barrage.

The Order of Battle Section was focused on how an enemy unit was organized on paper; the idea was to compare and contrast what reports indicated was a unit's actual strength, training status, numbers of replacements, and overall morale of its soldiers with a unit's original status. The differences reflected just how far the fighting capacity of a unit had deteriorated. Late in the war the methodology became increasingly sophisticated thanks to new insights gained from the French. Their analysts had discovered that when a German division was taken out of line during or after an operation, it could be assumed that the unit suffered an estimated 3,000 losses. Thus by calculating the number of divisions withdrawn every month by 3,000 and by adding 11 losses each day for those divisions situated in a quiet sector, an estimate could be made of the gross number of losses suffered by the enemy.

Based on a stolen report of the chief of the Health Department delivered to the High Commission of the Reichstag in April 1918, the French further refined its model; attributing 40 percent of the losses to capture, 12 percent to death, and the rest to wounds and sickness. Most of those suffering from wounds and illness recovered at varying rates; 10 percent proved fit to return in 30 days, 20 percent in 60 days, etc. For such a system to work there had to be a highly accurate base line and continual updating of files. The efforts of AEF intelligence were finally validated when in August their numbers began to track with recently captured documents, foretelling by several months the dissolution of enemy divisions.[38]

Closely aligned to the Order of Battle Section was another section solely devoted to monitoring the enemy's artillery organization and the movement of its heavy guns. From the beginning, obtaining reliable and timely information on enemy artillery proved an impossible challenge if for no other reason than that the batteries were located a long distance from the front lines and their lines of communications were faced to the rear. To compound matters, two-thirds of enemy batteries changed their numbers, battalions, and guns over time. The enemy often prepared several locations for its artillery and then moved them during the night. Additionally, there were only a handful of captured documents and knowledgeable prisoners to draw from. The French and British intelligence forwarded any and all information, but here too, there was little to send. Initially, AEF analysts attempted to plot enemy artillery, but because the data were at least a month old and so sketchy, the intelligence staff most often ended up destroying the maps. Only in sectors of the front where there had been little action for some time did the results come close to being accurate. One consequence of the information void was that the Germans only had to feed rumors that their heavy artillery was on the move to bring about a countermovement by French artillery reserves.

During the last eight months of the war, there were major changes in the various reports issued by the G2 at GHQ; these alterations occurred as a result of assignment of more personnel to the Order of Battle Section and the arrival of more intelligence collectors in the field. It had also taken some time before intelligence possessed a sufficient number of qualified analysts—individuals who dealt with facts, used deductive reasoning, and possessed a grasp of detail. The "Summary of Information," which was distributed down to division, initially included translated captured documents of interest, identification of enemy units, and intercepted German communiqués. In March 1918, the publications branch of the Information Division at the GHQ began a report titled "Summary of Intelligence" that covered a wide range of subjects, both combat and noncombat related, but in the summer, the publication effort would undergo a major shift. The Order of Battle Section would now publish the "Summary of Intelligence" and restrict its contents to a list of enemy units, intelligence produced from aerial reconnaissance and prisoners, and copies of important captured documents. Such subjects as political and economic updates would in the future be covered within the "Summary of Information."

In his estimation, Nolan sincerely believed that "the best intelligence document you can hand a noncommissioned officer and a platoon, company, battalion, regimental and brigade commander, is a good topographical map of the ground over which their unit is to attack."[39] Unfortunately, not all officers could read a map or even find their own location. To understand what type of area (hill, woods, ravines, etc.) the enemy would occupy after being driven from his first lines came from combat experience and years of study.

The only producer of maps for the Americans throughout the war remained the 29th Engineers, which enjoyed the initial luxury of having its ranks filled by skilled professionals drawn from civilian life and consequently requiring little training. For some unknown reason, as the deployment of AEF combat elements accelerated, the War Department decided to remove several companies of the 29th from its priority lists, leaving them behind in the States. This proved detrimental to the overall efficiency at the central plant; to compound the situation, the 29th was being forced to cannibalize its draftsmen, lithographers, and topographers in order to help meet the growing mapping needs elsewhere. For instance, it became necessary for the 29th Engineers to supply one officer and 36 soldiers to the *Geographique* in Paris in order to assist the French, who had previously expended a great deal of its resources in meeting the AEF's early demands for maps.

Divisions were responsible for updating their sector maps and forwarding all changes in enemy trenches and other military features so that army headquarters could incorporate the information in its battle maps. As a stopgap measure, an officer trained in photo analysis and four members of the 29th traveled to each of the divisions that had been training under the French. Here, they instructed both officers and enlisted personnel for topographical work. Inexplicably, this same arrangement was not repeated among divisions destined for the British and US sectors. At corps, the Tables of Organization allotted 1 officer and 23 topographic engineers, but like the divisions, there was no easy solution on how to acquire the necessary trained individuals. Although the first two received a full allotment, each of the remaining corps was able to obtain only one officer and four enlisted men. Consequently, they filled the empty slots from a variety of sources and relied heavily on on-the-job training.

The 29th Engineers would finally receive their last seven companies between July and October, bringing the total to 12, but when the 29th did eventually acquire its fill of personnel, the new arrivals often lacked the necessary skills. In one instance, Colonel Roger Alexander, the chief of the Topographic Division, arranged for the exchange of 60 to 70 incoming soldiers from western Pennsylvania where they had been coal miners in civilian life. These were transferred to the 23rd Engineers, a road-building unit, for much needed draftsmen and former students at the engineering colleges of Lehigh and Lafayette.

There were also shortages of equipment and materiel, often arriving late and in small amounts. Coupled with this were the normal logistical snafus; for instance, the 29th Engineers discovered one of their missing trucks with its lithographic presses near the city of Orleans where local units were using the specially designed vehicle to haul logs for the forestry service. Colonel Alexander indicated that his supply situation would have been far worse had it not been for his chief clerk Bryant, who did not have the appearance of your average soldier and spoke no French, but nevertheless proved invaluable. Upon reporting for duty, Bryant received his marching orders: "Don't tell me you can't do anything because of regulations. You tell me how a thing can be done."[40] Learning that the Topographical Section possessed only two typewriters, the supply clerk took the request and reappeared the next day with a dozen brand new Remingtons without saying how or where he had acquired them. Apparently, Bryant had found his calling because he would eventually end his career in logistics, having obtained the rank of major.

STARS AND STRIPES

Intelligence continued to address a number of peripheral issues. After arriving in France, General Pershing broached the subject of a newspaper for the members of the AEF as a means of boosting morale. Colonel Nolan took no action until Captain Guy T. Viskniskki, a newspaperman in civilian life and veteran of the Spanish-American War, was assigned to the Censorship Division. During a dinner conversation with Nolan at press headquarters, Viskniskki indicated how he had edited the newspaper *Bayonet* for the 18th Division at Camp Lee, Virginia, but had arrived at the conclusion that the AEF should seriously consider a newspaper for all the troops.[41]

In a follow-up memorandum, the captain set forth his ideas. Among the provisions, Viskniskki was most insistent that the soldiers of the AEF should be required to buy the newspaper at 10 cents a copy. In this manner, they would know that it was their newspaper. Viskniskki called the newspaper a soldier's link to home. For this reason, he also supported advertising in the paper. "It was good for AEF morale to know that Ivory Soap had not surrendered its floatability . . . and in the manufacture of chewing gum that the Wrigley flavor also was lasting through the war."[42] In spite of having several well-known sportswriters on staff, Viskniskki nixed the idea of a sports page. He refused to give publicity to million-dollar boxing bouts while the Doughboy was fighting for 30 dollars a month. Bottom line—Nolan would approve of Viskniskki's proposal and ran it by Pershing for his approval. Subsequently, on February 8, *Stars and Stripes* made its debut in Paris with Captain Viskniskki as editor-in-chief. For startup money, Viskniskki had to borrow from the Secret Service division's agent fund with the promise that it would be paid back as quickly as possible.

The goal of the newspaper was best described in a postwar editorial:

> The Stars and Stripes had and has but one purpose—to give the Army a voice and thereby to stimulate the morale of the American Expeditionary Forces. Here, at its start, was a green and none too self-confident Army, scattered to the winds of Europe, and in serious danger of losing all sense of belonging to a single Army. To write for the Yanks training with the British, the Yank brigades with the French, the Yanks loaned to Italy, and the Yanks venturing, a bit on their own, northwest of Toul—to tell each separate part and group that the others were helping—that was the idea. And as Yanks are all skeptics who can smell bunk a mile off, it was decided that the truth must and should serve.[43]

But Viskniskki was not above printing insensitive cartoons and jokes that may have reflected widespread prejudices back home but certainly were offensive to various groups of soldiers serving in France. On this and other matters, the editor proved impervious to any and all criticism.

The *Stars and Stripes* also communicated all new general orders that directly impacted the soldier and his status, but it did so in such a manner as to gain his attention. Instead of merely publishing the order word by word, the newspaper's staff would tell about its provisions and illustrate them through the use of stories. On at least one occasion, this would get Viskniskki in hot water and bring about a three-day detention. General William Wright Harts, the commander of the district of Paris where the paper was published, had proposed new uniforms for the US soldiers. Although the uniforms were certainly colorful, their style was anything but traditional, so *Stars and Stripes* came out with cartoons that ridiculed the suggested changes. The newspaper routinely received thousands of letters to the editor discussing the same subjects. The letters were often poorly written, and many contained nonacceptable phrases, so the *Stars and Stripes* editorial staff would frequently compose a representative letter and substitute it.

As a measure of its success, the paper's circulation reached 500,000 in less than a year, which more than paid for the expenses, thus allowing the *Stars and Stripes* to donate over 2 million francs to aid French orphans. Although truck availability was at a premium, the newspaper still was able to obtain 50 vehicles that, coupled with aircraft, were used to distribute the newspaper to the troops in the foxholes, hospitals, and rest areas. The newspaper's popularity owed much to the caliber of the individuals who worked for it, many of whom would go on to prominent careers in journalism, such as Lieutenant Grantland Rice, who became a widely read US sportswriter, and Private Harold Ross, future editor of the *New Yorker* magazine. Marine Private Abian Wallgren became the newspaper's cartoonist and created the character "Wally," who was very popular among the readership, but the primary reason for the newspaper's success was editor-in-chief Viskniskki, who faced the day-to-day strain of publishing a major newspaper, while ensuring that *Stars and Stripes* achieved its goals. As far as Nolan was concerned, no man worked harder.

COMBAT ARTISTS

World War I would be the first US conflict with an officially sanctioned effort to document it by photos, motion pictures, and paintings. Both France and Great Britain had dispatched combat artists to the battlefield; it was natural that the War Department would desire a team of its own. In March 1918, eight newly commissioned captains, who in civilian life were trained professional artists, arrived in France where they were assigned to GHQ intelligence and placed under the overall supervision of Colonel Walter Sweeny of the Censorship Division. With little instructions to guide them, "The Eight," as they were often called, established a home base in Neufchateau, east of Paris. From here, they immediately headed for the front lines, bearing passes from both the US and French commands that granted them unprecedented travel access. The artists also carried written orders that kept them on occasion from being arrested as spies, given their habit of stopping to draw in sketchbooks.

The local division intelligence officer was responsible for providing support to the artists, but this was not without precedent. The G2 also assisted another element tasked with shooting photos for historical purposes. The soldier artists did a great job depicting war in a realistic style, such as showing artillery and troops in the rain and mud as well as churches and villages that had suffered the scars of war. Unfortunately, when the paintings were sent back each month to Chaumont for an exhibit, the Army representative who was responsible for judging the art was quick to disapprove of many because he considered them drab when compared to the more heroic paintings of the French. Anticipating the use of the final paintings for propaganda purposes, the War Department shared its concerns in writing about the direction of the program. Consequently, on several occasions, Colonel Nolan intervened by dispatching letters that indicated his total support for the artists and their works. As for the artists themselves, they took solace in knowing that they had the approval of a combat veteran like Nolan.[44]

SECURING THE FORCE

While one arm of military intelligence focused on collecting the enemy's secrets, its other arm was busy keeping AEF's information, communications, and personnel safe from being exploited by enemy intelligence. The responsibility for carrying out the campaign against hostile intelligence forces was divided between the Signal Corps and the Corps of Intelligence Police (CIP). The former was responsible for creating and distributing codes and, eventually, for monitoring friendly communications in order to reduce the number of transmission violations. Elsewhere, counterintelligence worked to ensure that the US force remained loyal and to block efforts by foreign agents who were intent on taking advantage of weaknesses in AEF security.

From the beginning, counterintelligence faced a number of major problems. Perhaps the most significant was that the CIP was not a true corps and thus lacked the benefit of selecting its personnel, and in counterintelligence, the appointment of the right individual was most important. When the war came to a close, the CIP totaled only 452, nearly 40 percent short of its original goal; this was attributable to the suspension of recruitment on the home front and the high standards set by the AEF for those wishing to transfer into the corps. In the beginning, guidelines required any recruit not making the grade to be dispatched back to the States. Fortunately, this policy was quickly rescinded because other organizations could utilize that recruit's skills. The CIP also did not have older, more mature agents because there had been no policy to recruit such personnel. The average age of the British counterintelligence agent differed from the Americans by almost 10 years. It is interesting to note that on the home front, former policemen were often viewed as ideal candidates due to their investigating skills, but overseas the perception was just the opposite because ex-policemen possessed a mindset of wanting to arrest suspects immediately rather than waiting to observe them. Another problem was an absence of agents with suitable cultural background to enable them to blend with and work among the civilian population made up of lower or criminal classes.

Many commanders failed to appreciate the requirement for counterespionage as there was no precedent prior to the war and the prevailing belief was that the threat from enemy spies was highly exaggerated. Unfortunately, the time required to organize undermined the amount of time counterintelligence could devote to educating the Army. Counterintelligence also suffered because its personnel most often worked in the civilian world that surrounded the AEF, while the Army wanted to treat members of the CIP like other troops. This led to taking time off from more pressing matters to stand in military pay lines. An agent by the name of Elliott recorded some of the pitfalls: "in order to collect our pay, draw our clothing, travel . . . etc., we were constantly obligated to reveal our identity to Quartermaster, etc."[45] In return, they often received the greeting, "What outfit you in buddy, Secret Service?" CIP agents also lacked promotions that were in keeping with their peers—for instance, British counterintelligence had sergeant-majors of intelligence. Consequently, the Americans appointed acting sergeant-majors, who gained more privileges and responsibilities but still lacked the corresponding pay.

Counterintelligence training was at first left in the hands of foreign officers, but eventually, US officers assumed full responsibility. The first phase of instruction often consisted of studying various manuals on the subject of counterespionage and typing names to feed into the central file located in Paris. Advanced training varied greatly depending on the eventual assignment of the agent. For instance, in both the rear and front zones, new agents often began their careers working control points or serving at the ports of Le Havre or Marseille. A must for all agents was a thorough understanding of the most recent updates to the French pass system because German intelligence had stolen a large number of French labor authorization cards. Those destined for assignments within the First Army received additional training at one of the British corps.

Approximately one-third of CIP members wound up in what was called the front zone, where the United States was responsible for 123 miles of territory contiguous to the fighting. The headquarters for the CIP in the front zone was collocated with the GHQ and under the command of Colonel L. A. Sigaud; eventually, the majority of these same agents would come under the control of the First Army element at Seine-et-Marne. When the front was stable, intelligence officers used cars and motor bikes while enlisted agents pedaled from place to place. They were on constant alert for flashing lights, intermittent smoke, windmills, church clock faces, devices in haystacks or corn shocks, hidden wires or radios of any kind, and carrier pigeons—anything a spy might use to transmit a message. Once, a CIP sergeant saw a flickering light in a nearby church steeple so he naturally investigated, but all he discovered was a lone soldier looking for pigeons and a possible meal.

Counterintelligence had two fundamental missions in the front zone. The first was to establish mobile checkpoints. Within designated areas, agents asked to see identification papers in order to prevent entry to those civilians who didn't belong. Although it was virtually impossible to stop skilled spies at control points, one often could interrupt the flow of secrets by hampering their movements. Thus, enemy agents were rarely caught, but those who were proved most cooperative. They seldom were good sources when it came to timely information but often provided a sense of how Germany's overall war effort was progressing.

The search of a suspicious individual was not a simple task. Counterintelligence personnel knew that invisible inks and coded messages could be concealed anywhere, "written on the inside of envelopes, underneath a photograph, underneath a postage stamp and on the gummed edge of envelopes." There were even instances where words were written on the back of a woman in invisible ink. Hiding places for papers included "double collars or ties, hollow heels . . . hollow buttons and shoe laces. . . . Information has been discovered in the hollow stem of an artificial flower placed in the middle of a bouquet of real flowers or in a woman's hat." Missives also were "rolled up in very small pieces and carried in a gelatin sheath in the mouth or other parts of the body, in newspapers by marking certain words with a pinhole, written on parcels or boxes and the label pasted over the messages, written on bandages, indicated by embroidered stitches or in a hem, enclosed in coins which are sawed in half, hollowed out and soldered together again with the message inside."[46] Finally, some spies used more than one method in order to draw the attention of investigators away from the real means of conveyance.

Another mission of counterintelligence in the front zone was helping to secure France's borders with neutral and Allied countries because, as one Allied observer put it, "There is hardly a single place on the Swiss frontier from Basel to the extreme southeastern shore of Lake Constance which had not been occupied and organized by the Germans for espionage purpose."[47] Besides reducing the numbers of noncombatants from entering the AEF area of operations, the border mission was also a way to assist an ally, and the French appeared genuinely appreciative of the US support. A popular point of entry was Evian Les Bains on the southern shores of Lake Geneva and near the Swiss border. Here a joint British, Belgium, and US team labored to repatriate French citizens from occupied territory. The German government encouraged the policy in order to help reduce the number of noncombatants in its forward zone.

Besides screening French citizens to ensure that there were no enemy agents in the convoys, the intelligence officers also checked names against individuals who were known to have previously given aid to the enemy, and sometimes an expatriate proved a useful source for military, economic, and political information as well as insights on foreign intelligence organizations and their modus operandi. At Bellegarde and Pontarlier, personnel flowed the other way—US citizens wishing to leave France and enter Switzerland. If counterintelligence found anyone of a suspicious nature or if the individual was a potential source, agents alerted the military attaché in Bern and sent a report back to the GHQ.

Over the course of the war, the spy–counterspy game became increasingly sophisticated along international boundaries. On the French side of the border, a German spy routinely took a train bound for Switzerland; once aboard, he headed to a designated seat in the dining car. At the first stop past the border, a second person boarded the train and immediately found a seat next to his confederate. By this time, the first spy had finished his meal and was surreptitiously using his toothpick containing an invisible ink to write a secret message on the tablecloth. Once finished, he departed at the next stop for the purpose of catching a train back to France. A short time later, the second spy spilled wine on the message, using his napkin to cover his embarrassing accident. He then read the message while his napkin conveniently concealed the secret communiqué until it faded away.[48]

The Counter Intelligence Police assigned the bulk of its agents (58 officers, 305 enlisted, 14 clerks, and 58 civilians) to the rear zone and placed them under the overall command of Colonel Cabot Ward, who also served as the G2 of the Services of Supply (SOS). Ward and his staff of 8 officers and 15 enlisted operated out of the Hotel St. Anne in Paris until they relocated to more suitable quarters at No. 11 Avenue Montaigne in late March 1918. Their move was unceremoniously heralded by a large explosion in the nearby street; a shell had landed nearby from one of Germany's so-called Paris guns that fired projectiles from up to 75 miles away.

Throughout the war, Ward and his staff remained in Paris because of its close proximity to Allied counterintelligence and related agencies. Here, they conducted liaison with the Surete Generale, the French civilian secret service of the Ministry of Interior, and the Bureau Central des Renseignements of the Ministry of War, and, of course, with French military intelligence—in total, Americans worked with six independent French agencies. In addition, French counterintelligence was connected with numerous law enforcement offices throughout the country. In contrast, the British Expeditionary Force had only the Intelligence Service Line of Communications. As a rule, the CIP did not operate in areas covered by the British, but refused to sign a proposal that would have set this policy in stone. Although US agents were like the British in that they too were working in a foreign country and shared a similar system of command and control, they still found it surprisingly easier to deal with the French on a working level.

The rear zone CIP had two subheadquarters: one at Tours, which was the headquarters to the SOS, and the other in London; together, they fulfilled four major security missions—port, frontier, depot, and recreational areas. The London office oversaw port offices in Liverpool, London, and Cardiff, 12 American camps within the United Kingdom, and five troop docks in London. At Southampton, agents checked passengers traveling on the morning and evening cross-channel packets. To help man these offices in England, Ward commissioned several US citizens currently residing in the British Isles. Altogether, the three port operations refused to allow 189 undesirables to set foot in England and interrogated a number of seamen who possessed valuable information. The London office was also responsible for handling a serious breach of security involving a female German agent working as a code clerk in the office of the US military attaché.

Within SOS, port security was a high priority from the start because three transports carrying the 1st Division had been attacked off the coast of France. It was possible for German agents located within island coves that ran along the coast of western France to signal U-boats; the presence of numerous fishing vehicles further complicated policing the area. At Nantes, the CIP conducted surveillance of the many small towns and villages in the immediate area and along the mouth of the Loire River mouth to St. Nazaire. Le Harve was one of the first of the port offices, eventually having 40 agents. Regarding passengers departing and arriving, the port offices frequently experienced trouble with naval intelligence. The Navy officers had their own ideas on how to manage the mission but lacked the Army's resources and connections with French authorities.[49]

Finally, in March 1918, the largest of the counterintelligence port operations opened at Bordeaux because it had become the major site for transatlantic shipping. When military intelligence took the German agent Von Scheele into custody in the States, it forwarded information on his sabotage devices, which aided the CIP in their search of vessels arriving from US ports. As a result, they were able to discover undetonated explosives concealed among materiel destined for the front lines.

At each base port used by US troops, there was an element of at least two officers along with 12 Intelligence Police. The best way of reinforcing control of merchant seamen was for CIP agents to pay frequent visits to the various cafés and other establishments that catered to them. Agents also checked registration of guests in hotels and rooming houses where individuals who had eluded port authorities or control points often resided. Another security measure undertaken was to try to reduce the visibility of arriving units. For instance, when marching to their rest camps, regiments and divisions stopped parading with their normal flags and drums displaying the unit's designation.

Like ports, train stations were crucial checkpoints that presented many of the same challenges. Special attention was paid to the major train center at Is-sur-Tille, located en route to the front lines. Trains rolled through with the markings of each car's destination in plain sight; further compounding the situation, foreign laborers in transit could often be found waiting at depots. Colonel Ward noted that "a genuine spy would never attempt to go through a well-established and known railroad control point unless provided with carefully prepared papers," but spies did use train stations as drop points for pickup by another courier.[50]

There were 31 French cities with US supply, service, or training elements. Three to five CIP personnel were usually stationed in many of the cities so that they could monitor nearby supply and repair depots, storehouses, remount stations, prison camps, training areas, replacement depots, and tank depots. All instances of explosions or fires at such facilities were treated as suspicious unless proven otherwise. US counterintelligence took an important step when it convinced the French to establish "special reserved zones" around areas such as depots and ports that required extra vigilance; the city of Tours was the first so designated. That way, if undesirables attempted to enter within the zones, CIP personnel had the authority to deny their entry, or if discovered, the agents could take action to have them removed. Except for US military personnel or civilians in the Army's employment, the CIP still possessed no arrest authority.

In the rear areas, protecting against loose talk was a major focus. Hospitals were not a problem because most nonmilitary personnel were isolated from the wounded during the crucial three- to five-day initial period when soldiers possessed current information. Soldiers on leave from the front were a totally different matter. Here, contact with civilians was everywhere, especially with people associated with entertainment: hotel and casino staff as well as various troupes who traveled the country, all of whom provided excellent cover for German spies. Although the overall challenge was truly daunting, monitoring by observation and following up small leads were still considered the best courses of action. Acting on a tip, several CIP agents disguised themselves as insurance agents; to their amazement, they received all sorts of secrets while interviewing prospective clients. In response, counterintelligence had several varieties of "Shut Your Mouth" posters printed and distributed by the thousands.

All belligerents placed some of their most productive counterintelligence agents in the busiest hotels. The Americans had one particularly effective individual who worked at several French establishments well known for having a large military clientele. He served as a bellhop whose sundry jobs allowed him to become acquainted with the visitors and their luggage; occasionally, such agents resorted to steaming open mail of suspicious individuals. It was the lack of personal mail being received by the hotel manager that first alerted the US agent that the gentlemen might not actually be French. When the police approached him, the German spy made a dash for it but was soon apprehended.[51]

The SOS was very dependent on foreign labor. Because there were no regulations governing who was hired, local intelligence officers constantly tried to convince commanding officers to take independent measures to ensure that all laborers were who they said they were. To monitor the process, CIP agents disguised themselves as interpreters, laborers, and foremen so that they could mingle unnoticed among the workforce. In addition to laborers, the agents observed closely all foreigners, expatriates, persons in French uniforms, or persons in US uniforms in French areas and those who were supposedly mentally impaired. They also paid special attention to those purporting to be horse dealers, commercial travelers, wine merchants, caravan traders, fruit and other peddlers, prostitutes, and owners of canal boats and barges. To travel from place to place, most CIP agents walked. Bicycles would have been advantageous except the Quartermaster Corps only furnished Army-issue bicycles—not ideal for agents in disguise.

Sergeant Peter de Pasqua of the CIP was a master of several languages, giving him the freedom to move unnoticed as an interpreter for the American Red Cross. Counterintelligence agents often took work to supplement their $100-a-month allowance and pay; otherwise, their shabby apparel placed limits on what types of company they could keep, especially in a place like Paris. De Pasqua frequented the various eating and drinking establishments of the old French city of Beaune with his ears open to the sentiments expressed by the local clientele. While visiting a local bistro, Pietro, as Pasqua called himself, quickly befriended a Spaniard by the name of Diaz, who was openly uttering threats to the Americans. Diaz's companions included a second Spaniard who, like Diaz, worked as a laborer for the American SOS, and a third individual who was a disabled French veteran with radical political leanings. Under Diaz's leadership, the group planned various acts of sabotage and was in the process of making contact with a German spymaster in Spain. Having access to a censor stamp, Pietro offered to serve as the group's courier; this enabled him to learn firsthand of the conspirators' plans for destroying a major munitions depot. Just in the area of munitions alone, the AEF purchased from the French more than 5 million cannon shells and 5,000 artillery pieces. The gang's modus operandi was subsequently passed on to French authorities who proceeded to arrest the would-be saboteurs. For his part, Pasqua received the Citation for Meritorious Service, thus earning the distinction of being the first member of the Corps of Intelligence Police to be so decorated.[52]

The AEF required hundreds of laborers in the rear areas to build the depots and other infrastructure, but France had already exhausted its labor supply. Consequently, the most logical source was Spain, but German agents were successful in undermining the Allied recruitment of Spanish workers so that the AEF would never receive the numbers it desired. To demonstrate to what extremes they were willing to go, German operatives arranged for the poisoning of a group of Portuguese laborers destined for France. German agents also targeted supplies purchased from Spain, occasionally placing pieces of glass in canned goods and poisoning livestock destined for the US troops; they also encouraged labor strikes at a number of factories. After the war, German intelligence acknowledged that they had enjoyed far greater success in Spain than in the SOS. Unfortunately, the Americans were helpless in addressing the problem. Besides barring CIP specialists from traveling to Spain, the United States had its military attaché in the capital city of Madrid, far from the Franco-Spanish frontier where most of the action took place.

To compound the problem, most Spanish laborers evaded the control points and crossed the border after paying guides a small fee. The most effective means of dealing with illegal crossovers involved planting undercover agents in the various small villages and towns along the frontier. Colonel Ward labeled the overall effort a success, particularly in those towns that lay close to an official control point. In August 1918, offices opened at Hendaye on the Atlantic side of the Franco-Spanish border and at Cerbere on the Mediterranean side. Cerbere alone screened 3,000 laborers a month. Finally, in the fall of 1918, the rear zone opened a third office at Modane on the Franco-Italian border. Here, agents checked some 3,000 individuals over a six-month period.

At Selies-sur-Cher near Gievres, where the Americans had constructed a large refrigerator plant, rumors arose that a gang problem existed among Spanish laborers. Agent Pedro Padilla volunteered for the potentially dangerous assignment. Disguised as a worker, Padilla unfortunately was betrayed by his hands, which didn't reveal the normal calluses a laborer would have. He attempted to explain it away by saying that he had formerly been a painter. Unfortunately, the members of the gang didn't buy his story and escorted Padilla to a cellar where they planned on beating the truth out of him. Luckily, Padilla had spent the first seven years of his life in the same section of Madrid, where one of his tormentors had also once resided. By remembering details of an anti-American parade that had passed through the city at the beginning of the Spanish-American War, the American agent was able to dispel his comrade's suspicions. Using information supplied by Padilla, French authorities arrested several would-be saboteurs as well as placed newly discovered spy routes under surveillance.[53]

The possibility of using paid informants was first raised in April 1918, but Colonel Ward resisted the idea because in his mind, most counterintelligence officers were inadequately trained to perform such a mission. Unlike their French and British counterparts, US officers could not wear civilian clothes, and to obtain clothing allowances required filling out a mountain of paperwork to justify each and every expense. Consequently, it was not until October that Ward felt confident enough in his officers to allow them to undertake covert operations—by then it was too late to make a difference.

Sometimes threats to AEF's secrets came from the most unexpected sources. Captain Samuel Hubbard reported that while on assignment with French intelligence in Paris, he became convinced that some unknown person was rifling through his desk. Subsequently, he prepared a classified dummy report for Nolan's signature and purposely left the document in plain sight. Instead of retiring to his quarters after dinner, he returned to his office and found a hiding place from which he could observe the desk. Soon the door opened and in came an officer assigned to an Asian delegation. Out came an electric flashlight that he had hidden under his cap to search the premises. Upon finding the document, he slipped it under his coat and made a quick departure.

In the spring of 1918, the War Department issued "Counter Espionage Principles," which outlined the duties of a counterintelligence officer. Among other things, the instructions defined the relationship between counterespionage and criminal investigations: offensives and crimes "are of interest to Intelligence Officers only when connected with enemy activity . . . avoid the dissipation of energy in following cases of vice, liquor selling, fraud, draft evasion, and desertion unless these are traceable to enemy activity."[54] Segregating the two functions proved harder than anticipated, especially during the first months in the rear areas. Matters were not helped by the CIP having the word *police* in its title. In one instance, counterintelligence agents arrested a gang for monthly stealing $50,000 worth of supplies as the materiel was being transported between the wharves and railroad terminals. Although criminal investigations remained a distraction throughout the war, too often counterintelligence agents were the only ones who possessed the necessary skills to handle highly visible cases.

There were a number of occasions when investigating acts of crime led to uncovering serious security risks because enemy agents often used illegal activity to finance their activities. In April, the CIP learned that a professional group of drug dealers was working at a number of US aviation camps that serviced more than 700 airplanes. Follow-up uncovered an international ring of cocaine traffickers who were actually trading drugs for supplies and parts. The CIP also found out that the scheme was part of an enemy-financed effort to undermine the will of US soldiers to wage war. In several related cases, counterintelligence personnel discovered that airplanes had been sabotaged, with their wing struts practically sawn through. In response to these findings, French officials moved quickly to take into custody those responsible.

Near the war's end, Colonel Ward created a mobile unit comprising seasoned veterans to monitor difficult cases in order to provide advice and aid to less-experienced fellow officers. The senior professionals were also capable of providing on-site training when necessary. Ward felt that the approach was validated and had plans to expand the effort if the war had continued. Ward also foresaw the need for inspectors that would visit the various CIP elements to ensure that all functions were being done according to regulation, but this never progressed beyond the planning stage.

Besides agents who worked in either the front or rear zones, a handful of CIP specialists were assigned to the Counter-Espionage Section within the GHQ itself. Here, members of Special Projects helped to compile a central card file that ultimately contained 160,000 names and 3,500 dossiers. The Paris operation also possessed a list of 22,000 names from the American Registry Bureau, which oversaw civilian auxiliary groups, such as the Red Cross, that were connected with the Army. Among the lists of Americans was one containing the names of 7,000 young men living in France who were of draftable age and naturally of interest to authorities stateside.[55] Finally, the Paris operation maintained contact with the Passport Bureau, which controlled the movements of US citizens, checking more than 10,000 identification papers and denying 323 visas.

Almost all the agents within Special Projects had some form of specialty, ranging from performing surveillance to possessing knowledge of German espionage operations in Spain to searching for invisible codes and inks. Others provided security to VIPs traveling by rail; this led the CIP to detail one specialist to General Pershing's private train. Another agent was assigned to Pershing as his own personal bodyguard, who, on at least one occasion, was able to save the general from an assassination attempt at the hands of a distraught woman. Counterintelligence experts included an officer who worked exclusively on labor, socialism, and bolshevism cases; still another dealt with possible incidents of sabotage at Army construction sites. Agent Walter J. Goedeke, a former State Department employee from Baltimore, Maryland, received a commission as a first lieutenant and took charge of examining passports for forgery.

MAKING THE AIRWAVES SECURE

When Nolan first visited French intelligence, his hosts repeatedly emphasized the importance of using secure communications. They related attempting to convince the Russians of the same, but their ally had paid a high price on the battlefield for failure to take the warning seriously. After the war, General Erich von Falkenhayn, a member of the German general staff, validated the concerns of the French: "The intercepted wireless [Russian] . . . allowed us to follow accurately the movements of the enemy in the East from week-to-week and often day-to-day from the beginning of the war till far into 1915 and to take corresponding measures. . . . By this means, the war in the East assumed quite a different and much simpler character for us than that in the West." And Nolan had good reasons to listen to the French: "When we entered the war in 1917, we were at least no better than that of the Russians in 1914."[56]

There was a major difference between communications security on the home front compared to that overseas. The War Department faced the challenge of protecting certain types of information, whereas the AEF confronted a much larger problem of combat information across the board. Over the course of the war, there were a handful of major players. The Radio Intelligence Section initiated an education campaign to let everyone know that the enemy was indeed listening, and in the spring of 1918, it started to monitor periodically AEF's own transmissions to determine if the message was being received. Another major player was the Code Compilation Section, organized by the chief signal officer during December 1917. The Code Compilation Section initially consisted of a captain, three lieutenants, and a corporal; months would pass before it began producing codes in any sufficient quantities.

The problems that communications security specialists faced during World War I were largely the same challenges that would confront their successors in World War II through the Vietnam War. During these conflicts, thousands of lives were lost, and the element of surprise on the battlefield was compromised because of the inability to change human nature. Simply put, Americans loved to talk, and the telephone and radio seemed designed with them in mind. It didn't take long for security specialists to identify the telephone as the principal culprit. Monitored calls routinely revealed the order of battle and provided dates and places of planned attacks. It could not get much worse than the following evaluation given to one US headquarters: "radio stations and telephone operators have furnished information of vital importance to the enemy in regard to your battle order, the organization of your divisions, the location and form of training of divisions in reserve, the location of heavy artillery and tanks while preparing for the attack, and the date the attack was to take place."[57] Nolan further confirmed the overall lack of security by citing a captured German report that gave the Allied battle order over a large sector; the same report also contained an apology for allowing a whole week to pass without radio identification of a certain US division.

With the coming of modern warfare, command and control on the battlefield and necessity of rapid response seemed in many a commander's mind to justify open conversation. When given the choice between secure communications and the ability to communicate freely, most commanders chose the latter. As one division commander confessed, "The available means, therefore, for the rapid and full transmission of information are the radio, buzzer, and telephone, and of these the telephone was by far superior—provided it could be used without hindrance." A major reason officers communicated in the clear was that they simply did not believe the enemy was actually listening or, if they were, that they could respond fast enough. This thinking stood in stark contrast to reality; Allied intelligence acknowledged that the Germans were copying an astounding 75 percent of all radio transmissions.

There was also an ongoing reluctance by AEF communicators to follow established guidelines, especially those serving on the front lines. They easily discarded so-called foolish instructions for their own "just as good" approach. The troops would never see the necessity for changing the code, for putting in the nulls that were prescribed, and for keeping words in the clear out-of-coded messages.[58] They even naively believed that they could satisfy the security requirements by dividing a plain text message into groups of five letters. To counter such thinking, the Signal Corps tried to convince those entrusted with the task that it would be better to send messages in the clear than to transmit in both code and plain text, thus compromising the code. General Pershing signed off on the following letter sent to the commanding general, First Army: "Your attention has been called, by letter, to many cases of criminal carelessness in the use of our code and the transmission of messages in clear, or in a mixture of code and clear. Even messages entirely in code have, in general, been so carelessly prepared that the enemy will have no difficulty in solving the code."[59] The situation was often made worse because officers responsible for encoding messages changed assignments too frequently for them to become familiar with the various rules or even the absolute necessity of following them.

Finally, US soldiers have always demonstrated both ingenuity and a certain "can-do" attitude on the battlefield. Unfortunately, this carried over to communications and led to the creation of their own homemade codes. One of the most popular was the baseball code, that translated such terms as "stolen so many bases" (captured so many prisoners) or "Ty Cobb singled" (we bombarded). In some form or other, many of these would still be around 50 years later; for instance, the point-of-origin codes that relayed a location based on a deviation from a shared point of reference. Yet, time after time, Allied cryptanalysts demonstrated that homemade versions could be broken easily within a matter of minutes.

Solutions to the communications security problems took several forms. In December 1917, the newly formed Code Compilation Section found itself alone and largely dependent on its own limited resources. Its chief, Captain Howard R. Barnes, who had at one time worked in the State Department code room, put it this way: "At the commencement of the war, it is doubtful if any Regular Army officer had ever compiled a modern field code or assisted in its compilation. Indeed, when this Section was organized its files did not contain a single copy of an American Army field code."[60] Barnes also enjoyed no direct contact with the MI-8 and was soon made aware that he could not depend on the flawed Playfair cipher, which the British had already abandoned because it could be broken in less than 30 minutes. The only assistance offered by the Allies were the obsolete editions of their various codes. Captain Barnes did acknowledge one valuable source—the contribution of Colonel Parker Hitt, both as far as his writings and his availability for consultation while serving as the assistant chief signal officer for the AEF. "To him more than to any other officer of the American Army is due whatever success the American codes may have obtained."[61]

The staff's first attempt at cryptography was the Telephone Code, dated March 1918, often referred to as the "Female Code" because it utilized the first and last names of women. Its purpose was to disguise units and names of their key personnel; for instance, the chief signal officer of the First Army was dubbed "Mary Brown." Besides the telephone, wireless operators also initially used it to transmit messages. The next product was the American Trench Code, a small single-part code of some 1,600 words and phrases, designed for use in conjunction with a complex system of super-encipherment. Due to fear that the enemy might capture a copy, the Signal Corps never distributed it to regimental headquarters or below. To fill the gap, the Code Compilation Section created 3,000 copies of a smaller version for use down to the company level.

On May 5, the following report was delivered to the General Staff. "Actual use of our code [the Trench Code] has shown that after all the care of producing a scientific, practical and secure code, it is used very carelessly and thoughtlessly in the field. . . . It is, therefore, absolutely essential that before a man uses a code, he must be thoroughly familiar with all fundamental principles of code and with the means of communication he is going to use." If mishandling of Trench Code was a problem, then choosing not to use them at all was an equal concern. "Although it may seem a paradox, the most striking feature of the use of the Trench Codes was the general inclination to avoid them whenever possible."[62] The Trench Code's use of super-encipherment also turned out not to be a very good communications security tool. Being presented with 44 super-enciphered messages, one of the best AEF cryptanalysts took only five hours to recover the alphabet, all by simply making frequency counts of the various letters.

AEF cryptographers had one thing going for them: they were not burdened by precedent, so they could focus on determining what was actually needed—a system that was simple to operate, comprehensive enough to produce a good working vocabulary, and revised at regular intervals. The answer consisted of shifting as much of the burden from the communicators on the front lines to the Code Compilation Section in the rear. The staff members achieved this by moving to a two-part code not requiring any additional encipherment and by making provisions to replace the codes approximately every two weeks. The British code makers had concluded that there was a limit to the numbers of copies of code and to the number of days in use before either enemy intelligence broke it or friendly operators compromised the document. In previous wars, it would have been impossible to produce and distribute replacement codes with sufficient speed to guarantee the security of such a system, but the AEF had the technical and administrative capacity to undertake the challenge.

In June, the Code Compilation Section issued the Potomac Code—the first to include the two-part principle. The 47-page booklet, small enough to slip into a breast pocket, contained approximately 1,800 words and phrases in alphabetical order to make it user friendly. Designed for the First Army, the Potomac Code was the first in the so-called river series, with each code named after a US river; when the Second Army was later organized, it received a completely separate lake series. In total, the Code Compilation Section produced 14 replacement codes over a four-month period. Beginning in September, an Emergency Code, which contained 50 common phrases, was constructed for use on the front lines to supplement each river or lake code.[63]

The adjutant general at the GHQ assumed responsibility for printing the code in water-soluble ink for easy destruction in case of the threat of capture. The proofreading, printing, and binding took five days, but in case of an emergency, around-the-clock shifts required only 72 hours. To safeguard the process, two to three officers remained on hand during the printing to police all excess copies. During the 10 months of its existence, the Code Compila-tion Section produced 80,000 copies of numbered codes and pamphlets. The possibility always existed that the code could prematurely be compromised; thus several editions were held in reserve so that they could be issued at a moment's notice. The word group "DAM" was appropriately printed on the front cover in order to report a lost code.

Although Army regulations stated that code distribution belonged to the adjutant general, the Code Compilation Section of the army assumed respon-sibility for distributing the codes directly to all users and maintaining a central accounting of all obsolete or compromised books, but the growing size of the AEF soon would make this impracticable. Instead, the Signal Corps turned distribution over to the Radio Intelligence Section, which furnished them to corps, divisions, and below; on the back side, radio intelligence also retrieved outdated or compromised books. One consequence of this decentralized dis-tribution system was the inability to determine just how many codes were in actual use at any one time or even who actually issued them, when they were put into service, or when they were withdrawn.

The cryptographers also produced additional codes covering a variety of subjects: staff, telegraph, casualties, and aircraft; the French bilingual Carnet Reduit was for AEF officers performing liaison duties. In June, the section put out a Staff Code to replace the Telegraph Code. The new edition was the largest and most comprehensive ever attempted in the field, but regardless of the code in question, those who misused it often trumped the good work of the Code Compilation Section. Colonel Moorman could not have put it in stronger language: "There certainly never existed on the western front a force more negligent in the use of their own code than was the American Army. . . . My idea would be to hang a few of the offenders."[64]

Following a review that revealed a lack of overall communications disci-pline and transmission of too many messages in the clear, one last attempt was made to right the ship, and in the summer of 1918, all remaining portions of communications security within the G2 A-6 was transferred to the Signal Corps, which created the Security Service. The AEF was not alone in its decision; all belligerents were simultaneously taking actions of their own to stem the tide of compromised information. There was speculation that had the Germans enacted their security controls some six months earlier, the effec-tiveness of Allied signals intelligence would have been greatly diminished.

The Security Service placed their representatives (security or control of-ficers) at army, corps, and division headquarters where they exercised several different means of safeguarding communications. First, they continued with the security reminders. For example, the first page of the AEF telephone director warned users: "Your conversation is very likely to be overheard by the enemy Secret Service and our Security Service—both of these organizations are continuously on duty." This was followed up by the control officers reviewing the issuance of callsigns, helping to assign code names, assuming responsibility for distribution of codes, and notifying users when a code had reached the end of its life.

The most significant step taken toward ensuring that communicators obeyed the guidelines was implementation of an extensive monitoring system. At the GHQ and at the headquarters of both field armies, control officers used stenographers to monitor long-distance calls placed through the switchboards and to listen in on the trunk lines that ran between corps, army, and the GHQ for potential security leaks. To gain a picture of what the enemy might pick up by the telephone in the field, the Security Service assigned one monitoring station to every division in order to intercept all traffic sent in the clear. According to the report of the chief signal officer, "Nothing was so effective in inducing officers to be careful in the use of the telephone than to present them a few minutes of their own conversation."[65] In July, the Security Service established a second net of stations whose sole purpose was to monitor US radio communications.

Monitoring stations filed daily reports up the chain of command. Occasionally, interception of compromised information led to immediate steps to avert a disastrous course of action. A serious breach could also cause the Security Service to issue a reprimand to the offending organization along with an attached statement from higher headquarters. If a pattern persisted, the Security Service could propose changes. For example, numerous leaks led to installing buzzer phones exclusively at battalion headquarters and below to shield against possible enemy intercept. Security officers also began receiving training in the principles of cryptography so that they could recommend changes in the preparation and handling of codes.

Although the members of the Security Service felt that monitoring was the strongest incentive for change in their arsenal, the practice had a number of shortcomings. There were often significant delays between the initial monitoring report and the finding being communicated to the offending unit. Most commanders in the field chose to ignore such warnings as nothing more than another administrative distraction; this was because no violator ever faced punishment. Control officers also never followed up; it simply was not the gentlemanly thing to do when there was a war going on.

World War I was still a watershed in the development of US Army communications security. For the first time, the discipline came to mean more than simply codes and ciphers. It now involved monitoring of actual transmissions for the purposes of detecting security violations and correcting weaknesses in the codes themselves. Another new function seen for the first time was the use of security guidelines, coupled with published warnings against possible misuse of communications. Unfortunately, like so many efforts by successor organizations in future wars, the Signal Corps was in the end unable to address many of the human causes of poor security.

COURSE OF THE WAR

The German strategist General Erich Ludendorff summed up his army's plans for 1918: "The situation in Russia and Italy will make it possible to deliver a blow on the Western Front in the New Year." As troops moved west, Germany's ranks soon swelled to 136,000 officers and 3.450 million enlisted, making it the "the greatest army that the world has ever known." In Ludendorff's mind, Germany's foremost enemy was time. "Our general situation requires that we should strike at the earliest moment . . . before the Americans can throw strong forces into the scale."

The French and British leadership both believed that their troops would be the ones to bear the brunt of the German attack, and the divided Allied command failed to present a much-needed united front during this crucial hour. There was, however, increasing evidence that the German army would attack the British Expeditionary Force (BEF), simply because it had less backcountry in which to retreat. Of Germany's 192 divisions, 69 of them concentrated on the 70-mile front facing the British, whose own forces consisted of 21 divisions plus 12 others that resided either in reserve or in rest areas. To make matters worse, Britain's prime minister unilaterally agreed with the French to cover an additional 25 miles of the front, further stretching BEF's already thin force. General Sir Hubert Gough, commander of Britain's Fifth Army, accurately discerned from studying his foe that the enemy would launch its assault against him; aerial photos confirmed his conclusions. The final piece of the information came from trench raiders who took a number of German prisoners; they consistently pointed to March 21 as *Der Tag* or "The Day." Using persuasion, the general obtained an additional three divisions and took steps to fortify his position to include using tanks as defensive weapons.

When the Americans sent the 1st Division into the trenches at the first of the year, the Allies did not plan to mark the milestone. General Marie Eugene Debeney, who commanded the French First Army, specifically forbade US correspondents to witness the arrival of the division. He did not trust US newspaper, reporters and besides, it was prohibited by French press policy. Nolan immediately requested permission from General Pershing to speak to the chief of the French Mission. Within the hour, Nolan had received a phone call telling of General Debeney's decision to reverse himself and to grant press access.

Although the emerging AEF intelligence remained focused on the quiet sector that lay to its front, it showed signs of becoming a contributing force by providing the Allies with several crucial pieces of information. In March, the Germans placed into service an entirely new code; solving it became top priority for AEF cryptanalysts because the code was believed to be an indicator of the long-expected German attack. With all AEF radio intelligence focused on the problem, the break came on March 13—just two days after the German army implemented its new Schlusselheft code. Apparently a German station had yet to receive a copy, so its signal personnel asked for a rebroadcast of a message using the old code already solved by Allied signals intelligence. At midnight, AEF radio intelligence personnel at the Souilly station recovered several intercepted messages—the first in the new code and the next two in the old. The Americans had quickly recognized the phrase "OS," which stood for *Ohne Sinnz* or "message unintelligible," in a transmission requesting the original message to be resent; already having broken the old system, cryptanalysts easily decoded the new. As German communicators were just starting to make use of their new code, Allied intelligence stood ready to read their mail. Nolan speculated that in this case alone the adversary's carelessness in handling their codes had "undoubtedly cost the lives of thousands of German soldiers in this great offensive."[66]

Following two weeks of fighting known as Operation Michael, the Germans gained 1,250 square miles of shell-desolate countryside, captured 90,000 prisoners and more than 1,000 guns, and broke one British army and wounded another; they had now stretched their own front another 50 miles and suffered in casualties the equivalency of an army. On April 9, the Germans attacked the BEF again (Operation Georgette) during the crucial Battle of Lys. The Germans threw division after division into the fight, forcing the British to slowly withdraw while valiantly contesting every field in the process. Finally, on the night of April 29, Ludendorff called off the operation. The Germans had regained the ground and more that the Allies had won over the three previous years, but it came at a terrible cost. Together, the belligerents suffered nearly 450,000 dead and wounded and 300,000 captured.

On April 30, at Seicheprey, not far from St. Mihiel, the Germans decided to test the 26th (Yankee) Division. Leading up to the battle, AEF intercept operators copied four enemy messages warning of enemy attacks. The engagement that followed would prove that the American fighting spirit was alive, even if experience was lacking. During the counterattack, the Americans regained what was initially lost, but in the process, the New England unit suffered 634 casualties—the AEF's worst losses of the war to date. Still, the battle was hailed back home as a victory for the purposes of selling Liberty Bonds.

War often calls for improvisation, even for intelligence systems. When their cart overturned carrying communications gear and telescopes, an AEF observation crew quickly spotted a nearby baby carriage that proved to be more than an adequate replacement; because it was lightweight, it could be taken almost anywhere. The carriage soon became a familiar sight among troops of the 1st Division, and the observation element was widely known for having helped provide timely alerts during three recent counterattacks. The principal challenge was keeping the carriage out of sight from various Army inspectors who would have been hard pressed to find authorization for such a vehicle. The inevitable happened when an inspector had come to watch troops moving into action. An intelligence officer described what happened next. Suddenly, a soldier appeared around a corner pushing the carriage festooned with all sorts of odd-looking gear; 11 soldiers smoking cigarettes were walking not far behind. "The army inspector turned purple with rage and almost burst with anger. Audible were his oaths and remarks about court-martial. He did not realize that he was looking upon the most efficient and admired observation post in France."[67]

Under the leadership of Captain Samuel Hubbard, the Order of Battle Section at the GHQ was busily determining where the Germans would attack next. Consequently, intelligence analysts expended a huge amount of time focusing on the location of important fighting divisions that the Germans had withdrawn from the front line, referred to as Masses of Maneuver. Normally, this information was not easily available, and some of it depended on Allied intelligence that was busily engaged during periods of active combat. This would cause the Order of Battle personnel to spend sleepless nights awaiting news in order to adjust their reports and maps. Hubbard had become thoroughly familiar with a French document titled "A Study of German Operations against Riga and the Study of the German Operations in Picardy." It seemed evident that the enemy would attack where, if successful, it could straighten out its line and where an assault would be least suspected. The site selected by Hubbard's staff was Chemin des Dames. Here, the German Army could use 10 to 15 divisions to attack the fortifications, capture the Mountain de Reims, and then swing left, automatically forcing the French to withdraw from the Champagne and Verdun areas and to begin a new line along the Marne. The estimated date was sometime between May 25 and May 30. After having his section's conclusions checked and rechecked, Hubbard directed that the findings be presented to the entire intelligence staff for their input.[68]

Being a junior reserve officer, Hubbard did not find selling the report to senior leadership easy. Only after an entire day spent alone with Colonels

Nolan and Arthur Conger was Captain Hubbard finally able to persuade his superiors. Upon meeting with the US liaison officer who served at French headquarters, Hubbard repeated his findings. The liaison officer then reported back to Colonel de Cointet, subchief of the French Intelligence Section; Cointet immediately saw the logic of Hubbard's argument and called for a briefing. Although Cointet sold his chief of staff on the plan, the French commander of the Sixth Army, General Denis Auguste Duchene, dismissed outright Hubbard's premise. For those who had previously witnessed Duchene's decision making, his rejection came as no great surprise; someone had once compared the general's approach to that of an average French private who had no inkling of approaching danger until bullets started flying. The defeat of the French that followed on May 27 soon placed German forward elements on the road toward Paris, causing Parisians to begin fleeing their city. These dire circumstances forced General Pershing to reverse his position on maintaining US forces separate from the British and French; instead, he would offer up five divisions for employment in the Marne area.

The American 2nd Division moved 14 miles from the village of Bremoiselle; its orders were simple: stem the tide. Given the successful German advance in the spring of 1918, the French feared that their battle lines north of Paris might be broken, but no large-scale maps existed for ground south of the Marne should Allied forces have to occupy it. Given only 12 hours to produce a large-scale contour map so that the artillery could safely direct fire, French and US intelligence rushed their topographical specialists to the area of operations. Here, surveyors labored to complete their work while being subject to enemy barrages. To check the results of the topographers on the ground, the Air Service took photos that formed a mosaic for comparison. Besides successfully creating a map for the artillery, intelligence also placed into the hands of front line infantry through accurately drawn maps depicting potential defensive areas—all in just two days. The US cartographers were beginning to demonstrate their superiority to the other Allied services in two important ways: speed, due to the use of the latest equipment, and mobility, due to the use of printing presses mounted in trucks—all of which would lead to more requests by the Allies for assistance, along with orders for their own trucks.[69]

Major General James Harbord, Pershing's former chief of staff, now commanded the Marine Brigade of the 2nd Division. At dawn on June 1, the Marines and the 3rd Brigade moved up the Paris-Metz road to take their positions in the rear of the retreating French army. One participant remembered that many on the march were saying cynically, "Here we are heading toward Metz while the French Army is moving on Paris and we're supposed to be fighting the same war."[70] The road itself served as the dividing line for the two brigades. Although Brigadier General Edward M. Lewis's infantry would fight in several small-scale actions, the lack of artillery hampered them from accomplishing more.

What followed for the Marines would be known as simply Belleau Wood, a rough wooded area strewn with boulders covering approximately 1 square mile. Over the next week, the Marines showed themselves to be the most aggressive fighters on the western front, and in their honor, Belleau Wood was renamed Bois de la Brigade de Marine. By June 11, the Marines were finally relieved and others took up the battle, but in the interim, the single brigade had thrown back the enemy with heavy losses. During the German offensive, the 2nd Division captured 1,687 prisoners, more than the entire BEF for the month, but suffered 9,777 wounded and 1,811 dead. It was Ludendorff's fatal mistake that he did not broaden his front, and the Marines, the 2nd Division, and the AEF were able to help avert a disaster should the Germans had reached Paris, just 40 miles away.

Compared to other elements within G2, the Censorship Division received more than their share of "brickbats than bouquets"; Belleau Wood was a classic example. Early during the fighting, the Press headquarters gave the Marines all the headlines in US newspapers. A correspondent by the name of Floyd Gibbons had filed an interim report extolling the efforts of the Marines at Belleau Wood; this was followed by a premature announcement of Gibbons's death. While attempting to save a marine's life, Gibbons would lose an eye and receive several other serious wounds, but none proved fatal. As a tribute to the fallen correspondent, a friend who was a censor in Paris allowed Gibbons's account to go through as written. The swift approval was also facilitated by a censorship decision made prior to the battle—the term *marines* could be released but not the names of specific Army units. Subsequently, Colonel Walter C. Sweeny, in charge of the Censorship Division, had a hard time explaining what happened, and Nolan found himself in trouble with General Pershing, who was receiving an earful from his field commanders demanding to know why their units were not being mentioned in the news.[71]

NOTES

1. Dennis E. Nolan, "A History of Military Intelligence and the AEF: A Working Draft," chap. "3-2-35," 9.
2. Bruce W. Bidwell, *History of the Military Intelligence Division* (Department of Army, 1961), pt. II, chap. XIV, 34–36.
3. Nolan, "A History of Military Intelligence and the AEF," chap. "CA," 7.
4. C. S. Coulter, "Intelligence Services in the World War," *Infantry Journal* (April 1922): 376.

5. Nolan, "A History of Military Intelligence and the AEF," chap. "3-2-35," 7.

6. Shipley Thomas, *S-2 in Action* (Harrisburg, PA: Military Service Publishing, 1940), 1.

7. Coulter, "Intelligence Service in the World War," 377.

8. US Army Signal School, "T.P.S. and Listening Posts" (France: American Expeditionary Forces); War Department, *Report of the Chief Signal Officer* (Washington, DC: Government Printing Office, 1919), 317.

9. SCR originally stood for "set, complete, radio" but eventually was translated "Signals Corps Radio."

10. War Department, *Report of the Chief Signal Officer*, 18.

11. Ibid., 316.

12. War Department, *Report of the Chief Signal Officer*, 317.

13. War Department, *Report of Code Compilation Section, General Headquarters, American Expeditionary Forces, France* (Washington, DC: Office of the Chief Signal Officer, 1935), 37.

14. Maurer Maurer, *The US Air Service in World War* (Washington, DC: Office of Air Force History, 1978), Vol. IV, 196–198.

15. E. Alexander Powell, *The Army Behind the Army* (New York: Scribner's, 1919), 312–313.

16. Maurer, *The US Air Service in World War*, Vol. I, 138.

17. James J. Cooke, *The US Air Service in the Great War* (Westport, CT: Praeger, 1996), 47.

18. Maurer, *The US Air Service in World War*, Vol. IV, 199.

19. Diane Hamm, ed., *Military Intelligence: Its Heroes and Legends* (Arlington, VA: US Army Intelligence and Security Command, 1987), 48–49.

20. Ibid.

21. Terrence J. Finnegan, *Shooting the Front* (Washington, DC: NDIC Press, 2006), 329.

22. Ibid., 372–373.

23. Samuel T. Hubbard, *Memoirs of a Staff Officer, 1917–1919* (Tuckahoe, NY: Cardinal Associates, 1959), 162–163.

24. Ibid., 75–77.

25. Nolan, "A History of Military Intelligence and the AEF," chap. "C&C."

26. War Department, Office of the Chief Signal Officer, *Final Report of the Radio Intelligence Section, General Staff, General Headquarters, American Expeditionary Forces* (Washington, DC: Office of the Chief Signal Officer, 1935), 41; H. J. Round, "Direction and Position Finding," paper read at Wireless Sectional Meeting of the Institution, January 14, 1920.

27. War Department, *Report of the Chief Signal Officer*, 322.

28. War Department, Office of the Chief Signal Officer, *Final Report of the Radio Intelligence Section*, 7

29. Frank Moorman, "Wireless Intelligence," lecture delivered to the MID on February 13, 1920.

30. Nolan, "A History of Military Intelligence and the AEF," chap. "CA," 10.

31. Powell, *Army Behind the Army*, 250–251.

32. Nolan, "A History of Military Intelligence and the AEF," chap. "1-25-35," 1–2.

33. Thomas M. Johnson, *Our Secret War* (Indianapolis: Bobbs-Merrill, 1929), 220, 223.

34. War Department, Office of the Chief Signal Officer, *Final Report of the Radio Intelligence Section*, 7.

35. Moorman, "Wireless Intelligence."

36. Cooke, *US Air Service in the Great War*, 192.

37. During Colonel Mitchell's court-martial trial of 1925, General Nolan, who was serving as the deputy commander of the US Army, would be called upon to deliver the army's leadership response; it is unknown how Nolan felt as to the merits of the trial, but it is doubtful that he felt too much personal sympathy for the air commander.

38. Nolan, "A History of Military Intelligence and the AEF," chap. "MID," 16.

39. Ibid., chap. "3-4-35," 18.

40. Nolan, "A History of Military Intelligence and the AEF," chap. "C. A.," 11.

41. Viskniskki was familiar with the *Stars and Stripes* published during the Civil War because several members of his hometown of Carmi, Illinois, had actually worked on the original paper.

42. Ibid., chap. "S&S," 9–10.

43. Ibid., chap. "S&S," 22–23.

44. Peter Krass, *Portrait of War* (Hoboken, NJ: Wiley, 2007), 168.

45. Ann Bray, ed., *History of the Counter Intelligence Corps* (Fort Holabird: US Army Intelligence Center, 1959), Vol. III, 93.

46. Ibid., 36.

47. Ibid., 22.

48. Johnson, *Our Secret War*, 160–161.

49. Bray, *History of the Counter Intelligence Corps*, Vol. III, 32–33.

50. Ibid., 39.

51. Johnson, *Our Secret War*, 112–113.

52. Hamm, *Military Intelligence*, 59–66.

53. Bray, *History of the Counter Intelligence Corps*, Vol. III, 46–47.

54. War Department General Staff, War College Division, MI-3, "Provisional Counter Espionage Instructions" (February 1918), 33

55. Bray, *History of the Counter Intelligence Corps*, Vol. III, 54.

56. Nolan, "A History of Military Intelligence and the AEF," chap. 3, 15.

57. War Department, Office of the Chief Signal Officer, *Final Report of the Radio Intelligence Section*, 12.

58. War Department, *Report of Code Compilation Section*, 42; War Department, Office of the Chief Signal Officer, *Final Report of the Radio Intelligence Section*, 51.

59. War Department, Office of the Chief Signal Officer, *Final Report of the Radio Intelligence Section*, 12.

60. War Department, *Report of Code Compilation Section*, 32.

61. Ibid., 42.

62. Ibid., 32.

63. Assistant Chief of Staff, G-2, Army Security Agency, "Historical Background of the Signal Security Agency" (April 1943), Vol. II, 137–146; War Department, *Report of Code Compilation Section*, 6–7.

64. Moorman, "Wireless Intelligence."

65. War Department, *Report of the Chief Signal Officer*, 332.

66. War Department, Office of the Chief Signal Officer, *Final Report of the Radio Intelligence Section*, 19.

67. Thomas, *S-2 in Action*, 44–45.

68. Hubbard, *Memoirs of a Staff Officer*, 224–228.

69. Powell, *Army Behind the Army*, 239, 241.

70. S. L. A. Marshall, *World War I* (Boston: Houghton Mifflin, 1964), 378.

71. Nolan, "A History of Military Intelligence and the AEF," chap. "Press," 12.

6

Coming to a Close

"On the thirtieth of October we arrived at the city of Langres,
And hiked up to our barracks, the place we now call home;
But before we had a chance to show what Co. G could do,
The Kaiser and his dirty bunch cried: 'Komerad, We are through.'"

—Private William Thater, Company G, 29th Engineers

The summer months of July and August 1918 would prove to be the turning point of the war. On July 4, the American Expeditionary Forces (AEF) rose to a million troops in France, thanks to the growing numbers of combat forces that consisted of a mixture of regular, National Guard, and conscripted divisions or the so-called National Army. There were now three US corps and 20 divisions on hand; of the divisions, seven were in the area of the Marne, four were with the British, and the final nine were either training or, having finished training, were headed for the Vosges Mountains.

On July 14, the Germans launched their last great offensive, the crossing of the Marne, which began with traditional artillery barrage. During the battle, the American 38th Infantry Regiment, under the command of Colonel Ulysses Grant McAlexander, achieved that of which legends are made. The 38th assumed a defensive position along the south bank of the river for the purpose of protecting two important roads. On one flank, the 30th Infantry Regiment was beaten back from its poorly constructed positions, and on the other, the French 131st Regiment was also quickly pushed back. Still, for three days, the 38th held its ground. Although suffering heavy casualties itself, the regiment had rightfully earned the title of "The Rock of the Marne." More important, the Allies had stopped the attack along the Champagne front.

Because of the German Army's failure to break through for a decisive win, it had overextended itself in the long, narrow Marne salient, which ran from Soissons to Reims. Using his Sixth and Tenth Armies, French Marshal Ferdinand Foch laid out a plan to recapture Soissons; Lieutenant General Robert Lee Bullard would command the American III Corps. To gain the element of surprise, the Allies suspended traditional artillery fire. Had the Germans suspected the attack on July 18, they may have chosen to shell the roads, which would have been disastrous for the Allies because the thoroughfares were clogged with men and machines struggling in the rain to move to the front.

Two balloon units supported the 1st and 2nd American Divisions under the French Tenth Army during the counteroffensive to sever the Chateau-Thierry Road, but the companies quickly discovered that keeping up with advancing troops was a major challenge. During a typical offensive, each balloon company worked independently, moving between 5 and 10 kilometers a day under ideal conditions. Although the enemy aircraft brought down eight balloons and artillery damaged a ninth, the observation platforms were still credited with adjusting artillery fire and providing valuable hourly updates to the advancing infantry. The rapid movement of troops coupled with poor weather conditions also hampered aircraft, but patrols at dawn and dusk and a number of deep photographic missions were still able to provide essential information. For the first time, US intelligence took oblique photos of the front at low altitudes—a practice that would be repeated during the planning phase of future operations.

Just three days into the attack, the Americans discovered how difficult it was to turn an initial advantage into victory. The 2nd Division had moved seven miles, but at a terrible cost. Some of its units experienced 50 percent casualties that totaled over 5,000 dead and wounded. The 1st Division was left with even more losses, but the AEF could now boast of two battle-hardened divisions. In terms of the larger picture, the Franco-American counteroffensive pushed the German troops back from the Marne to the Vesle River. At last the Germans had begun their great retreat that would ultimately lead to the end of hostilities. Count George von Hertling, who served as German chancellor during this period, reflected on this crucial period: "At the beginning of July 1918, I was convinced, I confess it, that before the first of September our adversaries would send us peace proposals. . . . That was on the 15th. On the 18th even the most optimistic among us knew that all was lost. The history of the world was played out in 3 days."

Although the German leadership had acknowledged the expanding US presence on the front lines, they never fully grasped just how many troops were arriving daily in France as well as the total numbers in the rear areas. This was borne out at a conference held in Berlin that autumn; German intelligence estimated US troop levels short by a half million, and their projections for the future revealed that the information gap was growing. Throughout the war, German intelligence had calculated that only 6,000 soldiers were arriving aboard each troop ship, but in reality, the Americans were transporting 12,000 to 15,000 per vessel. The reason for the erroneous conclusions could be attributed in part to the failure of German analysts to consider that more-than-normal capacity would be attempted. Knowing the size of many of the ocean liners—once interned German ships that had been commandeered by the US government—only reinforced their flawed thinking.[1] This is just one of the reasons that the director of military intelligence at the War Office in London, General G. M. MacDonogh, would state, "I do not propose to tell you that intelligence won the war, but I would suggest the reverse, namely that it was bad intelligence that lost the war."[2]

US radio intelligence reached its high watermark in August when it intercepted 11,000 messages; this coincided with the Americans' experiencing a major break in reading Germany's mail. Although the enemy's Fifth Army used a code that was daily enciphered by a different key, the code itself was only 1,000 words long, meaning that many words had to be spelled out, and it was the spelling out letter by letter that opened the opportunity for a solution. For this reason, the intercept operators had to be extremely accurate in their copying. The Germans had an officer by the name of Jaeger, who relentlessly attempted to keep the usage of spelled words down to a minimum by reviewing and signing off on each edition. Ironically, because the code did not contain a word group for the name Jaeger, every time a message went out with his signature, the Americans immediately had 40 solutions toward breaking the key. Unfortunately, someone on the other side eventually caught on and Jaeger's name disappeared from all future transmissions.[3]

FIRST ARMY

During the pause that followed the so-called Second Battle of the Marne, General John Pershing acted to fulfill his long-standing vision—the creation of First Army on August 10 with its headquarters at La Fetté-sous-Jouarre. General Hugh A. Drum, chief of staff at First Army, selected Colonel Willey Howell from among Nolan's staff to serve as his G2. Now Pershing could demonstrate to the world that US fighters fought differently and better. At a ceremony to honor Pershing, the Allied leadership made one last appeal to the Americans to forgo their independent command—something that not only had Pershing insisted on from the beginning but a position that had the full backing of the White House. British Prime Minister Lloyd George, who spoke at the occasion, reminded those present how much his country had sacrificed in just helping to bring American troops to France and that it was done in anticipation that at least five of the divisions should be "put in training behind our lines." But the prime minister's appeal would fall upon deaf ears.

Pershing was also forced to address the steadily growing criticism on how the Services of Supply (SOS) was being managed. Secretary of War Baker asked "Why in Heaven's name does it take so long to unload these ships and to turn them around?"[4] There were also concerns being voiced about the slow pace surrounding delivery of supplies, rations, arms, and ammunition into the hands of the Allies. To keep Washington from creating a separate command within the AEF's communications zone, Pershing recalled from the front General James G. Harbord, now commander of the 2nd Division, and placed him in charge of the SOS. Not only was Harbord an able administrator, but his recent successes on the battlefield helped to blunt criticism from the home front.

ARRIVAL OF VAN DEMAN

Although AEF intelligence remained focused upon supporting forthcoming offensives, important issues were still being addressed at GHQ. Over time, there had been growing cooperation between the AEF G2 and the MID. If left up to General Dennis Nolan and Colonel Ralph Van Deman, this undoubtedly would have happened much earlier, but one of the sticking points had been General Pershing's jealously guarding his total command and control within the war theater. No other issue so illustrated the problem as AEF's attempts to intrude on the prerogatives of military attachés. This dated as far back as Pershing's departure for France. Although he had received a letter of instruction that contained a sentence specifically exempting military attachés from his command, Pershing was not long in theater before he began to take steps challenging the clause, such as ordering officers attached to the London delegation to be reassigned to his headquarters. These plans were quickly abandoned when the War Department resisted. Later, when an attaché to France proceeded to collect information without first coordinating with general headquarters (GHQ) intelligence, General Pershing dispatched a strongly worded protest to Washington.

The most important step toward greater cooperation between the principal intelligence players occurred when the War Department reassigned Van Deman to the AEF. Immediately, Nolan tasked him to coordinate with the Allies on various issues left unresolved over time and to look for new ways in which the Military Intelligence Division (MID) staff members could assist their

AEF counterparts. Van Deman's first priority was to address a matter that involved both the military attaché in Paris and the G2, SOS; it concerned the issuing of US passports and visas. Normally, a local embassy only provided its military attaché the courtesy of review, but given the wartime conditions, the AEF demanded a more central role. Colonel Van Deman transmitted a letter to the State Department in which he attempted to justify the AEF's position: "To allow unrestricted travel of enemy agents is to aid the enemy in the prosecution of the war and therefore add to the number of killed and wounded of our forces, and to the prolongation of the war."[5]

The matter was finally resolved when the State Department created a central Passport Control Office in Paris that fully represented the interests of the AEF. Specifically citing the new arrangement as a prototype, Van Deman wrote a letter pressing the State Department's security service to revise the existing passport controls within England, Europe's neutral countries (such as Switzerland and Holland), and even Cuba, China, Japan, and Siberia and to embrace a general policy of greater coordination between state and the military; but this time, his request wouldn't even be acknowledged. While still in Paris, Van Deman also worked to improve communications security guidelines among the GHQ G2, the French Second Bureau (Intelligence), and the French postal censorship organization.

Van Deman then traveled to England, where he arranged for a committee of US, British, French, and Belgian intelligence officers to meet routinely at The Hague in the Netherlands to resolve long-standing issues, such as agents, exchange of information, and greater coordination at the working level. The basic reason why nothing had been done in the past was that the Belgian military attaché believed himself to be the senior officer, and both the British and French harbored serious reservations regarding the ability of Belgian intelligence to keep secrets. As a solution, Van Deman encouraged the establishment of a second committee to convene in London to discuss matters that could not be addressed at the Hague, but Van Deman's visit to England would not be a total triumph. US Consul General Robert P. Skinner refused to budge on the matter of granting any authority to military or naval attachés on passport and visa applications.[6]

Arriving back in Paris in October, Van Deman continued to address unresolved problems and to make progress concerning operations in Switzerland and other nearby countries. During the summer months, the Secret Service division had established counterintelligence elements in all adjoining neutral nations for the primary purpose of following the movement of known enemy agents, but the effectiveness of these so-called information centers had suffered from a lack of coordination between the local military attaché and MI-4 in Washington. Subsequently, Van Deman met with Colonel W. F. Godson, the military attaché in Bern, Switzerland, and in a few weeks, he sent a message to General Marlborough Churchill at MID that an improved system had been agreed on; in the future, counterintelligence, not military attachés, would handle all related issues.

ST. MIHIEL

The St. Mihiel salient—a huge inverted triangle consisting of woods, rolling hills, small villages, creeks, and the Rupt de Mad River—had existed almost from the beginning of the war and had posed a constant fear that the Germans would use it to strike deep into Allied territory. Eleven German divisions, totaling 75,000 troops, defended the salient against 400,000 Americans and 48,000 French, but the Germans occupied some of the finest defensive positions on the western front that were reinforced with thick barbed wire. It had been long in Pershing's mind to slice off the St. Mihiel salient, thus demonstrating his army's power; the offensive would also be AEF's first involvement in a large-scale offensive. On August 16, Pershing issued preliminary instructions to assemble forces for an early September offensive, but parts of the intelligence system had already begun to collect information months earlier. Because of the need to help pinpoint enemy batteries, US intelligence had six months before they sent sound and flash ranging systems to work with nearby French artillery.

Meanwhile, the 29th Engineers were busy preparing maps for the upcoming offensive. When the planned allotment of topographical troops for First Army did not arrive from the States, the 29th Engineers dispatched Colonel C. L. Hall and 65 enlisted men on September 1 to fill staff vacancies and to move with the First Army. Utilizing their mobile printing presses located in trucks, Hall's detachment set out to prepare maps for the 16 divisions involved in the attack. Although the engineers brought with them battle maps of the Toul sector created at the Base Plant in Langres in anticipation of the upcoming offensive, they quickly discovered that some of the maps were too small and the locations of operations were constantly shifting. Immediately a call for assistance went out to the French armies occupying nearby sectors to provide copies of existing maps and updates of recent changes. Fortunately, the French were able to forward the needed items to Langres where they were copied and printed just in time for the attack on September 12.[7]

Distribution was not a simple task, given the 15 tons of maps necessary to cover all contingencies. By now it was becoming all too apparent that a serious mistake had been made by locating the main printing operation at Langres, which was situated farther and farther from the battlefield; delivery of maps was also complicated by bad weather, unpredictable telephone communications, and lack of motor transportation. Besides maps, Hall and his men copied over 2,300 aerial photos of the terrain over which the offensive would take place. To become familiar with the territory as well as to take much needed photos, US pilots and observers had flown French airplanes already operating along the sector to keep from arousing the enemy's suspicion.

In the rear area, US reconnaissance aircraft were being readied for the campaign. The air observation group assigned to First Army headquarters consisted of the 91st, 24th, and 9th Squadrons, but the 91st assumed the lead as it was the only one of the three with prior combat experience. All of the 91st Squadron observers had either served previously with the artillery or had attended the training center at Gondrecourt; as far as actual combat flight experience, no observer from any of the other sister squadrons had more than 10 hours' experience. In the area of photography, the 91st would also lead US squadrons in number of photos taken—some 3,700 during the course of the war. Plans called for four reconnaissance teams within the First Army Observation Group to be constantly ready to undertake all types of missions, while each corps had an observation group composed of both US and French squadrons.

The US sector north of Toul and facing the St. Mihiel salient was near enough to the region of Lorraine to have a mixed civilian population (speaking both French and German) with equally mixed loyalties. Most US soldiers found the locals a dour lot who sold their produce at fivefold the real value. On the eve of the St. Mihiel offensive in September 1918, the Corps of Intelligence Police (CIP) assembled a large number of its agents for the sole purpose of clearing enemy informers from the area of operations by setting up a system of travel controls; the effort was labeled a success when scores of refugees and line-crossers who lacked proper identification were stopped and questioned.

General Nolan gave orders that all US correspondents should assemble at Meaux until the evening before the attack so as not to alert German intelligence. It was during the St. Mihiel offensive that Nolan began the practice of laying out for newspaper reporters the overall plans of the upcoming campaign, and then going division by division and corps by corps to explain each of their objectives. Nolan also reemphasized to the reporters exactly what could and could not be printed. Looking back, he not only believed that his efforts led to more accurate news stories for the US public, but that the security reminders resulted in less censoring being required, thus allowing for more timely reporting. If the Americans were successful, Nolan anticipated that the press might raise the question of whether General Pershing had stopped too soon. Consequently, he went out of his way to reemphasize that the objectives of the operations were limited and what those goals were. While Nolan discussed the US order of battle with the correspondents, intelligence staffs at army and corps were busily distributing intelligence summaries on the location of enemy units. The printing of such reports were again held off to the last minute to minimize potential leaks.

Prior to launching the offensive, the Americans had undertaken a series of steps to conceal their intent; for instance, units sought natural cover by day and moved only at night. Their final resting places were to be out of sight from the enemy's observers, who were occupying the high ground, as well as from German aircraft. When the Germans sent a scout into the Americans' area to search for useful documents, two soldiers who witnessed the intruder returning to his lines were able to pursue him into the no-man's land where they used knives to kill the German and retrieve a stolen codebook. Regardless of all the steps taken to cloak the nature of the Americans' plans, the Germans knew full well the scope and object of Pershing's attack. The campaign was widely talked about up and down the supply chain, and the Paris newspapers were openly hinting at the time and place. Lieutenant John Clark reported on September 8, "That the Boche knew we are here is very evident, for yesterday a balloon message came over, which read—'To the 9th Infantry—we are ready for you.'"

The Signal Corps' Security Service found out exactly what the German intercept operators were hearing by establishing a network of stations to monitor US communications. Copied messages were then passed on for an analyst to see what specifics he could derive from them. Before the attack at St. Mihiel, it was quite apparent that the AEF communicators had provided the Germans with the complete AEF order of battle along with the location of divisions in reserve plus names of commanders and various directives. Without any aids, the security specialist quickly read the messages and even learned the point of attack, only the time was off by 24 hours because someone transmitting the message had been misinformed.[8]

From its headquarters at Ligny-en-Barrois, First Army radio intelligence would direct its multiprong approach to the campaign. Its radio intercept stations at Toul and Souilly, which lay between 15 to 20 miles from the St. Mihiel salient, picked up early signs that confirmed Germany was fully aware of the upcoming offensive. Monitors copied transmissions from the enemy observation post at Butte de Montsec; the abnormal level of traffic meant that German observers were busily sending out reports on US troop movements. During the St. Mihiel offensive, the Germans frequently used their trinumeral codes, even for important messages; this allowed radio intelligence to easily read most communiqués. Concurrently, AEF listening stations in the Bois d'Apremont were also hearing an abnormal amount of telephone chatter among various German elements.

Beginning on September 8, both radio and ground intercept saw signs of enemy nervousness and withdrawal in the southern portion of the salient. The listening sites at Flirey and Limey reported that the German telegraph was relocating to the rear—a typical move when an attack was anticipated. The Americans learned this not by what was heard from intercepted conversations, but by the increased volume of traffic. It was further confirmed by a German prisoner who informed his interrogators from the 77th Division that the narrow-gauged tracks were being removed and shipped to the rear. On the western side of the salient, enemy radio traffic remained normal. Thus, the Germans appeared to have been expecting the attack to come between St. Mihiel and the Moselle, not between Les Esparges and St. Mihiel.

Just prior to the launching of the attack, indicators confirmed that the enemy had suddenly withdrawn. Aerial observation was reporting explosions from artillery dumps, the absence of balloons, and increased fires in villages along the lines of retreat, and the aviators who were flying over the area of operations were not experiencing hostile fire. Now averaging only 30 intercepts a day, the number had dropped 25 percent during the four days leading up to the attack. Serious consideration was given not to launching a preliminary artillery bombardment but rather to advancing the infantry on its own. Still, AEF direction-finders were placing the enemy stations at their former positions. In fact, September would be direction-finding's busiest month with all eight stations taking more than 43,000 bearings. Having received no concrete information to the contrary, Lieutenant William Dearden of the Order of Battle Section agreed with radio intelligence that reporting should err on the side of caution and assume that enemy units had remained in place. Based solely on direction-finding, General Pershing ordered an intense bombardment from the ground and air, but a follow-up inspection determined that the falling shells had actually done little damage to either the barbed wire or entrenched positions.[9]

A surprise awaited the Allied troops when they went over the top and found that the Germans had indeed retreated, leaving behind only a token rear guard. The Germans had also retained a handful of signal personnel to operate a dummy communications net—a first. Scouring the area, intelligence personnel came upon a post office filled with undelivered letters from German soldiers. Also discovered were a number of useful scraps of paper that described the overall decline in morale of German forces plus a secret document that showed in detail the fortifications within the St. Mihiel salient. From these papers and interrogation of prisoners, it was learned that the Germans had originally planned a quick counterattack but had abandoned their position when they learned that they would be hit from both sides of the salient.

On the day of the attack, AEF reconnaissance benefited from the use of fast, high-powered pursuit aircraft that could fly in bad weather when it was almost impossible for the slower biplanes to take off. Although the pilots were not trained in surveillance work, they, nevertheless, brought back important updates.[10] Over the next two days, air operations continued to face terrible visibility with long periods of fog and low cloud cover, which prevented flying higher than about 1,000 meters and sometimes as low as 50 to 100 meters. Crews were able to fly artillery observation and long-range reconnaissance during breaks in the weather, going as far as 60 kilometers beyond the enemy's front line. Between infantry patrols and use of aircraft, the Allied commanders were still able to receive enough timely reports to track the enemy's changing positions.

Photo missions would be limited to targets of the highest priority—railroad stations and enemy artillery before and after being hit by Allied shells and bombs. Initially the chief of staff of the First Army sent his orders for photos through the G2 to the Observation Group, while the chief of Air Service sent his directly to the group commander. Upon receiving conflicting instructions, the First Army Observation Group complained, and the matter was resolved in favor of all orders going directly to the chief of Air Service for consolidation.

Together the belligerents deployed 33 balloons, of which 15 belonged to the US companies. Only two of the AEF companies were battle tested, and six others possessed less than a month's experience. Although high winds kept the balloons grounded during the first two days, all companies continued to move forward during the battle. Using a straight line measurement, the French and US balloon units totaled some 202 kilometers. Besides helping to direct artillery fire, the balloons also provided situation reports to the infantry.

St. Mihiel would showcase a more mobile signals intelligence effort. In the lead-up to the campaign, the Signal Corps had outfitted three radio-tractors with both goniometric equipment and receivers. Located at Coimievelle, Royaumeux, and Saiserais, the trucks were to move forward with the troops, but the assignment would prove anything but easy, the location being 75 kilometers from their home base. Somehow over shell-torn and gas-drenched landscape, the noncommissioned officers in charge of the mobile units kept them moving and operating—broken parts such as a busted clutch and steering gear notwithstanding.[11]

The final report of the AEF chief signal officer indicated that "Upon several occasions the efficient work of our intercept operators was cited in secret reports."[12] During the St. Mihiel operations, operators copied radio messages warning of a counterattack, as well as its strength and the time and place at which it would occur, three hours before it took place. Intercept station No. 4 at Toul filed the following types of dispatches being broadcast from a German brigade: "Twelve noon is time set to drive enemy out again by a counterattack." Two hours later, station No. 3 at Toul intercepted a coded message: "The enemy is pushing forward east of Soulevre Farm on left flank 351. Threatens the brigade. Reserve battalion is going to counterattack to the south of the division area. Battery correction and observation good."

For the first time, the Americans deployed their scouts in a more traditional role of keeping track of a retreating enemy. The scouts took with them pigeons to carry back messages alerting forces where the Germans were making their next stand. General Nolan and Colonel Arthur Conger followed closely behind the advancing Doughboys in an automobile. When they reported to General Pershing that the troops had been gallant, General Pershing responded, "I knew I could depend on them. There are no soldiers in the world to equal them." He also would release a separate communiqué in which he praised the efforts of intelligence and mapping, saying that no offensive operation had been better served.

In the end, the Allied forces would suffer only 7,000 casualties while capturing 16,000 prisoners and 443 of the enemy's guns. More important, they had reduced the front by 20 miles and set the stage for encircling the German fortress at Metz and helped to pave the way for an even larger offensive in the Argonne. Great euphoria followed the victory! Captured German officers were asking for French beer because theirs had been so watered down, and before departing the salient, the retreating Germans had informed the local citizens that they were finally going home. In response to the overwhelming victory, General Nolan directed that news censors should bend the rules and allow the correspondents great latitude. The United Press was typical when it cabled the following dispatch: "The Americans have completely flattened out the St. Mihiel salient." Nolan's rationale for loosening the normal constraints on news censorship was to give General Pershing and the AEF full credit, cheer up the Allies, and demoralize the Germans.

Following St. Mihiel, there was one intelligence story that continued to make the rounds, and it involved Colonel "Vinegar Joe" Stilwell's attempt at a practical joke. A certain colonel (believed to have been none other than the G2 at I Corps) persistently phoned Stilwell at II Corps for the purposes of determining if his intelligence staff had acquired any new information on the subject of poison gas. When operations in the St. Mihiel area came to a close, Stilwell replied to the officer that he had just acquired a prisoner in charge of chemicals for one of the German corps; this important source was a supposed expert in biochloride gas by the name of Otto Schmeerkase—pronounced as Smeargas by the Americans and obviously fictitious. Stilwell felt confident that his fellow officer would quickly see through the hoax. Just the opposite occurred: the officer sent someone to pick up the prisoner, forcing Stilwell to improvise. The prisoner had been here, but the system had now transferred him to another camp. Stilwell again miscalculated because the escort immediately departed to locate the prisoner. By phoning ahead and letting others in on the joke, Stilwell was able to keep his fictitious prisoner on the move, but Stilwell continued to miscalculate because the escort officer would not be distracted in his pursuit of the misplaced Smeargas. In fact, news of the capture would be picked up by a number of US newspapers. Soon every intelligence officer was in on the ruse; eventually, the story found its way back to the original requestor who was not amused and immediately recommended the court-martialing of Stilwell. Fortunately for the G2, he would escape discipline because General Pershing was in such a good mood in the wake of the US victory.[13]

MEUSE-ARGONNE

Prior to St. Mihiel, the British and French commands had unveiled new plans that would include the Americans. Once the AEF finished its offensive, it was expected to swing immediately 60 miles north and launch a second offensive in the Meuse-Argonne region no later than September 25. Unwilling to abandon the long-anticipated St. Mihiel offensive, Pershing had left a logistical nightmare for his army to solve. Colonel George Marshall shared his thoughts upon receiving the news: "I remember thinking that I could not recall an incident in history where the fighting of one battle had been preceded by the plans for a later battle to be fought by the same army on a different front, and involving the issuing of orders for the movement of troops already destined to participate in the first battle, directing their transfer to the new field of action." To compound the transportation problem, the railroad lines were limited, and the three narrow roads were badly shelled; the endless rain only compounded the problem of the movement of equipment and men. The abrupt change to a different area of operations also highlighted a major intelligence shortcoming—unlike St. Mihiel, intelligence was left with no time to conduct a study of the Lorraine front.

A deception plan was created to convince the Germans that an attack would come across the Rhine River from the southeast so they would draw more forces to that sector. It seemed a perfect situation as locals tended to be more German than French, both in terms of their language and loyalties. General Nolan dispatched confidential orders to Major General Omar Bundy to establish a corps headquarters at Belfort and to plan for seven divisions. To prevent leaks that the so-called Shine Offensive was not genuine, Bundy himself was not even informed about the subterfuge. While meeting with other members of the delegation in search of the phantom headquarters site,

Colonel Conger typed a letter to Pershing to alert him that all was ready for the attack through the Belfort gap. After depositing the carbon copy of the message in a wastepaper basket, Conger momentarily left the Hotel Tonneau d'Or in Belfort. Upon his return to his room, Conger would, to no surprise, find the document gone.[14]

A more sophisticated means of sending false clues to the Germans took place in the lobby of the Bellevue Palace Hotel in Bern, Switzerland. The establishment was widely known for hosting a cosmopolitan crowd and was a favorite haunt for a German spy whom the Americans dubbed Bella Donna. It would not take Bella long to spot the fresh American face, especially when he offered to buy drinks. After a while the couple moved to an out-of-the-way place where they continued to imbibe; eventually the gentleman conveniently fell into a stupor, allowing his companion to search him until she found the envelope that contained secret details of the upcoming offensive. Then off she went to steam it open and to read its contents, making a copy before hurrying back and replacing the original. The Secret Service staff back at Chaumont was pleased when informed that the bait had been taken.[15]

Besides a phantom headquarters, the Americans also dispatched messages, confirmed the presence of tank tracks and flew aircraft over the proposed area of operations—all for the purposes of deceiving the enemy. After studying incoming reports from his agents and observers, a German intelligence officer wrote to General Erich Ludenforff: "I recognize quite fully that all these preparations made for attack may perfectly well turn out to be a *ruse de guerre* intended to mislead us as to the real point of attack. However, there is nothing to indicate that it is not the real point of attack, and our danger there is so great that I deem it imperative to have these divisions." Upon receiving the memo, General Ludendorff ordered 36,000 troops be dispatched to Alsace and the Vosages.

The Meuse-Argonne offensive was a campaign along a 14-mile, well-defended front. The objective was to sever the Lille-Metz railroad and thus cut the Germans' ability to ship supplies and men, east and west. The initial battlefield was the 12-mile Meuse River valley, with heights on one side and those of the Argonne forest, and thick undergrowth on the other. In the valley, there were several natural strongholds: the heights of Montfaucon, Romagne, the Bois de Barricourt, and the Bois de Bourgogne. In addition, the Germans held four successive lines of defense, each defended by trenches, concrete emplacements, and barbed wire. AEF intelligence reported that the Allies should anticipate facing five enemy line divisions and that these would be reinforced by four more in the first 24 hours and two additional by the second day. It would be slow going for the Yanks as they moved down the throat of the enemy.

The French Fourth Army was to attack on the left flank and the American First Army on the right. The first assault wave consisted of 10 AEF divisions while another 8 were held in reserve—totaling 450,000 men. On Thursday, September 26, the Allies launched their coordinated campaign, but after only two days, the offensive began to stall. This brought General Pershing to the front where he attempted to urge his commanders forward. He told General Hunter Liggett, Commander of the I Corps, "that he must push on regardless of men or guns, day or night."

Nearby, Nolan was checking out the intelligence situation. Observing a handful of prisoners being sent to the rear, Nolan called out to the passing Germans, "Well, it looks pretty bad for you, doesn't it? We've been pushing you back steadily, 6 or 7 miles!" To this, a prisoner of war called back, "We'll soon stop that. We're the 52nd Division, and we've been in rest billets for a month. They sent us here to stop you Americans, and we're the boys who can do it. You may have captured a few of us but there are a lot more over there like us. More fresh troops are coming." With this latest bit of information, Nolan rushed off to brief Pershing.

Not only did Pershing welcome the update, but the appearance of his intelligence chief gave the general a way to help solve an immediate leadership problem facing the 28th Division of the Pennsylvania National Guard. Pershing easily convinced Nolan that it was essential that he take over the temporary command of the 28th Division's 55th Infantry Brigade. This was not totally unexpected because Pershing had previously informed members of his staff that they should anticipate being given troop commands, and Nolan knew that he was soon to be replaced by Van Deman as G2.

Under Nolan's personal direction, the soldiers from the undersized brigade successfully launched a surprised night attack that drove the Germans from the village of Apremont. One soldier remembered: "We were up there fighting we saw him going from shell hole to shell hole, never bending his head. This is what gives men grit. I never saw the general we had before outside of a dugout, the new one was always leading us."[16] Nolan then proceeded to order the construction of four strong points and the deployment of artillery in such a manner as to defend against the three counterattacks launched by two enemy regiments and accompanied by heavy bombardment. During the last assault on October 1, Nolan used tanks in pairs, which came from both the east and west sides of Apremont, to help crush the attacking forces, leaving more than 1,000 dead and many of their comrades in arms as prisoners. As one captured German officer told Nolan, "You forced every soldier to choose the manner of his death this morning, whether he would be killed by machine gunfire or whether he would be run over by tanks."[17] For his "indomitable courage and coolness" at Apremont and his role in securing Hill 244 to the south of Châtel-Chéhéry and capturing close to 250 Germans on October 7, Nolan would become one of only 11 US generals during the war to receive the Distinguished Service Cross—the army's second highest decoration.

During his time with the 28th Division, Nolan attempted to read the intelligence reports coming down the chain of command but soon discovered that he barely had time to open the envelopes, and when he did, he found himself annoyed at the repetition of the information and how much of it was not relevant to the division's immediate needs, for instance, knowledge of the current situation on the left and right. Portions of the documents that described the larger picture seemed to have been written for the purposes of prodding the troops to exert a greater effort. Nolan remembered thinking at the time that it was "a lot of bull" and saw no evidence of a lack of determination on the part of the troops. Instead, he believed that the summaries should have reemphasized why the Germans could not have afforded to withdraw from the Meuse-Argonne area of operations. Another shortcoming was that intelligence reporting reflected no awareness of local conditions, such as rain, fog, and rough terrain.[18]

On the ground, Nolan also found himself resorting to more traditional means of battlefield collection. Good field glasses and alert outposts became the eyes of the brigade and were absolutely essential to protect against being surprised. Nolan soon discovered that he would have to reconstitute his observers and scouts because of losses. This was not unusual; nearby, the 18th Infantry reported that due to heavy losses, they would have to rebuild their intelligence collection element seven and a half times over the course of the campaign. Nolan utilized a company of infantry to perform open warfare reconnaissance where it would routinely send out patrols to determine what lay ahead. Because few within the ranks of the 55th Brigade spoke German fluently, only a handful of prisoners were interrogated; the rest were quickly sent to the rear along with captured documents.

By October 3, the Allies had advanced only 4 miles, ending the first phase of the offensive. The First Army had suffered 45,000 casualties, and the whole campaign was threatening to fall apart. Influenza and pneumonia were sweeping the ranks, and the rain and cold were making it difficult to meet General Pershing's goal of "drive forward with all possible force." The next day, Pershing launched the second phase of the campaign (known as the Champagne Offensive). Again, US troops faced heavy resistance. To address the problems of command and control that the current situation exposed, Pershing formed the Second Army at Toul with General Robert Lee Bullard in charge. Another veteran of the intelligence staff at the GHQ, a Colonel Thompson, was named G2, but because the sector was a quiet one, Second Army would make no major contribution in terms of intelligence during the war's final days.

By October 16, the US troops had finally reached the so-called Hindenburg line—halfway to their ultimate objective but originally planned for the first of the month. A captured prisoner from Poland informed the Americans about the newly constructed defenses in the area. French Marshal Ferdinand Foch summed up the situation in which the AEF found itself: "there is no denying the magnitude of the effort made by the American Army. After attacking at Saint-Mihiel on September 12, it attacked in the Argonne on the 26th. From September 26th to October 20th, losses were 54,158 men—in exchange for small gains on a narrow front, it is true, but over particularly difficult country and in the face of serious resistance by the enemy."

SECURITY

Prior to the launching of the Meuse-Argonne offensive, the Censorship Division provided guidelines as to what the press corps could and could not write about, helping to speed up the ultimate process of censoring the dispatches. It also had key individuals, such as Major General Fox Connor, the chief of operations at the GHQ, to come and speak to the reporters. Nolan felt that the prebrief was well worth the effort as the correspondents did an outstanding job relating to their audiences that the terrain and defenses were extremely difficult—more than any other sector on the whole front—and for this reason German resistance remained unusually strong.

During the campaign, the AEF placed veteran information officers with each corps and army headquarters to serve as points of contact for the press and to convey the latest information from the front. They also maintained a book of various messages from the field that could be viewed by the press in order to obtain a feel as to how the battle was going. Information officers also provided copies of their units' news to the Field Press headquarters, where reporters who were unable to visit a particular corps could still obtain the information. Although the Field Press headquarters was responsible for accuracy, official communiqués being released daily to the US press told only half the story. They might describe in glowing terms the capture of a town or the launching of a successful attack, but the dispatches would conveniently leave out that the town itself was unimportant or the ground regained insignificant.[19]

In the lead up to the last campaign, counterintelligence took on a more active combat role because each of the corps had a 12-man CIP element and most divisions were assigned several sergeants. As the Allies reclaimed conquered territory during the Argonne operation and its aftermath, counterintelligence assumed control of the civil population, and under French guidelines, the CIP was given a number of duties, beginning with the detection and prevention of espionage. To perform its missions, CIP was especially indebted to a handful of agents who possessed firsthand knowledge of the region and its inhabitants. US agents also picked up individuals on their so-called black list and sent them back to French counterintelligence for further questioning; persons on the white list were given questionnaires to fill out.[20]

Prior to entering a city or town, the CIP attempted to find former residents of the community who could serve as guides for the troops and aid in identifying those who could be trusted. Possessing authorization from the French, CIP agents could order the replacement of an existing mayor. Germans had established what they called "Town Majors" in control of local communities. Some of the appointed officials had administered such basic regulations as curfew in a fair manner, while others had been quite abusive with their powers. Key members of the community were also able to provide details of atrocities committed by German commanders and soldiers. Counterintelligence personnel questioned citizens for order-of-battle information and searched buildings for documents, signaling devices, and wiretaps. Even laundry laid on the grass could be a sign from a spy to enemy aircraft.

Unfortunately, during the last stages of the war, the US combat units' failure to embrace communications security remained widespread. Colonel James Rhea, commander of an Infantry Brigade of the 2nd Division, told the story of having occupied a French farmhouse because a German commander had personally promised the farmer and his wife that the building would not be fired upon. Rhea no more than sat down at the table for supper when shelling quickly forced him to retreat to the cellar. The colonel then learned that the coordinates of the house had been sent out in the clear as the brigade's new command post. Testing a theory, Rhea had another message transmitted in the clear, saying the first one was in error and that, in reality, the command post was a building some 450 meters away. In less than five minutes, the firing stopped on the farmhouse and shelling began on the second building. Upon learning of this incident, Nolan lamented, "This was 18 months after we had declared war and we had not succeeded in getting in the minds of all our officers the danger involved in this type of communications."[21]

There was one silver lining to the lack of good security practices; it involved the first use of code talkers. As the 36th Division, a National Guard unit from Texas and Oklahoma, moved from St. Etienne to the Aisne, it became increasingly apparent that the enemy was listening to their conversations. Colonel A. W. Bloor, commander of the 142nd Infantry, wrote about one such instance: "our division had given false coordinates of our supply dump, and in 30 minutes the enemy shells were falling on the point." Apparently, the enemy was using the phone lines it had left behind as a means to intercept the Americans' conversations. Subsequently, Bloor and his staff reasoned that a solution to their communications problem might well rest with the Native Americans from southern Oklahoma who spoke some 26 different dialects, only 5 of which had a written language.[22]

The next step was to select 13 enlisted men and 2 officers from the Choctaw tribe. The Choctaws' first assignment was to order a staged withdrawal of two companies from Chufilly to Chardeny on the night of October 26. Following this success, the code talkers alerted units about the Germans' plans for an all-out assault on Forest Ferme. Captain Ben H. Chastaine described the results: "When the Germans rushed from their dugouts into the barrage and moved forward, they found the 142nd Infantrymen waiting for them with rifles, grenades, and trench knives in their hands. The Huns barely had time to realize what was happening before they were prisoners." Still, the Choctaws' initial vocabulary of military terms was limited. They could describe artillery by using the word for "big gun," but when it came to such military terms as regiment or ammunition, they were at a loss. During a lull in the fighting, the Choctaws began to fill in the vocabulary gaps. They settled on the word for "tribe" to represent regiment; other new terms included "scalps" for casualties and "stones" for grenades. "The number of grains of corn" was substituted for the numerical designator of a battalion.[23]

THE USE OF INTELLIGENCE

Mapping and copying of photos were divided among the Base Plant at Langres, the topography detachment with the First Army, and their French counterparts. As in the past, the French continued to provide high-quality aerial photos and teamed up with a US survey party to produce geodetic points for artillery fire. As the battle progressed, US forces were beginning to move in one day's time beyond territory that was covered by a 1:20,000 map. At the same time, mapping reproduction was unable to advance beyond Neufchateau, far to the rear of First Army headquarters. This placed a great deal of strain on Colonel Hall and his men to have updated maps in the hands of attacking troops by 0300 hours each day. Even more demanding was the requirement to copy photos.

The Air Photographic Section of the Air Service, which was responsible for printing photos used in assessing bomb damage, quickly stepped in to fill the void. Soon the Air Service had established three base facilities to handle mass production of photos: one at both the First and Second Army as well as the GHQ. In the field, it took only four days for the Air Service's 14 processing detachments to assimilate the 29th Battalion's day-to-day mission of producing photos for mapping and intelligence updates. A sergeant described life in the photo labs: "Sometimes our work would cover only three or four hours of darkroom work, but it usually was much more. Once we worked 36 hours straight. . . . We usually ran one or two print crews, but when our personnel increased, we used three. We used a bromide paper, which was very fast and exposure went from several seconds to a flash. At times a printer could turn out 250 prints an hour."[24] At the height of the war, the United States also had 75 mobile processing labs built on truck bodies—each equipped with a dark room, enlarging camera, printing apparatus, and drying fans. The greatest challenge was finding a reliable water source; often water would have to be carried in cans from nearby rivers to the labs.

Private Edward Trueblood of the Flash and Sound Ranging Service related his view of the battle beginning with the opening salvo.

> By the time the barrage started, all our light artillery had been brought up and put in place, and we were able to rain shells from the famous 75's upon the enemy in torrents. . . . We were counter-barraged by the Huns, and for a time they made it hot for us. But our superiority began to show after about an hour's firing. The men in the Flash Division worked hard to give our gunners the correct location of the German batteries. We worked hard and fast and the accuracy of our effort was shown by the silencing of the German guns. One by one they ceased firing, as the American artillery, with the data we supplied them, dropped shells on the Hun batteries.[25]

The accuracy was further borne out in a topographical survey conducted after the fighting stopped that showed the actual location of the artillery batteries varied only ever so slightly (10 to 12 meters) from where the flash and sound ranging effort had indicated. The worst error was 200 meters, but the average of the bad errors was only 40 meters.

Colonel Willey Howell, G2 at First Army, was able to obtain several pieces of valuable information from captured German officers. A tact that Howell used was to inform all high-ranking prisoners that they did not have to talk, but if they should choose to do so, then they were expected to tell the truth. Over time, a number of officers were caught in falsehoods; Howell responded by holding a ceremony signifying they were no longer to be treated as gentlemen, thus shaming them into cooperating. One officer found trapped in a cave gave good insights into the overall condition of the German army, and the search of another officer revealed a document that pointed to the location of the 5th Guard Division. When US forces apprehended their first Austrian officer, Howell took the occasion to have a full-length portrait of the lieutenant colonel painted so that it could be printed and circulated in case others were captured.

The small village of Vaux probably showed US combat intelligence at its best. Leading up to the operation, the staff of Colonel Conger, who now commanded the 56th Brigade, carefully studied aerial photos and reports from refuges and scouts as well as spent time looking through telescopes of various observation posts. The result was a carefully drawn map that showed the town in detail down to the individual houses and cellars; in addition, there were indicators as to the position of the German infantry and machine guns. The Americans were even prepared to close off the main underground water course extending the whole length of the town. Here, they found, as expected, German troops hiding. Because of the thorough preparation by intelligence, operations surrounding Vaux were promptly dubbed a "cut and dried show."

Overall, the Germans did not utilize communications to the same degree that it had at St. Mihiel; consequently, AEF radio intelligence did not enjoy the same level of success. In the days leading up to the launch of the Meuse-Argonne offensive, intercepted signals had demonstrated what intelligence liked to call "nervous chatter." Following the initial attack, the German stations reflected a reorganization that did not end until October 5; on this date, the newly constituted sites were heavily concentrated farther from the front, indicating a determination by the German leadership to hold the new position. As US troops moved forward, the radio intercept, air intercept, and direction-finding personnel at Souilly also relocated and took up a position on top of the citadel at Verdun—here they were afforded an excellent overview of the enemy's artillery and a direct link to First Army headquarters. But it came with a price: the Verdun site was continuously gassed and bombarded with shrapnel. Among the successes was locating two enemy corps headquarters— one at Stenay and the other at Beaumont. On October 15, the French shared a report that identified 28 German radio stations as well as unit designators. This information, coupled with the Americans' own intercept, led analysts to reason that the concentrations of enemy stations plus their attempts to mask their corps and division nets from identification meant that the Germans planned on resisting most strongly between Etain and the Meuse.

The week following October 17, enemy communications located between the Meuse and Aisne disappeared, but on October 24, they began reappearing west of the Meuse but farther to the rear. For a while, it seemed that a reorganization of radio nets had taken place and that they were forming along a new defensive line known as the Freya Stellung. American intercept could spot antiaircraft stations by their use of "KUK," which warned of approaching Allied planes; the most active of the stations was northeast of Buxieres. Radio intelligence also successfully followed the movement of German meteorological stations; for example, on October 22, station Z-34 was seen relocating to the rear, about 6 kilometers northeast of Metz. Although listening stations found it difficult to maintain contact with a retreating adversary, they were still able to monitor the increases and decreases in enemy volume. On October 27, the 13th Landwehr Division and the 94th Division showed their intentions of withdrawing in anticipation of a ground attack.[26]

Because of lack of visibility during the last 10 days, there were few aircraft communications to be targeted. For a week, air intercept averaged only 10 planes a day. This changed dramatically on October 30, when the enemy feared an attack between Etain and Pont-a-Mousson. During this one 24-hour period, intercept identified 33 enemy aircraft performing spotting duty for German artillery and was responsible for directing counter fire against nearly 150 targets.[27]

The Argonne offensive witnessed the first American use of electronic warfare—exploiting communications and signals not for the purposes of intelligence, but as an offensive measure to mislead the enemy. German prisoners captured in late October, east along the Meuse between Beaumont and Fresnes, indicated that the German command was afraid of a US attack in the direction of Briey and Metz. To divert the enemy's attention, AEF radio intelligence established a network of stations on October 23 opposite Beaumont and Fresnes. Immediately, the sites began to communicate with one another in a code that could easily be solved. To ensure that German operators were listening in, the Signal Corps carelessly laid telephone lines that carried news of the forthcoming offensive. This ruse was carried on until November 1 when the real attack was launched. Proof that the effort worked was reflected in reports by AEF listening stations that showed the enemy was continuing to broadcast alerts; this was followed by a pullback of their ground telegraph system, more evidence that they feared an attack.[28]

The US thrust on November 1 came close to spelling the end for radio intelligence; direction-finding was largely abandoned because of the continuous movement of the opposing forces. On November 3, US intercept operators copied the Germans, trying to reorganize their radio nets east of the Meuse, which was interpreted that the enemy would not make a serious stand until they reached the river. Two days later, the American III Corps crossed the Meuse, followed the next day by the I Corps, thus severing German communications.

From September 14 to November 11, clouds, rain, and smoke from the battlefield made aerial intelligence missions generally unfavorable. Further complicating matters, the landing field for the army observation group was located some distance away; visibility at the front might be fine, but conditions for takeoff were prohibitive. Photo intelligence was consequently limited to only the most important targets, such as railroad centers, but during the 10 clear days, there was an intensive effort to cover as many objectives as possible. Some of the most valuable missions occurred over a three-day period in October, when artillery targets at Montmedy, Longuyon, Spincourt, Dommary-Baroncourt, and Conflans were all photographed both before and after friendly fire to allow for adjustments, but anything that was always on the move, such as enemy batteries, proved hard to locate. Night flying was not possible for the most part because of the weather and lack of experienced personnel—the 9th being the only AEF squadron with qualified crews. On the few times that night missions were attempted, crews were able to bring back invaluable information on enemy movements. Weather also played havoc with air-to-ground radio communications; this forced aircrews to resort to dropping messages and film—the slowest form of communications. One side risk was that if not careful, the vibration of the airplane could hinder the writing of messages and make them unreadable. Despite all these handicaps, army and corps headquarters were still receiving some form of air intelligence updates almost hourly.

In the last year of the war, the Allies began to exchange their nonautomatic cameras for semiautomatic versions. During the Argonne offensive, First Army Observation Group utilized the De Ram camera for its initial baptism under combat conditions. The De Ram camera had been abandoned by the French, but the Americans liked what they saw and encouraged the manufacturer to improve the model. At 90 pounds, the camera was by far the largest used by the Allies and had the capacity of fifty 18-by-24-centimeter plates. Reports on the De Ram camera under actual combat conditions were mixed, especially when it came to the photos themselves. This was in part attributable to the pilot having to position his plane more precisely.[29]

When it came to the issue of safety, the semiautomatic cameras were winners. Unlike manual models, the observer was not required to crouch in the fuselage while changing plates and making exposures. Plus, the camera allowed the observer to keep watch, and during emergencies, to man his machine gun. Near the end of the conflict, the risk factor for reconnaissance planes had continued to rise, ultimately leading to the deployment of pursuit aircraft to fly cover. In one instance, two US aircraft equipped with the De Ram camera shot down seven enemy planes without interrupting their photographic assignments.

Regardless of the challenges, aerial reconnaissance units attached to the corps remained the number one source of information during the offensive and received credit for working very closely with the infantry. This was especially true beginning in late October when aircrews of the observation group assigned to the III Corps began to refer to themselves as "cavalry reconnaissance" patrols, harking back to an earlier period in army history when the mounted horseman was the primary provider of battlefield intelligence. As the infantry advanced, the low-flying air surveillance went ahead, sometimes at no more than 100 meters altitude, only to return to drop messages warning of machine gun emplacements and the location of the enemy's rear guards. On occasion, the planes even resorted to using their machine guns to take on enemy infantry—not a part of their assigned mission. Following their flights, pilots and observers often traveled to the front lines to communicate firsthand what they were seeing; conversely, infantry officers were from time to time taken up in planes to see the area of operations for themselves. Troops began making greater use of their signaling panels, and air crews painted the insignia of the supported division on the side of their planes—all evidence that at least to some degree greater bonding between the Air Service and the infantry was taking place. There was also a more practical rationale for starting to use division insignia—American small-arms and machine gunfire were routinely riddling their own observation airplanes, assuming they were German.[30]

To conceal their presence, the 13 US companies did not inflate their balloons until the day of the offensive. The two French companies assigned to the sector did little work because their crews were ill. Most notably, the balloon companies enjoyed better liaison than ever before with both artillery and intelligence; well-established telephone links at each stop helped immensely, but the Meuse-Argonne campaign did confirm that balloons were far more effective in support of divisions than corps because of the latter's distance from the front lines. The balloons were able to stay with the continuously moving front, keeping 5 to 6 kilometers behind the front lines; the 8th Balloon Company set a record of moving 32 kilometers in one day over the shell-scared landscape. An indicator of the overall value that both sides attributed to the balloons was demonstrated by the sheer number grounded by aircraft and shell fire during the offensive—50 for the Germans and 21 for the Americans. Throughout the entire war, the Americans suffered a total of 48 lost to enemy fire.

The most effective function that intelligence had in its arsenal during the last days of the war was one that had been used sparingly up to that point—propaganda. Nolan came to believe that propaganda was only successful when it further repressed the morale of an already defeated enemy, thus hastening the end. This was borne out during Meuse-Argonne. One enemy officer later wrote that "What caused most damage was the paper war waged by our enemies, who daily flooded us with some hundred thousand leaflets, extraordinarily well-arranged and edited."[31] They arrived by paper balloons filled with hydrogen, airplanes, launched grenades, or patrols who left them behind. The 9-foot-long paper balloons with their slow-burning fuses carried 4 pounds and released one-half pound of papers at a time, and the Meteorological Section of the Signal Corps carried out a number of experiments on when and how best to utilize the balloons. Regardless, the chief means continued to belong to the Air Service, which dumped nearly 30,000 leaflets a day during the last months of the war. In May, only 85,000 were distributed during the entire month, but from July on, the number totaled more than 500,000.[32]

Americans found that the key to effective propaganda was always to deal in facts, and a feel for which themes would be most effective came after officers first tried them on German prisoners, for instance: "Austria is out of the War," "A graphic showing the rising number of American troops," or "Germany's request in October for an Armistice and President Wilson's Reply." Other propaganda contained insights on what peace might bring for Germany and that Germany would not automatically be excluded from the League of Nations.

The leaflets also contained information appropriate for enemy units known to be suffering long tours, lack of proper food, and battle losses. Under Pershing's orders, Nolan read and signed off on all releases and was personally responsible for designing a particularly effective leaflet that listed the rations of the US soldier and indicated that the United States was duty-bound to offer starving German prisoners no less. Germany forbade its soldiers from reading the incoming propaganda and offered a small payment for all leaflets turned in to their chain of command, but when captured, many German soldiers were quick to produce the document that promised rations.

One of the last soldiers to die in the war while performing an intelligence mission was Private David Barkley, a member of the 356th Infantry, 89th Division. The 19-year-old Barkley and another soldier were dispatched to reconnoiter enemy troop strength and locations across the Meuse River near Pouilly-sur-Meuse. Upon returning from behind German lines with the sought-after information, Barkley had to once again negotiate the river on November 9, but seized with cramps during the crossing, the scout succumbed to the icy waters. For his having bravely undertaken such a dangerous assignment, Barkley would posthumously be awarded the Medal of Honor; the native of Laredo, Texas, would also hold the distinction of being only the third Hispanic American soldier so decorated.

PEACE TALKS

Going back to January, radio intelligence at the GHQ had conducted an ever-expanding effort to collect foreign diplomatic traffic. The AEF cryptanalytic section worked mostly on messages that concerned the western front, but from time to time, copied communiqués between Berlin and the Salonika front.

Diplomatic messages tended not to demand the same urgency, so cryptanalysts enjoyed more time, and this proved essential as these types of transmissions most often eluded an easy solution. Yet from time to time cryptanalysts were able to break coded messages that proved to be of great value to the General Staff, especially during the crucial last months of the war.[33]

A former reporter on the Baltimore *American*, Lieutenant J. Rives Childs was frequently assigned the daunting task of tackling the most difficult messages. Colonel Frank Moorman, chief of Radio Intelligence, had originally selected Childs for work in codes and ciphers because he mistook him for an amateur cryptologist from New York by the same name. Although Childs was not a great cryptanalyst, he had a very observant mind and often discovered mistakes in transmissions that would prove to be keys to unlocking the ciphers. For example, he was able to read messages to the German Foreign Office that told of growing cracks in the Turkish and German alliance—all because someone had forgotten and used an outdated cipher.

Childs is best remembered for reading a transmission that would alter the thinking of the Allied strategic planners at the highest levels. General August von Mackensen, who commanded enemy troops in the eastern Balkans, sent a coded message to the General Staff in Berlin on November regarding his proposed retreat from Romania due to the success of the recent Allied offensive. The final solution by Childs was placed in the hands of the Allied Supreme War Council at Versailles within 48 hours of its receipt in Berlin. The breaking of a combination of substitution and transposition ciphers was always difficult. Still, on at least this one occasion, a communicator had either gotten lazy or was in a hurry and sent it out with only a single transposition.[34]

From September on, Allied intelligence services focused on communicating to the German population that their army was on the verge of collapsing. By using their agents to spread by word of mouth updates on how the fighting was progressing, especially emphasizing recent German battlefield losses, they helped to fan the flames. French spies even distributed copies of newspapers specifically printed for German readership; elsewhere, Allied monies were used to help finance various underground propaganda. The Americans devised an idea for an *International Bulletin* in which news stories would be printed in parallel columns of both English and German, but time ran out before it could be fully implemented. Thomas Johnson, in his book *Our Secret War*, tells the story of a US agent, a woman in Austria, who conceived the idea of printing tickets to be used at the government-run stores. These were distributed to the starving population in one province, who immediately made a run on meat and bread. When the customers quickly emptied the shelves, the cry went up, "There is no more!" The fear of a real famine quickly spread, putting further pressure on the government to call for peace.

In the end, both sides were at a loss on the next move. Pershing was forced to acknowledge that the Argonne campaign had been mismanaged, especially when it came to artillery tactics, and that his troops were facing the strain of the harsh terrain and inclement weather. Yet the general strongly believed that the war must continue until Germany laid down its arms unconditionally. President Woodrow Wilson hoped his advocacy of the Fourteen Points would set the stage for a lasting peace. The other Allies, Britain and France, seemed to have been in full agreement in the need to grant an armistice. While they acknowledged the importance of neutralizing the military power of Germany, they also believed that the war must end. In Germany, it was a complete victory by the British on the battlefield near Valenciennes on November 4 and the fear of revolution that finally brought about the abdications of the Kaiser and Crown Prince. Word of Wilhelm leaving Germany came by way of a British spy who first reported that 20 trunks belonging to the Kaiser were seen being shipped to Holland.[35] On November 8, at 7:00 A.M., the German Armistice Commission met Marshal Foch in a railway car on a siding in the Compiègne forest. The Great War would finally come to an official end on November 11 at 11:00 A.M.—a date and hour that a generation of US school children would observe with a moment of silence while facing east.

FINAL EVALUATION

Several factors allowed AEF intelligence to accomplish as much as it did. The support of the Allies in terms of guidance, training, and hardware was crucial. It permitted Nolan's staff to spend their initial energy on imitating and duplicating rather than inventing. The time allotted for standing up and testing combat intelligence was equally generous. Some 17 months had passed between the declaration of war and the deployment of the systems in a major offensive. Finally, the abundance of qualified linguists in World War I set the stage for productive dialogue between the United States and its fellow Allies. Counterintelligence, interrogation, document exploitation, interception of enemy signals, cryptanalysis, and deployment of agents to nearby countries were all accomplished with minimum delay because there were few language barriers. Never again in any future war would US Army intelligence enjoy such an abundance of linguists from the start.

Military intelligence in World War I was unique in several other aspects. General Nolan was saddled with a variety of functions that had little to do with intelligence, for instance, public affairs duties connected with the publication of *Stars and Stripes* and liaison with the press. In future wars, no G2 would ever again become as involved with such a wide diversity of functions—propaganda, management of censorship, and deployment of spies outside the immediate theater of operations. While visiting Chaumont, British intelligence officers expressed to Nolan surprise at finding US intelligence officers busily engaged in gathering political and economic information. "What are you fooling with those for? That's a 'lot of lumber.' You shouldn't have those in GHQ intelligence."[36]

During the 20th century, the US Army fought in five major wars. In three of the conflicts, intelligence would play a crucial role in the planning and conducting of operations, but in World War I and the Korean War, much of the fighting occurred along a stalemated line where neither side possessed a monopoly on information. Under such circumstances, intelligence placed a strong emphasis on order of battle for the purpose of knowing what enemy units were on the other side of no-man's land, their capacity to attack, and their susceptibility to an offensive thrust. In World War I, the stalemated front meant that artillery was especially important because of its ability to reach behind enemy lines. This would lead to a number of intelligence systems, such as air intercept and flash and sound ranging, being devoted solely to spotting enemy batteries. According to Robert H. Ferrell in his book *America's Deadliest Battle*, artillery was the great killer of war, especially US soldiers during the Meuse-Argonne campaign.

In the spring of 1918, Germany began their last offensive, only to be followed in the summer by the Allied counteroffensive that would ultimately bring the war to an early conclusion. The use of mobile warfare would force the abandonment of several collection systems and diminish the effectiveness of others. In 1918, aerial intelligence had definitely become the primary source of information because of the superiority of the camera over simple observation, but as important as photo analysis was, it too had its limits, beginning with the Air Service leadership, who did not see intelligence as a priority. During the war's last two great battles, weather also offered only two weeks of clear days suitable for photography—further validating the thinking of the intelligence leadership who firmly believed that it should never come to rely solely upon just one source of information.

Despite all the advances in intelligence collection and reporting during World War I, there remained a divide between corps and above and division and below during periods of active combat. Timely intelligence reports that originated at the GHQ or army headquarters seldom made their way past corps, especially during the Argonne-Meuse campaign, when the analytical base at the GHQ found itself far from the battlefield. Consequently, commanders at division and below were forced to rely heavily on their organic collection systems, which usually meant observation and scouting. This would not only hold true for World War I but also for divisions in World War

II and Korea where commanders often remained dependent on their organic collection and security resources. It was not until the Vietnam War when improved, secure communications links would allow for the timely delivery of accurate intelligence from corps and army to commanders on the ground.

Regardless of any shortcomings, AEF intelligence was able to achieve important milestones thanks to the talent and dedication of both the specialists and officers who led them. What Colonel Moorman said of those assigned to radio intelligence could equally apply to other intelligence personnel. They "have given their Government the very best they had of brains, energy, and good faith."[37] A number of high-ranking US officers who observed firsthand the collection and processing of information went out of their way to emphasize that undoubtedly the most powerful motivational factor for the typical intelligence specialist was the intellectual challenge—the satisfaction of having trumped the enemy.

Attempting to judge the impact of US intelligence support as a whole is difficult, if not impossible. Perhaps the most measured evaluation came from General Nolan himself, who wrote the following testament to the overall effectiveness of the organization under his command: "The information that our intelligence services gained enabled it at all times, and especially at crucial moments, to make diagnoses and estimates of the enemy's situation that subsequent information has shown were correct in their essentials and, to a large extent, in their details."[38]

The contribution of security is even more difficult to calculate than intelligence. There is simply no way to judge the full impact of education and monitoring, the effectiveness of codes, or even how many enemy agents were turned back. General Johnson Hargood later wrote, "As Chief of the Services of Supply . . . I fully realize the importance of this service [counterintelligence] in time of war."[39] The SOS alone was responsible for handling 3,706 cases that resulted in the neutralization of 229 foreign agents, half of whom were either imprisoned or interned and the other half expelled. As far as contributing to the force protection of US combat units, General Nolan cited the following example: "after the Armistice, one of the senior intelligence officers of the Germany Army said he would like to ask a question. Why the 41st Division had never appeared in the line? The fact that the Germans did not learn that [the 41st had been made a base division] until we told him showed their spies were either poor or our system was pretty effective."[40]

Although the Americans arrived late and began new, some of their intelligence specialists would ultimately show themselves to be superior to one or more of the Allies. The US cryptographers were able to solve a long-term problem—how to provide user-friendly codes to communicators in a timely manner to compensate for compromised versions. The highest form of compliment often is imitation; this was clearly evident in cryptography when the British changed the format of their codes to mirror the Americans, and after capturing one of the river code books, the Germans did likewise. The Allies had at first resisted General Nolan's proposal to establish spy networks in nearby countries, but time would alter their thinking. Unlike the Americans, the French had a large number of their train watchers rolled up by German intelligence and their spies compromised in Switzerland. Sir Basil Thompson, head of Scotland Yard, was quoted as saying, "The Americans had established an excellent system of intelligence throughout Europe, and as we had been closely associated before, we agreed to pool our information. . . . We worked as one organization, and when they had had time to extend theirs until it reached all over Europe, I thought sometimes that it was the better of the two."[41]

The men of the 29th Topographical Engineers used their exceptional skills, brought with them from their civilian lives, to produce superior products. They copied more than 4.6 million maps—two-thirds of which were printed during the August to December time period. Only the late arrival of a full contingent and the distance of the base printing plant from the front lines prevented them from achieving more. The 29th Engineers were also ground-breakers, becoming the first of the Allies to deploy mobile presses inside trucks.

However impressive the achievements of AEF intelligence had been, all of the equipment, personnel, and organizations would be swept away in a fraction of the time it had taken to acquire and assemble them. Unfortunately, it would take another global conflict on a much larger scale before the Army would once again recognize its need to create a viable intelligence and security system to support US forces in the field.

NOTES

1. Dennis E. Nolan, "A History of Military Intelligence and the AEF: A Working Draft," chap. 2, 7; chap. "Ger Mil Intel," 2–7.

2. M. W. MacDonough, "The Intelligence Service," *Infantry Journal* (1922): 256.

3. War Department, Office of the Chief Signal Officer, *Final Report of the Radio Intelligence Section, General Staff, General Headquarters, American Expeditionary Forces* (Washington, DC: Office of the Chief Signal Officer, 1935), 11.

4. S. L. A. Marshall, *World War I* (Boston: Houghton Mifflin, 1964), 406.

5. Ann Bray, ed., *History of the Counter Intelligence Corps* (Fort Holabird: US Army Intelligence Center, 1959), Vol. III, 38.

6. Bruce W. Bidwell, *History of the Military Intelligence Division* (Department of Army, 1961), pt. II, chap. XIV, 31.

7. Nolan, "A History of Military Intelligence and the AEF," chap. "G-2-C," 11.

8. War Department, Office of the Chief Signal Officer, *Final Report of the Radio Intelligence Section*, 12; Frank Moorman, "Code and Cipher in France," *Infantry Journal* (June 1920).

9. War Department, *Report of the Chief Signal Officer* (Washington, DC: Government Printing Office, 1919), 335.

10. Maurer Maurer, *The US Air Service in World War* (Washington, DC: Office of Air Force History, 1978), Vol. I, 269–271.

11. War Department, *Report of the Chief Signal Officer*, 323.

12. Ibid., 321.

13. Samuel T. Hubbard, *Memoirs of a Staff Officer, 1917–1919* (Tuckahoe, NY: Cardinal Associates, 1959), 81–83.

14. Thomas M. Johnson, *Our Secret War* (Indianapolis: Bobbs-Merrill, 1929), 318–319.

15. Ibid., 320–323.

16. Karen Kovach, *The Life and Times of Dennis E. Nolan: The Army's First G2* (Fort Belvoir: US Army Intelligence and Security Command, 1998).

17. Nolan, "A History of Military Intelligence and the AEF," chap. "2-23-35."

18. Ibid., chap. "1-31-36," 8.

19. Ibid., chap. "Press," "1-17-35," 18.

20. Bray, *History of the Counter Intelligence Corps*, Vol. III, 24.

21. Johnson, *Our Secret War*, 44–45; Nolan, "A History of Military Intelligence and the AEF," chap. "C&C."

22. There are various conflicting accounts, but based on personal research, this is as close to the truth as I was able to come. A letter from the Oklahoma Historical Society, the 142nd Infantry Memorandum, and unit records from the USA Center of Military History were all used.

23. In 1989, the French government presented the Chevalier de l'Ordre National du Merite to the Choctaw nation in honor of the first code talkers.

24. Terrence J. Finnegan, *Shooting the Front* (Washington, DC: NDIC Press, 2006), 443.

25. Edward A. Trueblood, *Observations of an American Soldier during His Service with the AEF in France in the Flash Ranging Service* (Sacramento, CA: News Publishing, 1919), 48.

26. War Department, Office of the Chief Signal Officer, *Final Report of the Radio Intelligence Section*, 24.

27. Ibid., 25.

28. War Department, *Final Report of the Radio Intelligence Section*, 35.

29. Finnegan, *Shooting the Front*, 589.

30. Maurer, *The US Air Service in World War I*, Vol. I, 254.

31. Propaganda Nolan; Nolan, "A History of Military Intelligence and the AEF," chap. "1-24-35," 12.

32. Johnson, *Our Secret War*, 56.

33. David Kahn, *The Codebreakers* (New York: Macmillan, 1967), 337–339.

34. Ibid., 339–340.

35. Following the war, Colonel Edward Davis, US attaché to the Netherlands, was able to arrange for interviews with a number of high-ranking officials in the royal retinue.

36. Nolan, "A History of Military Intelligence and the AEF," chap. "Cmb. Int.," 16.

37. War Department, Office of the Chief Signal Officer, *Final Report of the Radio Intelligence Section*, 21.

38. Nolan, "A History of Military Intelligence and the AEF," chap. "3-4-35," 12.

39. Bray, *History of the Counter Intelligence Corps*, Vol. III, 55.

40. Nolan, "A History of Military Intelligence and the AEF," chap. "Counter-Espionage," 7–8.

41. Johnson, *Our Secret War*, 186.

7

The Aftermath

"Simply because the war is over, we cannot stop preaching that intelligence gospel. Everyone who knows anything about intelligence has to keep preaching that national doctrine so that when we begin the next war, we won't begin it like the last."

—B. G. Marlborough Churchill

At the conclusion of the fighting, two divisions of the Second Army occupied Luxemburg, where Corps of Intelligence Police (CIP) personnel rounded up several German stay-behind spies and subsequently turned them over to authorities. US counterintelligence was also responsible for alerting General John Pershing to rumors that the French were considering annexing the small kingdom; consequently, the US command took swift action to block any and all forces from entering the country. To monitor the unfolding situation, two US agents posed as newspaper reporters so they could transmit updates on the debate being held within the Luxemburg parliament. One, a former detective from New Orleans, and the second, an architect in civilian life, particularly appreciated the wine and use of the casino that came with their assignments. While in their undercover status, they were even presented to the Grand Duchess herself.[1]

The American Third Army became the Army of Occupation and originally consisted of nine divisions and 200,000 men; Colonel Richard Williams, who had left general headquarters (GHQ) intelligence to serve as the I Corps G2, was now named G2 for the occupation forces. As agreed upon, the army stayed two days behind the retreating Germans; as far as intelligence, Williams's staff utilized various collection resources, such as air reconnaissance and truck-mounted intercept stations, to verify that the enemy was withdrawing on schedule. By way of Luxemburg, the Army of Occupation reached the Rhine at Coblenz, eventually entering Germany and establishing its headquarters at the Fortress Erhenbreitstein. Over the next nine months, it would steadily draw down to only 6,800, eventually lowering its flag for the final time in January 1923.

One of Williams's first actions was to establish a political section under the direction of Colonel Newbold Morris, a former journalist. During the occupation, monitoring the evolving political situation in Germany was deemed of upmost importance. Morris reassigned several officers to the Berlin commission involved with the exchange of prisoners; Major General George Harris who headed the US delegation was informed by Morris that "you have nothing to do with them, except that they will live with you at the Hotel Adlon."[2] Although the US officers had not been trained as espionage agents, they were still able to establish low-profile contacts and make discreet inquiries with various bureaus within the German government. To aid them in their assignment, the agents were in possession of the so-called pocket code, which had been specifically designed by MI-8 in Washington for use by attachés and spies and contained 13,000 code groups, words, and phrases.

Perhaps the G2's most effective human source was a US officer turned spy whose cover designation was "A-1." Over time, he gained the confidence of the so-called Workman's Council and other radical groups in northern Germany and eventually found himself in Berlin. Here he used his talents as a former newspaperman to become an outspoken champion of several extremist elements, but his greatest contribution was acquiring documents that showed in some detail the Republic of Germany's plans for its new army—a force that was decidedly larger than what was publicly being discussed. Upon his return, the American Expeditionary Forces officer was formally decorated for his efforts.

Colonel Williams and his staff remained heavily focused on counterintelligence; in the early days of the occupation, the mission benefited from the dozens of CIP sergeants scattered among the combat units. Throughout the war, Coblenz had been a popular route taken by various German spies; consequently, Colonel Williams reassigned 20 CIP enlisted men and officers to that city alone. A typical case involved the search of two laborers; not only were their credentials forgeries, but the individuals themselves turned out to be members of the German foreign office. As the numbers of suspicious visitors continued to grow, US agents steered all suspects to the local hotel Riesenfuerstenhof, where they were placed under constant surveillance until the purpose of their travels could be fully ascertained. The hotel telephone operators and staff worked for the Americans, and many of the rooms were bugged with a dictograph. From these recorded conversations, counterintelligence first became aware of the extent of the city's active black market that was manipulating the sale price of war surplus goods; US authorities would take subsequent action to have it shut down.[3]

The GHQ remained at Chaumont with General Dennis Nolan still in charge of intelligence and security matters; a forward G2 element was soon organized at Trier on the border of Germany. As the intelligence staff at the GHQ began to dissolve, one of the first to depart was Captain Guy Viskniskki, editor of the *Stars and Stripes*. When the guns of war went silent, his staff finally had had enough of his heavy-handedness and refused to publish another edition. This was not uncommon within a major newspaper but was unprecedented in the Army. As a member of General Pershing's staff observed, "You cannot expect these men to be soldiers just because they have put on a uniform. They are newspaper men and nothing you can say or do will make them anything else."[4]

Besides the disgruntlement of staff members, there was a culmination of complaints by various parties over the previous nine months, mostly from officers who could not persuade Viskniskki to print their articles. For instance, the story was told of a Catholic chaplain who showed up with such a demand. Captain Viskniskki ordered his fellow officer to get out immediately and then proceeded to follow him down the stairs, cursing how dare he try and "get propaganda in *The Stars and Stripes*." To heap further abuse, the editor returned to his office, leaned out the window, and sang Methodist hymns directed toward the departing chaplain. After the incident, Viskniskki himself believed that he had finally crossed the line and told everyone that the incident would be reported to Nolan, who was Catholic, and that he fully expected to be fired shortly. To the contrary, when Nolan did learn about the incident, he was more amused than offended, but in the end, Viskniskki had simply made too many enemies inside and outside of the newspaper, forcing the general to release him.[5]

Subsequently, Viskniskki did offer up a final proposal that Nolan and General Pershing readily endorsed. The former editor suggested that members of the US press corps be given a grand inspection tour so they could see firsthand what the AEF had accomplished. Three special trains with 200 newspaper reporters on board traveled from various ports and bases in the Services of Supply (SOS) to Chaumont, where they received briefings from key staff members. Then it was on to the various battlefields where officers conducted walking tours to show firsthand what each division had accomplished. Finally, they were sent to Coblenz to visit America's Army of Occupation. Besides the briefings, they were given pounds of mimeographed papers to take back with them. Intelligence also released captured documents in which German generals praised the fighting spirit of the US soldiers, but held back those with comments that were less than complimentary or that questioned General Pershing's decision not to follow through at St. Mihiel.[6]

Besides being free for the first time to write without the threat of censorship, America's news reporters had ended the war on a positive note. General Nolan and others had hoped that the effort would lead to future stories acknowledging the role of the Army and its soldiers, but memory of America's sacrifice on the battlefields of France soon faded away. Twenty years later, General Nolan acknowledged that veterans were always asking him why the American people did not remember the Meuse-Argonne battle. How could Americans so quickly forget their country's deadliest battle that cost 120,000 casualties to include 26,000 dead? Nolan confessed to having no ready answer; his only explanation was that the emergence of the dreaded Spanish influenza on the home front had occupied the nation's attention.

Some of the printed materiel given to the correspondents came by way of the one intelligence element whose workload would remain at a very high level until June 1919—the 29th Topographical Engineers. After the Armistice, all forward presses stopped copying battlefield maps, and the mobile printers of the Second Army began to pour out copies of small-scale maps covering the Meuse to the Rhine to aid troops advancing into enemy territory. At Coblenz, a printing plant was established to handle the larger-scale maps that covered portions of France, Belgium, Luxembourg, and Germany. Eventually, the Army of Occupation requested maps depicting all roads leading to Berlin, should such a move become necessary. On top of this, the Base Plant at Langres handled an avalanche of requests for copies to be included in final reports of all armies, corps, and divisions as well as elements belonging to the SOS.

The shortness of the war had scuttled Colonel Ralph Van Deman's promotion to general officer and his plans for assuming the position of G2. Still, he continued in his capacity as an observer assigned from the War Department to assist Nolan, especially in matters pertaining to counterintelligence. The same concerns about Bolsheviks and other radical elements that were making headlines back in the States were also holding the attention of US intelligence officers in Europe. In response to the worldwide social and political turmoil, Van Deman cabled the War Department and suggested that it coordinate with the Justice Department regarding Americans in Europe who had been involved with various revolutionary movements. He went on to add that the "whole matter should be kept as quiet as possible."[7]

As far as an immediate threat to the remaining troops in Europe, Van Deman pointed out the need "to ascertain how far this propaganda has permeated our troops and next to take any measures possible to eradicate what exists and counteract future efforts of the Bolshevik-Internationalist group."[8] In January

1919, Allied intelligence became aware of circulars being distributed among the US and British soldiers encamped along the Rhine that called for mutiny. Although printed by an element named Spartacist, which advocated an armed strike against the new Weimar government, the author of the documents was Robert Minor, a US correspondent whose ancestors had links to such notables as Thomas Jefferson and Sam Houston of Texas. More important, his father, being a judge, had political and personal contacts inside the Woodrow Wilson White House. During 1918, Minor had traveled to Russia where he held extensive talks with Lenin; following the Armistice, he used his newspaper credentials to move freely throughout Europe including Berlin.

US intelligence had first learned of Minor's role when it had authorized one of the agents attached to the American Commission in Berlin to infiltrate a local Bolshevik organization. Here, the agent recorded damning quotes by Minor, such as the time was "ripe to spread the doctrines of Lenin and Trotsky among the American soldiers." Subsequently, intelligence dispatched a second agent to confirm that it was indeed Minor who had been placed in charge of manufacturing the propaganda for the communists. Although he corroborated the news of Minor's role, the agent failed in accomplishing the second half of his mission—the enticement of the US writer back to France.[9]

By now, Colonel Van Deman had become personally involved in the hunt for Minor and was able to arrange for a German American officer by the name of Siegfried to go to Berlin disguised as a disaffected soldier. There he made contact with Minor and his fellow conspirators. Four months later, Siegfried finally pursued Minor to travel back with him to the border area where they planned on distributing pamphlets. At Coblenz, military intelligence had the US journalist placed under arrest. Unfortunately, the recently assigned intelligence officer to the area had not been prebriefed and knew nothing about Van Deman's plans for Minor, so he proceeded to call the US Embassy in Paris for guidance. Consequently, US foreign officials immediately demanded that Minor be turned over to them.

Although Minor was imprisoned, he received the treatment of a VIP. Outside the building where he was confined, there was a constant circus, with the media, social reformers, prominent writers, and members of the White House all calling for Minor's immediate release. Carrying with him the evidence that the Army had gathered, Colonel Williams traveled back to the States where he met with various governmental officials, including members of the US Senate, in order to try to persuade them that Minor should be brought to justice, but in the end, political pressure would force General Pershing to release the propagandist. Upon his return to America, Minor would continue to gain notoriety by serving as editor for the *Daily Worker*, the news organ of the Communist Party, and to devote his life to supporting the causes of the Soviet Union.

Chapter 7

PEACE CONFERENCE

The SOS assigned 40 of its counterintelligence agents to help protect President Wilson during his attendance at the Peace Conference. Allied intelligence had picked up the rumor that radicals funded by the Bolsheviks planned an uprising at Brest to coincide with the president's arrival on the ocean liner *George Washington*. Other rumors were circulating that there might even be an assassination attempt. To counter these threats, CIP agents joined forces with the French to work undercover as journalists or as activists sympathetic to the Bolshevik cause. Their objective was to convince protest leaders that Wilson might be simply ignorant of their proposals and that petitions, not bullets, should be extended. Traveling with the president was General Marlborough Churchill, who was assigned the innocuous title of general military liaison coordinating officer; Churchill was accompanied by 20 officers from the Military Intelligence Division (MID) who were specifically chosen for their language skills in order to provide support to the conference.

Meanwhile, Van Deman was given overall charge of security for the American Commission; his staff worked out of Number 4 Place de la Conference, which housed the offices and members of the delegation. Counterintelligence spent much of its time focused on site security; this began with a thorough examination of the residence where the president planned on staying, plus all the surrounding buildings. Telephone and telegraph wires leading in and out of the building were shielded from potential wiretapping, and counterintelligence personnel in plain clothes patrolled the nearby streets. In addition, all persons associated with Wilson's residence or having anything to do with nearby buildings had to undergo a thorough background check before responsibility for the area was transferred to the Secret Service.

The examination of personnel was hindered by an earlier decision that General Nolan had made when the G2 office of the SOS was closed. Van Deman had argued that its suspect card file should be left with the local military attaché, but Nolan didn't think that such sensitive information should be placed in the hands of unknown persons unfamiliar with counterintelligence procedures. This meant that there were no records available for quick checks in response to inquiries of the Peace Conference and General Passport Bureau. It also hindered future counterintelligence operations being conducted by Americans in Paris and nearby areas.

Van Deman's staff was responsible for granting clearances for the assigned orderlies, messengers, telephone operators, hotel employees, clerks, typists, and laborers and for creating a system of passes to facilitate monitoring of everyone's comings and goings. Counterintelligence routinely swept vacant living quarters to ensure that secure documents were not left out in the open, and guards were placed on round-the-clock surveillance of the map and document rooms. Steps were taken to ensure that the contents of wastebaskets were collected by cleared personnel and burned daily. The CIP removed all suspicious persons hanging around Number 4 Place and occasionally monitored the outgoing switchboard calls. Van Deman also took it upon himself to warn, in a discreet manner, military members of the US delegation should they be seen being approached by individuals with possible ulterior motives. Despite the many tasks, only a fraction of the 60 CIP personnel assigned to the Peace Conference found themselves engaged full time in security work; the majority fulfilled roles of interpreters, translators, and bodyguards or as one of the counterintelligence noncommissioned officers described it, we were employed "as a species of bellboys, ladies maids, and hall men."[10]

In addition to his normal counterintelligence duties, Van Deman once a month issued a country-by-country summary on the state of bolshevism to the secretary of the US delegation. Van Deman also coordinated with the British on keeping track of representatives and others who were promoting a radical political agenda; the rationale was that they also posed an espionage threat. A highly placed member of the US delegation, William C. Bullitt, had journeyed to Russia and returned with a rosy picture of the new workers' paradise. To refute Bullitt's claims that the revolution had been largely bloodless, the secretary of the American Commission requested that Van Deman issue a rejoinder. Regardless, Bullitt would go on to become America's first ambassador to the Soviet Union during President Franklin Roosevelt's administration; he would later alter his favorable outlook on the Soviets and attempt to warn the White House of their geopolitical designs on Eastern Europe.

Colonel Van Deman along with Major Royall Taylor were the Army representatives on a small intelligence committee led by Ellis L. Dresel of the State Department. Its chief purposes were to collect and evaluate updates on all aspects of the political and economic conditions in Germany. The group arranged to attach their own observers to a number of special commissions being created; their purpose was to send delegations to various parts of Europe in order to determine the local situation. It helped that several of the more important commissions were led by Army generals. For instance, General James Harbord was appointed chairman of a mission bound for Armenia in October 1919. The American businessman and humanitarian Herbert Hoover was approached about allowing intelligence officers to accompany his relief efforts, hoping they could return with a political and economic assessment of conditions throughout Europe. This Hoover adamantly refused to do. Yet unbeknown to the US statesman, a way was found so that a handful of Army representatives were sent incognito on some of the aid missions.[11]

The conference also allowed Van Deman a number of private opportunities to obtain valuable background information. Van Deman used his position to hold discussions with the likes of Lieutenant Colonel T. E. Lawrence who had returned from the Middle East and Sir Basil Thompson of Scotland Yard and also debriefed Colonel Sherman Miles, back from his recent tour of the Balkans. Given his past experiences in the Far East, Van Deman was particularly interested in the latest information about Japan and their efforts to acquire copper, mercury, and antimony.

Major Herbert Yardley was selected by the US peace delegation to handle all cryptologic duties; this included preparing a code for use by the president's inner circle of advisors for their transmittal of secret communiqués back to Washington, D.C. Yardley would choose as his assistants Lieutenants Frederick Livesey and J. Rives Childs, both of whom had served as cryptanalysts for the AEF.[12] As work demands decreased, they began to refocus more of their energies on partying. Childs and Yardley finally abandoned the Hotel Crillon for less expensive rooms so they could spend their limited funds on wine and women, and when both decided they deserved a break and trip to Brussels, they simply signed each other's travel orders. In March 1919, both General Churchill and Major Yardley would be ordered home to attend to their organizations, which were now in a state of disintegration.

SIDESHOWS

The Allies feared that arms and supplies, once intended for the Russian government but now sitting on the docks in northern Russia and Siberia, would fall into the hands of the Bolsheviks and that they might try to sell them to the Germans. There were also 55,000 Czechoslovakians, former deserters of the Austro-Hungarian Army, who now wanted to return home in hopes of forming a new nation; their only way out was to travel by railroad to Vladivostok. President Wilson based his decision to assist the Allies on information provided him solely by the British; he would receive no known input from US intelligence. Yet, in the spring of 1918, the military attaché to China had journeyed to Vladivostok where he filed a report on local conditions. At the same time, the Philippine Department also had dispatched a three-man team of its own to survey the situation in Siberia. In committing to join forces with the British and French, the president also went against the wishes of members of his own cabinet, including Secretary of War Newton Baker and Army Chief of Staff General Peyton March.

Apart from long and cold winters, the AEF, northern Russia, which landed on site in late summer and early fall 1918, had little in common with the

US element later established in Siberia. To begin with, the northern Russia regimental group of 5,000 was half the size and technically remained under the administrative control of General Pershing. This led to much resentment among the troops because they were at one time stationed in France and now were not being allowed to return home with their fellow comrades-in-arms. Another irritant was that they were a part of a multinational force and under the operational command of the British. Even more troubling was that the Allied force in northern Russia would become embroiled in a protracted battle against the Bolsheviks in order to maintain a beachhead. Meanwhile, the intelligence reports being prepared at MID in Washington, D.C., were raising concerns that the whole effort might turn out to be another ill-fated adventure similar to Gallipoli.[13]

In northern Russia, there were three players in the intelligence picture: the small intelligence element that was part of the regiment; the American Section within GHQ intelligence that was run by the British; and the military attaché team that was a part of the US Embassy. It also should be noted that the officers within the US Military Mission, the military attaché office, and the American Section at GHQ intelligence were one and the same. Early on, it was decided that the American Section at GHQ would provide the situation reports regarding the political and military situation as well as coordinate the US portion of the counterintelligence effort being financed by the British. The regimental team would only deal with matters of a local and immediate interest to its commander during times of actual combat.

Soon, the increasingly hostile Bolsheviks were flooding the US troops with propaganda literature; it did not take long for Allied counterintelligence to realize that many of the complaints being raised by soldiers were mimicking the same words contained within the leaflets. During the course of the US stay in northern Russia, some 13 mutinous actions occurred; among them, the refusal of a US infantry company to pack its sleds in response to a movement order. To no one's surprise, the leader of the rebellious act was a disaffected agitator working for the Bolsheviks.[14] Relief finally came in April 1919, when General Wilds P. Richardson arrived to take over the US Army troops. Accompanying Richardson were members of his staff, among them Captain W. N. Thomas, who would serve as the new G2, but Thomas would no more than find a place to billet when the Americans were ordered to pack their bags for home.

The War Department gave Major General William S. Graves command of the 9,000-strong AEF, Siberia, which was deployed in August 1918; the bulk of which would come from the Philippines. Besides guarding local military stores and protecting the Czechs, the Americans were to assist the local Russians if requested. The problem was that such terms as "Russians" were not precisely identified, and Graves did not seek clarification. Instead, he committed the US force to a rigid policy of noninterference. Graves would take the parting instructions given by Secretary Baker literally: "Watch your step; you will be walking on eggs loaded with dynamite."[15] All of the expedition officers received handbooks on Russia and Siberia, courtesy of the MID in Washington, D.C. The books even contained blank pages for the officers to record their own observations, but at the conclusion of the expeditions, no one would bother to collect the documents.

Lieutenant Colonel David P. Barrows, who had been one of the three officers sent to survey Siberia during the spring, was selected to serve as the chief of the intelligence element. (In the civilian world, Barrows was an international traveler and had received his PhD in anthropology from the University of Chicago.) Barrows soon organized his detachment into three divisions—human intelligence, codes and ciphers, and counterintelligence—the last element being the largest. Regardless, General Graves had his own ideas and promptly dispatched eight officers into separate areas of Siberia to serve as military observers; this meant that Barrows's staff would address only the local situation.

In addition to the 5 officers and 30 enlisted personnel assigned to Barrows, the Military Intelligence Division in Washington, D.C., had decided to deploy a detachment of its own that consisted of 16 officers and 15 enlisted. A good number of the intelligence personnel were selected based on their linguistic abilities—very prudent, given the numerous foreign armies in the area. The MID also created the only English map of the Trans-Siberia Railway to send with the expedition along with monographs on the food and raw materials status; the MID followed up by sending a weekly update on the economic situation in Russia and its Asiatic territories.

The intelligence mission failed for numerous reasons, beginning with a clash of personalities between Barrows and the command leadership. Graves forbade any direct communications between the intelligence personnel and the War Department despite the MID element possessing specific instructions to do so. When the intelligence officers objected, the general promptly dispatched a message to Washington saying that he was having a hard time dealing with them. If Washington needed information on conditions in Siberia, Graves reasoned that the State Department and its representatives would be the ones to gather it. As far as collection of local information, the general prohibited the intelligence staff from using the services of anti-Bolsheviks or so-called white Russians.

The one positive note was in the area of counterintelligence; the eight-man team assigned to the problem reported: "Attempts on the part of the Russians to spread Bolshevik propaganda among our troops were promptly discovered.

At no time were the Americans found to be influenced by Bolshevism. There were a few cases of desertion to the Russian Partisan or Bolshevik forces but in every instance the soldiers were found to be Russians who had apparently enlisted in the United States for that purpose."[16] Private Anton Karachun was one of those expatriates who was already sympathetic to Bolsheviks and would eventually go AWOL to join their cause. Witnesses testified that it was Karachun who helped to lead a group of partisans in an attack against US troops that resulted in the deaths of 26 of his comrades; he eventually was arrested, court-martialed, and returned to the United States, where he was imprisoned.[17]

In accordance with War Department directives to discharge all reserve officers, Barrows was forced to return home in March 1919. (Soon thereafter, Barrows would assume the presidency of the University of California at Berkeley.) Upon his departure, Barrows surrendered his position as the G2 to former Plans and Training Officer Colonel R. L. Eichelberger, who would gain fame in World War II as commander of the Eighth Army. Both officers would file separate after-action reports. In his, Eichelberger lamented that the entire affair had been conceived in an atmosphere of inaccurate intelligence information.

In November 1919, Colonel Benjamin B. McCroskey arrived, bearing personal orders from General Marlborough Churchill back in Washington; McCroskey, whose mission was to serve as an observer, was assigned to the consul general. In response, General Graves immediately protested to the War Department that McCroskey was carrying a paper that countered standing orders. Although McCroskey proceeded to delete the offending phrase from the document, Secretary of War Baker still ordered McCroskey to submit all future reports to Graves's staff for approval. Under his authority, Consul General E. H. Harris instructed McCroskey to monitor the changing military situation in a certain locale, but almost simultaneously, Colonel Charles H. Morrow, Commander of the 27th Infantry, received orders to evacuate all US troops in the same vicinity, including McCroskey. When McCroskey protested, he was promptly placed under arrest and forced to return to the States, where the whole matter was quickly swept under the rug.[18]

In March 1920, AEF Siberia itself finally departed. The situation of the Czech soldiers had resolved itself; they did not require special protection because the Bolsheviks were more than happy to see them leave. Prior to the Americans' redeployment, the military attaché in Tokyo sent a message to the MID in Washington in which he requested that Colonel Eichelberger be instructed to turn over all case files on local sources. The attaché proposed to set up an intelligence branch that would continue to work out of Vladivostok under the direction of Lieutenant John R. Northrup, who was especially gifted in languages. Upon learning of the plan, Secretary Baker cabled all concerned that the "Secretary of War prohibits intelligence personnel from operating in Siberia or Vladivostok. . . . Relieve them at once!"[19] The United States had based their decision to go into Russia without the aid of intelligence; unfortunately, as troops departed Siberia, the War Department saw no need to reverse the information vacuum—an omen that intelligence was expected to retreat to its prewar status.

AT HOME

The counterintelligence threat from Germany and those who supported its cause disappeared overnight. With it went most of the MID, which in the next nine months drew down from 1,259 staff members to only 274 persons, and by December 1919, the Army had only 18 military and civilians devoted to the counterintelligence mission. Of those few who remained, most were engaged in graft and fraud cases that had emerged at the end of the war. Besides handling hundreds of investigations themselves, the Army worked with the Department of Justice on one high-profile case that involved a $25 million airplane scam. Finally in 1920, all criminal investigations were turned over to either the Army inspector general or the attorney general.

Although wartime-related dangers of sabotage, espionage, and subversion had disappeared, new perils to the nation's peace had taken their place. To the casual observer, the United States, like the rest of the world, seemed on the verge of political and social upheaval. Federal troops were dispatched to suppress riots during the Boston police strike and to restore order in West Virginia between coal workers and the mine owners. Walter Lippmann reported that "The people are shivering in their boots over Bolshevism, they are far more afraid of Lenin than they ever were of the Kaiser." In the fall of 1919, one overwrought MID officer ominously predicted that the situation in the United States was on the verge of revolution.

Incoming reports reflected the headlines of the day and often cited radical activities and labor unrest, and the inbox on the desk of General Marlborough Churchill, chief of the MID, contained correspondence that also warned of potential dangers. Huge wall maps at the MID highlighted potential trouble spots in the United States and around the world, multicolored pins denoting whether they were bolshevism related, social and political disturbances, labor strikes, racial tensions, disease, and so forth. Given this background, the MID would assist in drafting the War Department's Plan White, which provided for the deployment of Army troops in times of domestic disorder.[20] On the other hand, an important exception was the content and tone of the

"Intelligence Summaries" themselves, which tended to be far more tempered and often went overboard to emphasize that the actual threat was either overblown or misplaced.[21]

Although there was much smoke and few immediate dangers, the spread of communism did pose a threat to America's Army. The Soviet Union had already dispatched its first spy to the United States. More important, the newly created Communist Party in the United States issued the following instructions: "one of the most important aims at present is the organization of communist 'nuclei' among soldiers and sailors," with its primary goal being "the fanatical persecution of officers."[22] Another intelligence report warned that the communists were planning to infiltrate the Army for the purpose of undermining morale, especially among the wounded soldiers still being cared for within hospitals.

Regardless of the current climate, the War Department had determined that Army counterintelligence would play no future role in addressing domestic threats, even those directed at the military. Secretary Baker wrote, "It is very obvious that the American people are very sensitive with regard to any military interference in their affairs. Harmless and even readily justifiable inquiries arouse suspicion, and opponents of the Army are very apt to quote such acts as forms of Russian or Prussian military supervision."[23] In response, the Army dismantled the final pieces of its counterintelligence structure by recalling all regulations on the subject and closing the doors of MID's Negative Branch in 1921.

This policy was reinforced the next year when Lieutenant W. D. Long, an intelligence officer assigned to Vancouver Barracks, Washington, sent a letter to all nearby county sheriffs informing them that it was the intention of his office to conduct surveillance on radical groups. Among the organizations listed by Long were World War I veterans, socialists, and the American Federation of Labor. The contents of Long's letter were soon leaked to newspapers, and the subsequent outcry from readers led to the dismissal of the lieutenant and MID's reiteration for a second time of its ban on surveillance of nonmilitary personnel. Army counterintelligence would never again in its history have the same widespread powers regarding the home front as it enjoyed in World War I.

The threat of social upheaval would take care of itself when the Communist Party overplayed its hand by engaging in an intensive propaganda campaign and isolated incidents of violence. This led the Department of Justice under Attorney General A. Mitchell Palmer to announce his determination to drive from America's midst the agents of bolshevism; in the process, some 249 undesirables, including a handful of anarchists, were deported. The absence of a visible threat on the home front meant that Army counterintelligence would not be a factor again until the eve of World War II. Although on paper the Army retained 45 CIP positions scattered among the newly created corps areas across the continental United States and within the Panama Canal zone, Hawaii, and Philippine Departments, they would, for the most part, remain unfilled or assigned nonsecurity-related duties.

A GLIMPSE INTO THE FUTURE

For the next 20 years, military intelligence by and large would retreat into a state of dormancy. The Army leadership failed to learn from the war that a viable intelligence effort was essential for contingency planning during peacetime. No steps were taken in preserving existing systems as evidenced by the unwillingness to maintain the highly efficient network of spies that was in place in Europe, and as far as military attachés, they would once again be dispatched abroad without proper training or guidance. Furthermore, much of the progress that had occurred in the area of collection had been made by Army personnel not normally assigned to intelligence—topographical engineers, signal corps personnel, and members of the Air Service. Once the fighting had ceased, they were removed from the control of the G2, and whatever future development took place occurred largely apart from intelligence oversight.

The three leaders of military intelligence during World War I all shared a similar vision for the future. Before leaving as chief, General Churchill wrote that the MID staff should be constantly ready to address the political status of nations worldwide: "What is the situation today and what is it likely to be tomorrow?" Upon his return to Washington, D.C., where he served briefly as the last chief of the Military Intelligence Division, General Nolan echoed many of the same sentiments. His wartime experience led him to conclude that intelligence should constantly be preparing monographs on both potential enemy and allied countries; of special interest was their armies as well as emerging strategies and technologies. Unfortunately, these ideas would quickly fall victim to a lack of resources.

The Army also failed to recognize the need for professional intelligence personnel. Nolan was able to organize the Military Intelligence Officers Reserve Corps to identify intelligence specialists who had acquired unique skills and training over the course of the war. But in time, it would amount to little more than a fraternal organization where veterans gathered occasionally to maintain social connections and swap war stories. As far as Van Deman was concerned, the Army could never have a really efficient intelligence service until it created a career service for its intelligence officers.

As far as educating the future Army, the General Staff College would limit the subject of intelligence to just one course. Apart from classroom study, General Churchill concluded that there was something lacking even more fundamental. All career officers should become self-educated in international affairs, current events, and emerging changes in a variety of technological fields. "We failed to realize that it is the duty of every army officer to follow the example set so many years ago by the Navy, and make himself not only a fighting man, but also a well-informed man of the world."[24]

Despite the shortcomings, the intelligence cause did emerge from World War I with several important links, albeit small strands that would serve as a bridge to the future. The assistant chief of staff for intelligence (ACSI), who replaced the chief of the MID within the War Department, would for the first time become a permanent fixture, but his junior status within the Army hierarchy was reflected in the non-general officer rank of the majority of chiefs. The ACSI was also saddled with oversight of nonmission-related functions, such as performing public affairs duties for the General Staff, and just like in the past, also continued to lack either administrative or operational control of intelligence and security personnel in the field.[25] Too many within the US Army's leadership shared the viewpoint of British Field Marshal Sir Douglas Haig, who wrote: "intelligence is rather a special kind of work and has a very small place in the army in peacetime."[26]

Cryptology would benefit from not only having served the War Department well but also for providing crucial support to the State Department during World War I. Together the departments secretly funded Yardley and his so-called Black Chamber in New York City, where for the next nine years a small team of cryptanalysts worked clandestinely to break diplomatic codes and provide American decision makers with insights on other nations' plans. Yardley's most singular achievement occurred during the 1921 Washington Disarmament Conference held in the District of Columbia. By deciphering the incoming mail of the Japanese delegation, the Black Chamber successfully put into the hands of US negotiators what concessions Japan was willing to make. This would allow America to force Japan's representatives to accept an inferior amount of naval tonnage (aircraft carriers and battleships) in the Pacific when compared to that of the United States and Great Britain.[27] Despite this and other successes, the New York operations would eventually be closed by members of the incoming Hoover administration only to be picked up again by the Army's newly formed Signal Intelligence Service under the control of the chief signal officer.

The Signal Corps once again assumed the total responsibility for securing the Army's communications. Thanks to the capable leadership of now civilian William F. Friedman, Army cryptographers moved from codes to machines to electromechanical devices and in the process ensured that the United States remained in the forefront. Colonel Moorman had called for the Signal Corps to have code and cipher officers placed within all army and general headquarters and for the instruction of personnel in radio intelligence work, but more than 15 years would pass before the corps began to take small steps in organizing intercept units based at home and within US territories abroad.

The final area to witness progress in the years leading up to World War II was aerial photography. As the Army Air Corps grew more independent, focus of its work during peace time shifted from using photos for intelligence purposes to creating maps for largely civilian uses and to pinpointing bombing targets more accurately. In the future, airplanes would fly faster and higher; one indirect consequence was the abandonment of the position of observer. Still, the development of new technologies and cameras to prepare high-altitude photographs and nighttime photography would eventually serve intelligence gathering.

In light of the Army's failure during its first 125 years to recognize the need for a viable means of collecting secrets, it is easy to see why many have labeled World War I the beginning of military intelligence. The introduction of myriad new disciplines, such as technical intelligence and counterintelligence, and the linkage of technology with intelligence, (i.e., radio intelligence and imagery intelligence) have made the war an important milestone. Along these same lines, intelligence became much more mobile, taking full advantage of trucks in the areas of printing maps, developing photos, or conducting intercept and direction finding. Equally unprecedented was the deployment of thousands of intelligence specialists on both the home and overseas fronts. In their own way, the changes that intelligence experienced were as dramatic as the introduction of the machine gun and tanks to ground warfare.

Unfortunately, too often the burst of activity during World War I has been equated with the achievement of actual progress in the advancement of intelligence within the US Army. In reality, only a handful of small, isolated efforts remained in the war's aftermath, requiring that an even greater endeavor be undertaken on a much grander scale 20 years later. A more accurate description of what had transpired during the Great War was that America's military intelligence had turned a very important corner in its history. The legacy of military intelligence in World War I is that of having created a clear demarcation with the past and having established a precedent upon which the next generation of intelligence professionals could draw as they faced the challenges of World War II and the Cold War.

NOTES

1. Ann Bray, ed., *History of the Counter Intelligence Corps* (Fort Holabird: US Army Intelligence Center, 1959), Vol. IV, 12.
2. Thomas M. Johnson, *Our Secret War* (Indianapolis: Bobbs-Merrill, 1929), 255.
3. Bray, *History of the Counter Intelligence Corps*, Vol. IV, 12.
4. Dennis E. Nolan, "A History of Military Intelligence and the AEF: A Working Draft," chap. "S&S," 20.
5. Ibid., 21–22.
6. Ibid., 28; chap. "Press," 23.
7. Ralph H. Van Deman, *The Final Memorandum* (Wilmington, DE: Scholarly Resources, 1988), Appendix F.
8. Ibid., 173.
9. Bray, *History of the Counter Intelligence Corps*, Vol. IV, 12–14.
10. Ibid., 5–6.
11. Ten years later, when Hoover became president of the United States, his administration would again assume an anti-intelligence position by shutting down the United States' most viable form of strategic intelligence—breaking diplomatic codes. The rationale at the time would be that "Gentlemen do not read each other's mail."
12. After the war, Childs would go on to a distinguished career in Foreign Service and eventually serve as ambassador to Saudi Arabia, Yemen, and Ethiopia; he also would become a world authority on the Italian adventurer Giovanni Giacomo Casanova.
13. Richard D. Challener, ed., *United States Military Intelligence 1917–1927* (New York: Garland, 1979), Vol. 5, vi.
14. James Gilbert, with John P. Finnegan and Ann Bray, *In the Shadow of the Sphinx* (Fort Belvoir, VA: US Army Intelligence and Security Command, 2003), 16.
15. Bruce W. Bidwell, *History of the Military Intelligence Division* (Department of Army, 1961), pt. II, chap. XVII, 2.
16. Gilbert, *In the Shadow of the Sphinx*, 16.
17. Robert L. Willett, "Anton Karachun: The Story of a Turncoat," *Prologue* (National Archives and Records Administration, 2005), 37, no. 4: 32–38.
18. Bidwell, *History of the Military Intelligence Division*, pt. II, chap. XVII, 32.
19. Ibid., 51.
20. Bray, *History of the Counter Intelligence Corps*, Vol. IV, 17.
21. Challener, *United States Military Intelligence 1917–1927*, Vol. 9, vi–vii; Vol. 6, vii.
22. Bidwell, *History of the Military Intelligence Division*, pt. III, chap. XXI, 10.
23. Bray, *History of the Counter Intelligence Corps*, Vol. III, 8.
24. Marlborough Churchill, "The Military Intelligence Division, General Staff," *Journal of the United States Artillery* 52, no. 4 (1920): 298.

25. In response to congressional pressure to limit the number of general officer positions, General Pershing, who had returned to serve as chief of staff, would ironically be the one to diminish the G2 position and to impose on it public affairs duties.

26. Kenneth Strong, *Men of Intelligence* (New York: St. Martin's Press, 1972), 34.

27. Herbert O. Yardley, *The American Black Chamber* (New York: Bobbs-Merrill, 1931), 312–314.

Appendix A

Military Intelligence
Division in the War Department

Sections noted with an asterisk (*) belonged to the Negative Branch and those with the pound sign (#) to the Positive Branch. Ann Bray in her book on counterintelligence suggests that some of the missing letters of the alphabet, such as MI-4D and MI-4K, were so "hush-hush" that no records were kept.

MI-1 Administration (original)
    1A Personnel
    1B Office Management
    1C Publications
#MI-2 Collection, Collation & Dissemination of Foreign Intelligence (original)
    Combat (Dec. 1917)
    Economic (Dec. 1917)
    Political
    Psychological (Feb. 1918)
    Geographical Monographs (Apr. 1918)
*MI-3 Counterespionage in the Military Service (original)
    3A Executive
    3B Line Troops (Mar. 1918)
    3C District of Columbia (June 1917)
    3E Air Service and Signal Troops (Jan. 1918)
    3F Foreign Speaking Soldiers (Jan. 1918)
    3G Office Administration (Mar. 1918)
    3H Investigation of Personnel (May 1918)
    3I Auxiliary Organizations (May 1918)
    3K Plant Protection (July 1918)
    3L Field Administration (Mar. 1918)

3M Graft & Fraud (Aug. to Sep. 1918)
3O Special Staff Units (Feb. 1918)
American Protective League Liaison (Apr. 1918)
*MI-4 Counterespionage among Civilian Population (original)
4A Executive (Nov. 1917)
4B Geographic Departments
4C Enemy Finance & Trade
4F Foreign Countries (Sep. 1918)
4G Legal Matters (June 1918)
4H Special Cases (June 1918)
4I Labor & Sabotage (Apr. 1918)
4L Research & Collation
#MI-5 Military Attachés (Mar. 1918)
#MI-6 Translation (Jan. 1918)
#MI-7 Graphics (May 1918)
#MI-8 Cable & Telegraph (original)
Code & Cipher Solution
Code & Cipher Compilation
Shorthand
Communications
Secret Inks
#MI-9 Field Intelligence (July 1918)
*MI-10 Censorship (July 1918)
10A Executive
10B Postal
10C Prisoner of War
10D Telegraph &Telephone
10E Radio Interception (Jan. 1918)
10F Press
10G Foreign Language Press
10H Compilation of Press Comments
10I Books (Aug. 1918)
10K Official Photographs & Motion Pictures
10L Commercial Photographs & Motion Pictures
10M Photograph Permits (Sep. 1918)
10N Precedents & Legal Aspects
10O Miscellaneous Propaganda
10P Clipping Bureau (Sep. 1918)
*MI-11 Passport & Port Control (Sep. 1918) Replaced Subsections of MI-3 & MI-4
*MI-12 Graft & Fraud (Sep. 1918)
*Military Morale Section (Feb. to early Nov. 1918)

Appendix B

Radio-Tractor Units

There was also a direction-finding and intercept site in Houlton, Maine, and even a covert site in Mexico City. Sites with more than one RTU had both direction-finder and radio intercept units.

RTU-31 McAllen, Texas
RTU-32 McAllen, Texas
RTU-33 Laredo, Texas
RTU-34 Laredo, Texas
RTU-37 Del Rio, Texas
RTU-38 San Antonio, Texas
RTU-39 Sutherland Springs, Texas
RTU-42 San Antonio, Texas
RTU-43 Pecos, Texas
RTU-44 Fort Bliss, Texas
RTU-45 Las Cruces, New Mexico
RTU-46 Las Cruces, New Mexico
RTU-47 Lordsburg, New Mexico
RTU-48 Lordsburg, New Mexico

Appendix C

G2 Organization at GHQ

G2-A Information Division
    A-1 Battle Order
    A-2 Artillery Materiel [Technical Intelligence], Economics & Translations
    A-3 Enemy Works
    A-5 Artillery Intelligence
    A-6 Radio Intelligence
    A-7 Air Intelligence
    A-8 Dissemination and Filing
G2-B Secret Service Division
    B-1 Administration
    B-2 Positive Intelligence
    B-3 Counterespionage
    B-4 Suspects and Circulation
G2-C Topography Division
    Maps
    Aerial Photographs
    Sound and Flash Ranging
G2-D Censorship and Press Division
    Communications
    Publicity
    Propaganda
    Visitors and travelers

Appendix D

First Army Observation/Photo
Air Service, November 1918

First Army Observation Group
    9th Aero Squadron
    24th Aero Squadron
    91st Aero Squadron
    186th Aero Squadron
First Army Balloon Wing
    11th Balloon Company
    43rd Balloon Company
I Corps Observation Group
    1st Aero Squadron
    12th Aero Squadron
    50th Aero Squadron
I Corps Balloon Group
    1st Balloon Company
    2nd Balloon Company
    5th Balloon Company
III Corps Observation Group
    88th Aero Squadron
    90th Aero Squadron
III Corps Balloon Group
    3rd Balloon Company
    4th Balloon Company
    9th Balloon Company
    42nd Balloon Company

V Corps Observation Group
    99th Aero Squadron
    104th Aero Squadron
V Corps Balloon Group
    6th Balloon Company
    7th Balloon Company
    8th Balloon Company
    12th Balloon Company

Appendix E

First Army Signals Intelligence Stations, November 1918

Goniometric Tractor No. 121	St. Morel
Goniometric Tractor No. 122	Mon Frencon
Goniometric Tractor No. 123	St. Juvin
Intercept No. 1 (short wave)	Verdun
Intercept No. 2 (long wave)	Verdun
Intercept No. 5 (intermediate wave)	Verdun
Aero Intercept No. 11	Verdun
Press Intercept	Souilly
Goniometric No. 13	Hattonville
Goniometric No. 14	Euvezin
Goniometric No. 15	Saizerais
Goniometric No. 16	Bratte
Goniometric No. 17	Tomblaine
Intercept No. 3 (short wave)	Euvezin
Intercept No. 4 (long wave)	Euvezin
Aero Intercept No. 1	Euvezin
Aero Intercept No. 2	Tomblaine
Undamped Wave Intercept No. 2	Euvezin
Press Intercept	Toul
Listening (Group Hq)	Dommartin
Listening No. 1	Saulz
Listening No. 2	Fresnes
Listening (Group Hq)	Bois de Creus
Listening	Le Souche, Louiseville Ferme
Listening	Le Rebois, Boise de Haudenvilles Hautes
Meteorological Intercept No. 1	Colombey les Belles

Appendix F

First Army Security Service
Monitoring Stations, November 1918

Undamped Wave (Army Hq) No. 2	Souilly
Army Headquarters	Souilly
Undamped Wave No. 1	Euvezin
Undamped Wave	Euvezin

Bibliography

There is little new about intelligence in World War I that has not already found its way into print. (If one wants to search original records of the America Expeditionary Forces (AEF), go to National Archives & Records Administration II located at College Park, Maryland, and pull documents from Record Group 120.) To provide context for both military intelligence and the Signal Corps, the Center of Military History's lineage series is a great place to start: John P. Finnegan's *Military Intelligence* and Rebecca Raines Robbins's *Getting the Message Through*. For an organizational history of the Military Intelligence Division (MID) read Bruce W. Bidwell's *History of the Military Intelligence Division, Department of the General Staff, 1775–1941*. Intelligence reports produced by MID are contained in *United States Military Intelligence 1917–1927*; the multivolume work has an introduction by Richard D. Challener. Generals Dennis E. Nolan and Ralph H. Van Deman were the two principal architects of intelligence; biographical material can be found in Karen Kovach's *The Life and Times of Dennis E. Nolan* and Marc Powe's article on Van Deman, "American Military Intelligence: A Sketch of a Man and His Times." Nolan wrote several drafts telling of his experience as the G2 of the general headquarters (GHQ) of the AEF; he borrows heavily from both official histories of the various branches within the G2 and personal accounts of participants. (Because much of the document is a cut-and-paste job, it also contains information drawn from documents of the intelligence staff of the AEF GHQ.) Nolan's papers can be found in the archives of the US Army Heritage and Education Center at Carlisle Barracks, Pennsylvania. Van Deman's account of the creation of an intelligence staff within the War Department, along with various pieces of correspondence, is contained in his *The Final Memoranda*, which was edited by Ralph E. Weber. There are several excellent books that trace the development of aircraft and its early use as an intelligence platform, such as James Cooke's *The US Air Service in the Great War*, but I would direct everyone's attention to both Maurer Maurer's *The US Air Service in World War I* and Terrence J. Finnegan's *Shooting the Front*. Regarding the use of cryptology, there is only one

235

classic—David Kahn's *The Codebreakers*; Herbert O. Yardley's *The American Black Chamber* and David Kahn's *The Reader of Gentlemen's Mail* provide accounts of Yardley's role as chief of MI-8. (It should be noted that Yardley's book was written for public consumption and that he often dramatized and exaggerated the accomplishments of MI-8.) Signals intelligence and communications security under the AEF can be found in three official histories: War Department, *Report of the Chief Signal Officer*; *Final Report of the Radio Intelligence Section, General Staff, General Headquarters, American Expeditionary Forces*; and *Report of Code Compilation Section, General Headquarters, American Expeditionary Forces, December 1917–November 1918*. Ann Bray's edited volume, *History of the Counter Intelligence Corps*, covers counterintelligence at home and overseas; for an overview of counterintelligence I suggest *In the Shadow of the Sphinx* by Bray, Finnegan, and myself. *Our Secret War* by Thomas M. Johnson shares accounts of US agents in both Europe and the United States. For the German threat on the homeland, I was dependent on Frederick Katz's *The Secret War in Mexico* and Chad Millman's *The Detonators*. Clarence Clendenen does an excellent job relating the intelligence portion of the Punitive Expedition into Mexico in his book *Blood on the Border*. Of all the personal accounts, one of the most valuable was Samuel T. Hubbard's *Memoirs of a Staff Officer, 1917–1919*. Finally, doing research you sometimes come across a small diamond; I recommend Alexander E. Powell's *The Army Behind the Army*. Written only a year after the war, it provides an excellent overview of intelligence, although important pieces are missing. I used it for insights as to the workings of the Sound and Flash Ranging Service.

52nd Infantry Brigade, 26th Division Bulletin. No. 1, April 17, 1918.
142nd Infantry Memorandum. "Transmitting messages in Choctaw." January 23, 1919.
Assistant Chief of Staff, G-2, Army Security Agency. "Historical Background of the Signal Security Agency." Vol. I & II, April 1943.
Bernstorff, Johann Heinrich. *Memoirs of Count Bernstorff*. New York: Random House, 1936.
Bidwell, Bruce W. *History of the Military Intelligence Division, Department of the General Staff, 1775–1941*. Department of Army, 1961.
Bigelow, Michael E. "The First Steps: Battalion S2's." *Military Intelligence* (March 1992): 26–31.
Bigelow, Michael E. "Van Deman." *Military Intelligence* (December 1990): 38–40.
Bloor, A. W. Memorandum from Commander, 142nd Infantry to Commanding General, 36th Division. "Transmitting Messages in Choctaw." January 23, 1919.
Bray, Ann, ed. *History of the Counter Intelligence Corps*, Vols. II, III, & IV. Fort Holabird: US Army Intelligence Center, 1959.
Browne, Joseph E. "The Origination and Evolution of Radio Traffic Analysis: The World War I Era." *Cryptologic Quarterly* 21–38.
Carlson, Peter. *Roughneck: The Life and Times of Big Bill Haywood*. Toronto: McLeod, 1983.
Chiles, James R. "Breaking Codes Was This Couple's Lifetime Career." *Geneva Quarterly Magazine* 2 (Fall 1988): 16–17.

Churchill, Marlborough. "The Military Intelligence Division, General Staff." *Journal of the United States Artillery* 52, no. 4 (1920): 293–315.

Clendenen, Clarence C. *Blood on the Border: The United States Army and the Mexican Irregulars.* London: Macmillan, 1969.

Cooke, James J. *The US Air Service in the Great War.* Westport, CT: Praeger, 1996.

Coulter, C. S. "Intelligence Service in the World War." *Infantry Journal* (April 1922): 376–383.

Crouch, Tom D. *The Eagle Aloft: Two Centuries of the Balloon in America.* Washington, DC: Smithsonian Institute Press, 1983.

Crouch, Tom D. *Wings: A History of Aviation from Kites to the Space Age.* New York: Norton, 2003.

Dwight, Eleanor. *Edith Wharton: An Extraordinary Life.* New York: Abrams, 1994.

Ferrell, Robert H. *America's Deadliest Battle.* Lawrence: University Press of Kansas, 2007.

Finnegan, John P. *Against the Specter of a Dragon: The Campaign for American Military Preparedness, 1914–1917.* Westport, CT: Greenwood, 1974.

Finnegan, John P. *Military Intelligence: A Picture History,* 2nd ed. Fort Belvoir, VA: US Army Intelligence and Security Command, 1992.

Finnegan, John P. *Military Intelligence: Army Lineage Series.* Washington, DC: USA Center of Military History, 1998.

Finnegan, John P. "US Army Counterintelligence in CONUS—The World War I Experience." *Military Intelligence* (January 1988): 17–21.

Finnegan, Terrence J. "Military Intelligence at the Front, 1914–18." *Studies in Intelligence* 53, no. 4 (December 2009): 21–40.

Finnegan, Terrence J. *Shooting the Front: Allied Aerial Reconnaissance and Photographic Interpretation on the Western Front—World War I.* Washington, DC: National Defense Intelligence College Press, 2006.

Foulois, Benjamin D., with C. V. Glines. *From the Wright Brothers to the Astronauts: The Memoirs of Major General Benjamin D. Foulois.* New York: McGraw-Hill, 1968.

Fox, John F., Jr. "Bureaucratic Wrangling Over Counterintelligence, 1917–18." *Studies in Intelligence* (2005): 9–17.

Friedman, William F. "The Use of Codes and Ciphers in the World War and Lessons to be Learned There from." *Signal Corps Bulletin* 101 (September 1933): 35–48.

Friedman, William F. "The Use of Codes and Ciphers in the World War and Lessons to be Learned." *Signal Corps Bulletin* (July 1938).

General Headquarters American Expeditionary Forces, Chief of Liaison Service. "The Enemy Is Listening!" A translated German document, No. 30231, January 26, 1918.

Gilbert, James L. "US Army COMSEC in World War I." *Military Intelligence* 14 (1988): 22–25.

Gilbert, James L., with John P. Finnegan and Ann Bray. *In the Shadow of the Sphinx: A History of Army Counterintelligence.* Fort Belvoir, VA: US Army Intelligence and Security Command, 2003.

Hamm, Diane, comp. *Military Intelligence: Its Heroes and Legends.* Arlington, VA: US Army Intelligence and Security Command, 1987.

Hannah, Theodore M. "The Many Lives of Herbert O. Yardley." Center for Cryptologic History, National Security Agency.

Hatch, David. "The Punitive Expedition: Military Reform and Communications Intelligence." Center for Cryptologic History, National Security Agency, 2007.

Hewes, James E., Jr. *From Root to McNamara: Army Organization and Administration, 1900–1963.* Washington, DC: Center of Military History, US Army, 1975.

Hinrichs, Ernest H. *Listening In: Intercepting German Trench Communications in World War I.* Shippensburg, PA: White Mane Books, 1996.

Hitt, Parker. *Manual for Solution of Military Ciphers.* Fort Leavenworth, KS: Press of the Army Service Schools, 1916.

Hoehling, A. A. *Women Who Spied: True Stories of Feminine Espionage.* Lanham, MD: Madison Books, 1993.

Hubbard, Samuel T. *Memoirs of a Staff Officer, 1917–1919.* Tuckahoe, NY: Cardinal Associates, 1959.

Infield, Glenn B. *Unarmed and Unafraid: The First Complete History of Men, Missions, Training, and Techniques of Aerial Reconnaissance.* New York: Macmillan, 1970.

Jensen, Joan M. *Army Surveillance in America 1775–1990.* New Haven, CT: Yale University Press, 1991.

Johnson, Thomas M. *Our Secret War: True American Spy Stories 1917–19.* Indianapolis: Bobbs-Merrill, 1929.

Johnson, Thomas M. *Without Censor: New Light on Our Greatest World War Battles.* Indianapolis: Bobbs-Merrill, 1928.

Kahn, David. *The Codebreakers: The History of Secret Writing.* New York: Macmillan, 1967.

Kahn, David. *The Reader of Gentlemen's Mail: Herbert O. Yardley and the Birth of American Codebreaking.* New Haven, CT: Yale University Press, 2004.

Katz, Frederick. *The Secret War in Mexico: Europe, The United States and Mexican Revolution.* Chicago: University of Chicago Press, 1981.

Kovach, Karen. *The Life and Times of Dennis E. Nolan: The Army's First G2.* Fort Belvoir: US Army Intelligence and Security Command, 1998.

Krass, Peter. *Portrait of War: The US Army's First Combat Artists and the Doughboys' Experience in WWI.* Hoboken, NJ: Wiley, 2007.

Lengel, Edward G. *To Conquer Hell.* New York: Holt, 2008.

Luebke, Frederick C. *Bonds of Loyalty: German Americans and World War I.* DeKalb, IL: Northern Illinois University Press, 1974.

MacDonough, M. W. "The Intelligence Service." *Infantry Journal* (1922).

Mainwaring, Marion. *Mysteries of Paris: The Quest for Morton Fullerton.* Hanover: University Press of New England, 2001.

Marshall, S. L. A. *World War I.* Boston: Houghton Mifflin, 1964.

Maurer, Maurer, ed. *The US Air Service in World War I,* Vols. I–IV. Washington, DC: Office of Air Force History, 1978.

May, Ernest R. *Knowing One's Enemies: Intelligence Assessment Before the Two Wars.* Princeton, NJ: Princeton University Press, 1986.

Mead, Gary. *The Doughboys: America and the First World War.* Woodstock, NY: Overlook Press, 2000.

Military Intelligence Division. *History of the Philadelphia Branch.* 1918.

Millman, Chad. *The Detonators: The Secret Plot to Destroy America and an Epic Hunt for Justice.* New York: Little, Brown, 2006.

Moorman, Frank. "Wireless Intelligence." Lecture delivered to the Military Intelligence Division, General Staff. February 13, 1920.

Moorman, Frank. "Code and Cipher in France." *Infantry Journal* (June 1920).

Morgan, William A. "Invasion in the Ether: Radio Intelligence at the Battle of St. Mihiel, September 1918." *Military Affairs* (April 1987): 57–60.

Morrow, John H., Jr. *The Great War in the Air: Military Aviation from 1909 to 1921.* Washington, DC: Smithsonian Institution Press, 1993.

Nolan, Dennis E. "A History of Military Intelligence and the AEF: A Working Draft."

Nolan, Dennis E. "Military Intelligence Division of the General Staff." Lecture delivered to the Army War College, September 1921.

Powe, Marc B. "American Military Intelligence: A Sketch of a Man and His Times." *Military Review* (December 1975): 17–30.

Powell, E. Alexander. *The Army Behind the Army.* New York: Scribner's, 1919.

Raines, Rebecca Robbins. *Getting the Message Through: A Branch History of the US Army Signal Corps.* Washington, DC: Center of Military History, 1996.

Round, H. J. "Direction and Position Finding." Read at Wireless Sectional Meeting of the Institution, January 14, 1920.

Rowan, Richard Wilmer. *The Story of Secret Service.* New York: Literary Guild of America, 1937.

Shannon, James A. "With the Apache Scouts in Mexico." *Cavalry Journal,* Ch. XXVII (April 1917).

Stevens, Philip H. *Search Out the Land: A History of American Military Scouts.* Chicago: Rand McNally, 1969.

Sweeney, Walter C. *Military Intelligence: A New Weapon in War.* New York: Frederick A. Stokes, 1924.

Thomas, Shipley. *S-2 in Action.* Harrisburg, PA: Military Service Publishing Company, 1940.

Trueblood, Edward A. *Observations of an American Soldier during His Service with the AEF in France in the Flash Ranging Service.* Sacramento, CA: News Publishing, 1919.

Tunney, Thomas J. *Throttled!* Boston: Small, Maynard, 1919.

US Army, Air Service. *History of 91st Aero Squadron.* Koblenz, Germany, 1919.

US Army Signal School. "T.P.S. and Listening Posts." France: American Expeditionary Forces. France.

US Army War College, Historical Section. The United States Army in the World War, 1917–1919. 14 parts. Washington, DC: Department of the Army, 1931.

United States Military Intelligence 1917–1927, Vols. 1–22. Introduction by Richard D. Challenger. New York: Garland, 1979.

Van Deman, Ralph H. *The Final Memoranda.* Ed. Ralph E. Weber. Wilmington, DE: Scholarly Resources, 1988.

Vassallo, Virginia G. *Unsung Patriot Guy T. Viskniskki: How the Stars and Stripes Began.* Danville, KY: Krazy Duck Production, 2007.

Wagner, Arthur L. *The Service of Security and Information.* Kansas City: Hudson Kimberley, 1893.

War Department. Office of the Chief Signal Officer. *Final Report of the Radio Intelligence Section, General Staff, General Headquarters, American Expeditionary Forces.* Washington, DC: Office of the Chief Signal Officer, 1935.

War Department. *Report of the Chief Signal Officer.* Washington, DC: Government Printing Office, 1919.

War Department. *Report of Code Compilation Section, General Headquarters, American Expeditionary Forces, France.* Washington, DC: Office of the Chief Signal Officer, 1935.

War Department General Staff, War College Division, MI-3. "Provisional Counter Espionage Instructions." February 1918.

Willett, Robert L. "The Story of a Turncoat." *Prologue* 37, no. 4. Washington, DC: NARA, 2005.

Williamson, Royden. "CIP in the Early Days." Paper at NARA Section 319.21 UD.

Witcover, Jules. *Sabotage at Black Tom: Imperial Germany's Secret War in America 1914–1917.* Chapel Hill, NC: Algonquin, 1989.

Wood, Junius B. Letter to BG Dennis E. Nolan, AEF, G2. July 6, 1919.

Yardley, Herbert O. *The American Black Chamber.* New York: Bobbs-Merrill, 1931.

Yardley, Herbert O. "A History of the Code and Cipher Section during the First World War." 1919.

Ziska, George W. Paper "T.P.S. and Listening Posts." American Expeditionary Forces, Army Signal School.

Index

About the Author

James L. Gilbert graduated from the University of Oklahoma in 1965 with a B.A. and in 1967 with an M.A. in history. From 1967 to 1980, he served as historian with the Army Security Agency, at first in a military capacity and later as a civilian. In 1980, he became the command historian for the US Army Intelligence and Security Command. Under his direction, the office was credited with publishing numerous books on military intelligence and helping to put the subject on the historical roadmap. Most recently, he co-authored *In the Shadow of the Sphinx: A History of Army Counterintelligence* and authored *The Most Secret War: Army Signals Intelligence in Vietnam.* He has also co-edited *US Army Signals Intelligence in World War II: A Documentary History.*